JAPAN'S OPTIONS FOR THE 1980s

Japan's Options for the 1980s

RADHA SINHA

ST. MARTIN'S PRESS NEW YORK

Printed in Great Britain
First published in the United States of America in 1982

Library of Congress Cataloging in Publication Data

Sinha, Radha.
    Japan's options for the 1980's
    Bibliography: p.252.
    Includes index.
    1. Japan – Economic policy – 1945 –
2. Japan – Economic conditions – 1945 –
3. Japan – Politics and government – 1945 –
I. Title.
HC462.9.S576   1982   338.952   81-13619
ISBN 0-312-44067-7   AACR2

CONTENTS

Preface

Acknowledgements

List of Tables

We have seen the young man mutilated,
The torn girl trembling by the mill-stream.
And meanwhile we have gone on living,
Living and partly living. . .

Building a partial shelter,
For sleeping, and eating and drinking and laughter.
God gave us always some reason, some hope; but now a new
    terror has soiled us, which none can avert, none can
    avoid, flowing under our feet and over the sky.

T.S. Eliot,
Murder in the Cathedral,
(1935)

PREFACE

No one can be more aware of my limitations in venturing to write this book than I am. It is not easy for a foreigner to capture the basic essence of a society which is not his own, from a distance, and primarily through foreign language sources. However, in my view this book, in a wider sense, is not about Japan alone; it is about the future of humanity in which I have as much at stake as a Japanese or a European or an American. In a more limited sense it is about the trade conflict between the West and Japan. But the Japanese reaction to the Western pressures may force Japan towards alternatives which may have serious consequences for the world.

There is enormous evidence to suggest that not many of the current Western grievances are justifiable by the very same 'rules of the game' which the West formulated in the past for the domination of the world economy and polity. It is widely acknowledged, even in the West, that many of the economic problems emanate not from foreign competition but their inability or unwillingness to restructure their economy to suit rapidly changing international realities. Nor is there a willingness to change their anachronistic attitudes towards non-Western people. It is not indefensible to suggest that Western anger with Japan is, at least in part, born out of frustration resulting from a recognition that the Western pre-eminence in science and technology, and ultimately their economic and political power, is being undermined by a non-Western people.

So far Japan has tried to placate the West, although not always successfully. The important question for the world today is 'what will Japan do if it is pushed too far?' It is primarily with this question that the book is concerned. It attempts to look into the current debate and to assess whether Japan will again fall into the same trap as she did in the 1930s and become a military power. The book argues that militarisation of Japan increases her vulnerability, and in this sense a Japan-US alliance is now a liability rather than an asset for Japan. It is further argued that Japan, as a leader of the non-aligned world, can play a major role in averting the impending nuclear holocaust which the Western 'prejudices' are set to ignite.

But is it not pretentious for an outsider to say what Japan ought or ought not to do? Being an economist, am I not getting into disciplines about which I know relatively little? And does not 'moralising' vitiate the analytical content of the book? I am fully aware of the limitations and shortcomings of the book but when the world is galloping towards the precipice of self-destruction rather than maintaining 'intellectual purity' and remaining 'value-neutral', I would like to register my protest, however modest it may be. I would like to repeat the warning a British astronomer, Arthur Eddington, had given in 1935. Writing on 'Subatomic Energy' he said:

> in the present state of the world it is rather a threat which it would be a grave responsibility to disparage altogether. It cannot be denied that for a society which has to create scarcity to save its members from starvation, to whom abundance spells disaster, and to whom unlimited energy means ultimate power for war and destruction, there is an ominous cloud in the distance though at present it be no bigger than a man's hand. (*New Pathways in Science*, 1935)

The 'ominous cloud' which seemed distant in 1935 was not that distant after all. And in the 1980s the cloud is certainly much 'bigger than a man's hand'.

RADHA SINHA
GLASGOW UNIVERSITY
DEPARTMENT OF POLITICAL ECONOMY

ACKNOWLEDGEMENTS

This book would not have been completed without the support and encouragement of my friends and colleagues in various countries over a number of years. I am deeply indebted to Martin Bronfenbrenner, Sydney Crawcour, Ron Dore, Johannes Hirschmeier, Masami Kita, Chris Mason, Michio Morishima, Hajime Ohta, Ramon Myers, Alec Nove, Alan Whitworth and Tom Wilson for reading the first draft of the book and making valuable suggestions. I am grateful to Yutukai Kosai, Tsuneo Nakauchi and Yo Otani for sending me Japanese publications whenever I needed them. My thanks are also due to Maureen Graves, Mike Atkin, Naresh Dayal and Anoma Kumarasuriyar for helping me with my researches into Japanese and English language periodicals and newspapers during my stays at Cornell University, during 1979 and 1980.

Among the institutions, I am thankful to the Hoover Institution at Stanford, for some financial support and for providing hospitality during my short stay in the summer of 1979. I am also thankful to the Centre of Asian Studies at Adelaide University and its Director, Andrew Watson, and to the Australian National University, particularly the Japan-Australian Economic Relations Research Project and its Director, Peter Drysdale, and to D.P. Chaudhury, D. Etherington and R Sundrum of the Centre for Development Studies at the Research Institute of Pacific Studies. Various drafts of the manuscript were typed by Joyce Stillie and Jo Finlayson for which I am most grateful. Last, but not the least, I owe my deep sense of gratitude to Gerry Mueller for his intellectual and moral support throughout, and for the patience with which he is always prepared to discuss with me my evolving ideas.

Above all I cannot forget my stay at the Nanzan University and Hitotsubashi Economic Research Institute in 1970 where my interest in the Japanese economy and society was so greatly stimulated in the company of Shozaburo Sakai, Kazushi Ohkawa, Miyohei Shinohara (who at that time was with the Economic Planning Agency) and particularly Shigeru Ishikawa and Johannes Hirschmeier, whose work and friendship has continued to inspire me over the years.

None of my friends and colleagues nor the institutions which were kind enough to offer their generous facilities are in any way responsible for the views and any errors contained in this book.

TABLES

1 INTRODUCTION

> In the light of an analysis of its resources, the Japan of the next
> three decades appears likely to have one of two aspects if its
> population continues to grow to 100 million or more. (1) It
> may have a standard of living equivalent to that of 1930-34
> if foreign financial assistance is continued indefinitely.
> (2) It may be 'self-supporting', but with internal political,
> economic, and social distress and a standard of living gradually
> approaching the bare subsistence level. Either of these
> alternatives seems more likely than that of a Japan which will
> have made itself self-supporting at a 1930-34 standard through
> foreign trade and improved resource utilization.[1]

This prognosis for the Japanese standard of living was made in 1949 by
E.A. Ackerman, a member of General MacArthur's staff. It was assumed
Japan would continue at virtually subsistence level for thirty years. Not
many Japanese thought differently. The indiscriminate bombing of their
cities by the US Twenty-first Bomber Command based in the Mariana
Islands had started in early 1945, only three weeks after the saturation
bombing of Dresden by the British. The very first air raid on Tokyo
killed 130,000 people and destroyed half the city in one night.[2] The
campaign was carried out with the same ferocity for the next three
months and paused on 15 June 'because they had run out of cities to
burn'.[3] The final blow came with the dropping of the nuclear bombs
on Hiroshima and Nagasaki. Japan was forced to surrender on
15 August 1945.

The Pacific War had not only taken a huge toll of human life (deaths
are estimated at 2.8 million), but had also destroyed a major part of
the economic and industrial base of the Japanese economy. Nearly
40 per cent of Japan's capital stock was lost during the war.[4] Industrial
production was drastically reduced to nearly 20 per cent of the
1934-6 average; even by the end of 1948 it had revived to only 32
per cent of the peak level attained in 1941.[5] Agricultural production
around the time Japan surrendered was only 60 per cent of the 1934-6
average.[6] On top of all this came the loss of the empire, as usual a
cheap source of raw material. Korea became independent, Manchuria
and Taiwan were restored to China, the Southern Sakhalin and the
Kurile Islands were given to the USSR and the Ryukyu Islands were
kept under direct US occupation. This disintegration of the empire

meant that over 6 million Japanese had to be brought back home to a shattered domestic economy. A drastic reduction in productive capacity together with rampant inflation had brought the standard of living down to almost pre-World War I levels.[7] In fact, with a view to teaching the Japanese a permanent lesson, the US occupation administration had explicitly decided to keep the future standard of living in Japan at the 1930-4 level.

The Far Eastern Commission, in a policy decision on 23 January 1947, had clearly stated that 'the peaceful needs of the Japanese people should be defined as being substantially the standard of living prevailing in Japan during the period of 1930-34. Data about the standard of living of 1930-34 should for present purposes be used to make an estimate of Japan's peaceful needs in 1950.'[8] These decisions were never implemented because of a change in attitude towards Japan during the second half of 1948. With the loss of China to the Communist fold, Japan became a crucial part of American anti-Communist policy in the Far East, which meant that the United States had to assist the industrial recovery of Japan to make her into a self-supporting nation. Once this decision had been taken the US provided considerable help to make this happen.

However, even in their wildest dreams, the US leadership could not have thought that Japan would, within thirty years, not only catch up with Western standards of living but also challenge the West's industrial and economic supremacy. In fact, the post-World War II performance of the Japanese economy has consistently surpassed the expectations of their own economic planners. Since the early 1950s the Economic Planning Agency of the Japanese government has issued a number of medium-term plans. The actual rate of growth has always surpassed the planned rates within the initial two or three years of the plans' implementation.[9]

The causes of such an outstanding achievement have been analysed at great length by many scholars, both Japanese and foreign. Without going into detailed analysis of the various factors we shall summarise the main reasons, some of which are important in the context of understanding the background of the present controversy between Japan and the West.

The Legacy of Pre-War Japan

In spite of the ravages of the war Japan had a number of advantages over her neighbours. It had a well-trained, well-motivated and disciplined labour force, now greatly augmented by the repatriation of mostly able-bodied Japanese from the colonies. Although some sort of basic minimum living was ensured through radical land redistribution imposed by the US occupation administration, there was still a large reservoir of underemployed labour in agriculture, small-scale industries, domestic trade and the distribution network. The labour supply was further augmented, as in the case of the European war-affected countries, by 'the unusual hump of births in the immediate postwar years'.[10]

Traditionally, Japan had no shortage of entrepreneurial talent or industrial dynamic. Even from 1900 to 1935 the rate of growth of Japanese manufactured exports far outstripped the West. While world exports of manufactured goods increased by only 20 per cent, the volume of Japanese exports of these goods increased by almost 600 per cent. Partly this was the result of starting from a low base, but by the mid-1930s Japanese export in manufactured goods constituted nearly 6 per cent of the world total.[11] Even the large-scale purge of the *Zaibatsu* officials, consisting of 2,500 high ranking executives and major stockholders and 2,210 officers, was not enough to undermine the post-war revival.[12] Most of those dismissed were replaced by younger and more dynamic people and as such the purge was probably a gain for the economy.[13]

It is true that the *Zaibatsu* system, the vanguard of industrial modernisation in pre-World War II Japan, did not survive the onslaught of the US occupation, at least in its original form. The major holding companies were dissolved and the owning families were deprived of their shares in the holding companies and of a part of their ownership of the component firms.[14] However, the loyalties of the component units continued, and, soon after the occupation ended, the three leading *Zaibatsu* – Mitsui, Mitsubishi and Sumitomo – regrouped (often in informal ways), and quickly recovered much of the lost ground. Together with some of the newly created independent companies such as Hitachi, Honda, Matsushita, Sony and Toyota they were soon once again the prime agents for dynamic growth.

Post-war Japan also inherited a reasonably honest and efficient bureaucracy.[15] Admittedly, in the immediate post-war years many bureaucrats, together with army personnel, capitalists and party bosses, were 'enriching themselves by allowing illegally hoarded supplies to be diverted into the black market and industrial channels'.[16] However, many such unscrupulous bureaucrats were dismissed in the course of the Illegal Transactions Investigations Committee appointed by the Katayama Cabinet.

Furthermore, although both the basic industries and infrastructure were badly depleted and needed modernisation, a minimum base for recovery remained. For instance, coal production in Japan in 1946 was around 20 million tons, which was a little less than half of the wartime peak of 57 million tons. By 1948 it had already recovered to 38 million tons. Electric power even in 1946, at 26 billion kilowatt hours was seven and a half times as great as that of India. By 1950 it was 57 per cent greater than in 1936.[17] The 1936 pig iron and ferro-alloys production was exceeded by 11 per cent in 1950; however, the production of steel ingots and casting had only recovered to just over 90 per cent and finished steel to only three quarters of the 1936 output.[18] The overall production index for machinery of all kinds had fallen from 146 in 1936 to as low as 61 in 1946, but by 1949 it had recovered to 115; the index for transport equipment fell from 152 to 48 in 1947 but recovered to 97 in 1949.[19] The production of chemicals, which had touched an all-time low of 27 in 1946 (1932-6 = 100), had already recovered to 81 by 1949.[20] The recovery in heavy chemicals was much faster, and the 1936 production was nearly achieved in 1949.[21] In 1947-8 Japan had 25,678 km of railway lines against 24,441 in 1938. The number of locomotives in 1947-8 was estimated at 6,283 against 4,735 in 1938.[22] Japan had 920,000 km of highways in 1947 against 940,000 in 1939.[23] In 1947 motorised passenger cars were only 20,000 against a total of 35,000 in 1937, but the number of commercial vehicles during the same period had increased from nearly 78,000 to 89,000.[24] However, there was a severe decline in shipping, as a result of wartime loss of vessels as well as damage to harbours, which took considerably longer to recover. Thus Japan had the basis both in terms of physical capital, technological know-how and skills together with managerial and leadership capabilities to act decisively towards what Tsuru calls 'regaining one's own normal weight'.[25] According to Tsuru, if the average of 1934-6 is taken as the 'pre-war normal' in terms of real income per capita, Japan's recovery was completed by 1953: but if one takes 1938 or 1939 as the norm then the rehabilitation would be seen to be completed in 1957.[26]

The International Environment

Japan was also helped by the contemporary international situation. Even before the post-war recovery was completed, the onset of the Korean War and the resulting 'special procurement' (military purchases) came as a distinct boon.[27] In 1952 and 1953 this was equivalent to nearly two-thirds of commercial exports.[28] Similarly, in the 1960s the Vietnam War boosted Japanese exports. Krause and Sekiguchi estimate that the Indo-China war added over one billion dollars to Japanese exports in 1971.[29] The period between 1953 and 1964 saw an unprecedented growth in world trade, particularly in the export of manufactured goods. During this period, the value of total world exports increased from $78 billion to $168.7 billion,[30] equivalent to an annual growth rate of 7 per cent. Exports in manufactured goods grew by 9.5 per cent per annum during the same period. Similar rates of growth of world trade and trade in manufactured goods continued almost until the mid-1970s. According to a World Bank estimate, the rate of growth of world trade between 1960 and 1977 was around 7.2 per cent, and trade in manufactured goods rose by almost 9 per cent per annum.[31] If Japan had simply succeeded in regaining her pre-war share in the present world trade of manufactured goods this would have added quite substantially to her export earnings. But Japan did much more. She improved her share of world trade by raising labour productivity substantially, with a corresponding price competitiveness of exports. In this context, the role of the undervalued yen remained quite significant almost until the collapse of the Bretton Woods System. Initially, the value of the yen in terms of dollars, fixed at a time when Japanese productivity was well below its potential, seemed to be harsh[32] and it continued to be overvalued during the 1950s, but in the following decade it became significantly undervalued. In the summer of 1971, after Canada, the Netherlands and West Germany abandoned the fixed exchange rate and allowed their currencies to float, the yen was described as 'the most undervalued major currency in the world'.[33]

The Role of the USA

The direct role of the USA in the economic revival of Japan should not be underestimated. Admittedly, there were some funnier sides to MacArthur's crusade. He not only wanted to turn Japan into 'the Switzerland of Asia' but also prepare her for 'formal conversion to the Christian faith' and eventually utilise Japan as 'a natural base from which in time to advance the Cross through all of Asia'.[34] However, some of the US efforts to democratise Japan such as the undermining of the *Zaibatsu*, the enactment of anti-monopoly legislation, a radical land redistribution, an encouragement of trade unionism, the enfranchisement of women, the reform of the educational system and the establishment of a parliamentary democracy must be considered as positive contributions, even though their direct economic benefits or costs cannot easily be assessed. The contribution of US aid to the Japanese post-war rehabilitation is well recognised by Japanese scholars.[35] Between 1946 and 1951 Japan received just over $2 billion from the US government (largely in the form of grants), to buy essential raw material, food and engineering goods.

In an estimate published by the Japan External Trade Organisation (JETRO) in 1966 it was shown that the total of current account deficit of Japan in the eighteen years between 1946 and 1964 amounted to nearly US $10.3 billion. During the same period Japan received $2.1 billion in terms of US aid, $7.3 billion in receipts from US special procurement (military purchases in a wider sense), and a net capital inflow of $2.7 billion in the form of long-term credit from the World Bank and the US Export and Import Bank, and long- and short-term private capital inflow, chiefly from portfolio investments. This has led Matsumura to conclude that: 'In retrospect . . . we owe our foreign exchange accumulation [1946-64 period] to three main factors, each of which is closely connected with specific American situations, that is American generosity [US aid], American Far East Policies [special procurements] and American profit-and-loss calculations [capital inflow].'[36] In addition to direct economic aid, between 1951 and 1968 the USA provided military aid to Japan totalling $1.6 billion.[37] Nearly two-thirds of the 2,545 technical agreements signed by Japan with foreign countries between 1950 and 1963 were with the USA alone. The pre-eminence of the USA in technology transfer to Japan continued in the 1960s.[38]

Moreover, the indirect effect of US support on the Japanese economy was substantial. The US government not only saved Japan from the post-war dismemberment suffered by Germany but it sponsored Japanese membership of the United Nations in 1952. Because of US support, Japan was allowed an observer status against the wishes of the Soviet Union,[39] who consented to this only in 1956. This provided Japan not only with a much-needed respectability but also with access to a number of UN agencies and their resources. When Japan joined the General Agreement on Tariffs and Trade (GATT) the USA extended to them the most-favoured-nation treatment. Other, richer countries such as the UK, France and Australia and their dependent territories (fourteen of them in all), did not extend similar treatment.[40] So far as the USA was concerned, Japan's membership of the UN was basically legitimising what was already being practised. Japanese access to the US market remained virtually unlimited at least until the mid-1960s, while Japan was allowed to keep its domestic commodity and capital markets virtually closed to foreigners. However, some opposition in the USA to Japanese products had already started in 1955, when Japan was persuaded to accept a 'voluntary' export restraint on cotton blouses.[41] Such protests gathered momentum in the 1960s. By the middle of the decade as many as 73 products were subject to voluntary export controls.[42] Another issue with economic implications is the Japan-US security arrangement and the US nuclear umbrella. It is often argued that such an arrangement has enabled Japan to escape excessive military expenditure and to concentrate on economic growth. As we shall see later, this expenditure, though small in terms of the proportion of Gross National Product, is not insignificant in absolute terms. The armed forces, the so-called Self-Defence Forces (the SDF), are much more sophisticated than those of her neighbours except the USSR, and the military build-up in Japan originated (and is likely to accelerate) under the direct inspiration (now political pressures) of the US government.

Besides, as Patrick and Rosovsky stress: 'Even if as much as 6 or 7 per cent of GNP has been allocated to defense, it would have reduced the growth rate by at most only two percentage points, even assuming no beneficial spillover effects of defense expenditures.'[43] Under the circumstances, the economic contribution of the Japan-US security arrangement would not be substantial. Moreover it is highly debatable as to which of the two countries gains from such an arrangement in the long run. After all, by becoming the front line of defence for the USA, Japan is probably more susceptible to pre-emptive Soviet nuclear attack. Besides, Japan's vulnerability to a Soviet threat has enabled the USA to obtain economic and trade concessions from her under the implied threat of abandoning their security commitment in the Far East.

Japan's Social System and Value-Orientation

Nevertheless, the success of Japan after World War II was largely the result of efforts by the Japanese elite — the political leadership, the civil service and big business. It was a repetition of the 'social engineering' that had made Meiji Japan into a feared member of the clan of imperial powers of the late nineteenth and early twentieth centuries.

The Japanese elite, in their efforts to 'catch up with the West' and eventually to supersede them, were greatly helped by the Japanese social system and value-orientation. Like many other societies, Japanese society is quite complex, and is composed of a great variety of elements. Besides, it has been undergoing rapid change, in the course of which old values are disappearing and new ones are taking their place. On the other hand, with growing affluence, the self-assertiveness of the Japanese people is increasing. Visible signs of a revival of ultra-nationalism can be occasionally discerned in Japanese literature. This trend is reflected in books like *The Logic of Evil* by Morimichi Kuramae, *The Method of Intellectual Life* by Shoichi Watanabe and Hideo Kobayashi's work on Norinaga Moto-Ori. In view of such complexities, no 'model' would be a true representation of reality of Japanese society today. However, one can construct an approximate picture — not an ideal one — clearly acknowledging that there may be considerable deviations in some cases. There may also be differences of opinion on the relative importance of the components of such a picture. As Dore suggests, 'one man's stereotype is almost as good as any other's'.[44] However, we feel that there are some special features in Japanese society — much more so than in other societies — which seem to have helped rapid economic growth and structural change without major social dissensions. In this context one can draw attention, for example, to Japanese group-consciousness. Quite simply, a Japanese feels more comfortable when he works in a group. This is well described in Dore's comparison between the average Japanese and the average Englishman in this respect. He suggests that the 'Japanese are lesser individualists, are more inclined to submerge their identity in some large group to which they belong, and more likely to be obsessed by a sense of duty'.[45] Against this the 'British are more selfish, more irresponsible, more inclined to tell Jack that they are personally all right'.[46] According to Dore, the 'Japanese care less about what happens outside their own group, and have less sense of social responsibility to correct abuses in their own society' whereas the 'British are more given to busybodying, less willing to live and let live'.[47]

To a Japanese an individual is not identified as a person possessing certain skills (what Nakane[48] terms 'attributes') such as a teacher, a joiner, a truck-driver or a soldier but he is perceived as a member of a group (in Nakane's terminology a 'frame') — a university, a company or a government department. This identification of an individual with his workplace is almost total. To a Japanese the place of work is his *uchi* ('my house') and the company his *kaisha* ('my company' or 'our company') and these have a pervasive influence on all aspects of his life.[49] In such a situation the relationship between worker and employer is not so much a contractual one but an emotional one. This sense of belonging lies behind the exceptional loyalty of Japanese workers, both blue and white collar, to their company. It reduces absenteeism, disregard for quality and industrial strife. Since workers identify themselves with the company and not with a craft, unions have developed along company (enterprise) lines encompassing all the workers — blue collar, white collar and junior executives.[50] As a result, Japan has escaped the misfortune of Britain, where work is often disrupted by demarcation disputes between competing unions within the same company.[51]

A sense of identification by the workers is often reciprocated by the employers. This is distinctly reflected in the 'lifetime employment system'. As is commonly known, the company not only provides conventional fringe benefits such as housing, maternity and hospital benefits and nurseries for children but also monetary gifts from the company on the occasion of marriage, birth or death.[52] Since employers do their best not to lay off their permanent employees during recessions or in the course of a structural change, the workers and their unions do not oppose technological change as much as their Western counterparts. Such a humane treatment of the workers by the Japanese companies is, however, limited only to a small proportion of the labour force. Under the Japanese system of wage employment there are several types of workers engaged by an enterprise.[53] They are the *committed standard workers*, who are employed immediately after graduation from school or university. After an intitial period of training, which may extend up to three years, such recruits are assigned to an appropriate job. These workers enjoy 'lifetime employment', and even after retirement the company helps them in finding another job with a subsidiary or in establishing their own business. They are the main beneficiaries of the fringe benefits provided by the company.

Another group of workers, called the *non-standard commited workers*, are recruited in mid-career by large enterprises from among the smaller companies. Under normal conditions such recruits enjoy a permanent job until retirement, but their terms of appointment — such as seniority-linked wage increases, transfers, promotions, etc. — are not as favourable as those of the *standard* worker.[54] Unlike the *standard* workers, they run the risk of being unemployed if the company is forced to reduce its number of workers. In addition to these two categories of permanent workers, large enterprises have a considerable number of temporary workers, who have neither job security nor are their wages and other benefits as attractive as those of the permanent workers. There is a further category of workers engaged by an enterprise through labour contractors. Such workers are formally the employees of the subcontractors who are responsible for their wages and terms of employment.[55] Workers in the last two categories are more liable to lose their jobs in times of recession. They are not even entitled to join a union, thus finding it difficult to protect themselves against unfavourable treatment by the enterprise. Thus lifetime employment is not a universal phenomenon in Japan. In a survey conducted in 1972 it was found that nearly 51 per cent of all male employees in the non-agricultural private sector belonged to small enterprises employing less than 100 people; another 21 per cent were employed by enterprises of intermediate size with 100 to 1,000 workers; and only 28 per cent were employed in large firms.[56] Lifetime employment was the general rule only for the last category and was only partially applicable for the intermediate category. By and large, most women and the workers in small retailing and industrial enterprises do not have the security of lifetime employment or the seniority-linked wage scale.[57]

It is this group of non-unionised workers without security of employment which suffers most during any serious slowdown of business, and it is primarily this group of workers on whom the main burden of a structural change will fall. Without union power they cannot fight a major retrenchment resulting from structural or technological change. On the other hand, their privileged counterparts, the workers enjoying the guarantee of lifetime employment, have no reason to fear such changes, because they know that their employers would retrain them and place them in an affiliated company. As we shall see later, the conglomerate nature of big business in Japan, covering several fields, makes this absorption of retrained labour easier.

Contrary to popular belief, the lifetime employment system of Japan and the concept of the firm as a community of which both management and workers are members is a clever device which was developed around the turn of the century by large companies anxious to secure a steady supply of skilled and semi-skilled labour for industry, commerce and banking.[58] The system did not have its roots in the Japanese tradition: long-term wage employment was uncommon in traditional industrial enterprises at that time and most industries were organised on a small-scale and on a putting-out system, under which payment was on piece rate.[59] The closest historical example of the present lifetime employment system was that practised by a few large commercial and financial houses of pre-modern Japan such as Mitsui, who recruited workers as apprentices at an early age and supervised their progress. Such employees, in theory, could rise to higher levels of the job hierarchy and some did, but the majority quit their jobs within a few years.[60]

In the early years of Japan's industrialisation, while the supply of unskilled labour was plentiful skilled labour was in short supply. Employers often attempted to lure skilled labour away from their competitors. Associations of employers, through co-operative action, were not effective in reducing the poaching of skilled workers and competitive bidding up of their wages. It is in this context that the system of recruiting young unskilled workers and providing in-job training within the firm was evolved. The seniority-linked wage scale and the fringe benefits were seen as a means for counteracting or minimising the need for organised labour or even a Factory Act. As a result of the employers' opposition, the Factory Act, which was first drafted in 1883, was not enforced until 1915.[61] Labour organisations for collective bargaining and strikes were illegal under the Police Regulations of 1900.[62] It was only after the establishment of the International Labour Organisation in 1919 and Japan's joining the Organisation that labour unions began to find their voice.[63] But the scope of their activities continued to be restricted under the Peace Preservation Act of 1925. The *Zaibatsu* were careful to maintain a common front to stifle the growth of a vigorous trade union movement. As Lockwood stresses, 'the weakness of collective bargaining, even at its height in the twenties, and especially Japan's lagging progress in factory and social legislation, must be attributed in large measure to the intense opposition, led by business interests, which greeted every proposal for advance in these fields. Whatever the business rivalries of big firms, here they closed ranks and presented a solid front.'[64] Managements of large enterprises continue to harbour 'dislike and suspicion of union leadership. Union activists are often punished by being given unimportant jobs and positions that do not lead to rapid promotion.'[65] Befu mentions the case of the Japan National Railway (JNR) which has its motto of *Kokutetsu Ikka* ('JNR, One Family') where the management has, in the past, used 'sanctions against union leaders — ranging from outright firing through docking of wages to reprimand'.[66]

Seen in this light, lifetime employment and the so-called philosophy of harmony and co-operation between employer and employees was a ploy to combat the emergence of a radical trade union movement.[67] In this they ultimately succeeded in the immediate post-World War II period with the help or at least the connivance of the occupation authorities.[68]

Apart from job security and seniority-linked salaries we should consider some other features of the Japanese employment system which have directly or indirectly helped the process of economic growth. Japanese employers make a lump-sum payment to their employees on retirement. This is in lieu of a pension and is equivalent to one or two months' wages in the terminal year of employment for every year of employment with that firm.[69] If a worker retires after 35 years of employment he may be entitled to a lump-sum equivalent to three times or more of his wage for the last twelve months of his work. Because of the tax-exemption provisions (except for the highest salaried executive) such a lump sum is untaxed.[70] For the retired worker, this provides ready capital if he wishes to set up his own business.[71] His previous company may often help him in this by selling him old tools and equipment and by providing technical help and some extra capital, if needed. The former employee, reborn as a small entrepreneur, may easily become a subcontractor for his former employer and continue as a member of the 'family'. However, there are exceptions. In many cases retirement pay is far from adequate for subsistence.[72] Sometimes large enterprises may dismiss permanent workers on the grounds of a recession and later employ the same people as temporary workers.[73]

In Japan the institution of subcontracting is more widespread than in other industrialised countries. For example, in Japan six major car-producers subcontract an average 70 per cent of their material cost against only 30 to 40 per cent by their US and European counterparts, with the only exception of Volvo, which subcontracts almost as much as the Japanese firms.[74] The wide prevalence of the system of subcontracting explains not only the competitiveness of Japanese firms but also their ability to introduce technological change rapidly. Many subcontractors are small or medium-sized firms, where wage levels are lower than those in the larger enterprises. Such firms do not often provide their workers with fringe benefits, and as a result their wage cost per unit of output is lower. Under normal conditions their productivity would also be lower, but Japanese parent firms take complete control of design, specification and quality control.[75]

Rejection ratios are high — often exceeding 20 per cent.[76] The parent firms can also, by transferring the effects of a recession to their contractors, retain their permanent employees. For example, instead of throwing away their used equipment and tools parent firms can often sell them to their subcontractors. This, in effect, means that a part of technological change is also transferred to the subcontractors. For all his services, a subcontractor is allowed only a small margin of profit. Subcontractors can, of course, be independent and work for more than one firm, but many prefer a 'tied' arrangement, as an unaffiliated small enterprise has a rather risky life. As Bronfenbrenner suggests, an 'untied' or 'unaffiliated small business man is by definition neither a favored subcontractor, a favored supplier, or a favored sales outlet for any of the big companies, *Zaibatsu* or otherwise. He suffers because it is his line of credit which is fragile, and sensitive to the slightest hint of credit rationing or tight money. In any recession, he is bankrupted by the thousands, while his workers lose their jobs and seniority.'[77]

Another important feature of the Japanese employment system concerns the payment of bonuses. Most Japanese employers, including the government, pay fairly large bonuses twice[78] a year, in July and in December. This system has some obvious advantages. First, bonuses are not considered a part of the regular wages, therefore the retirement lump-sum calculations do not include them. As such, the bonuses become a device to reduce the pension burden on employers. Second, employers can reduce the labour cost during recessions by adjusting bonuses more easily than seniority-related wages. (But the degree of flexibility is probably much less than is commonly supposed.[79]) Finally, the system of providing employees with a lump sum at six monthly intervals ensures a stable demand for durable consumer goods.

This tendency to obtain durable goods is aided by the Japanese attitude to conformity. 'Keeping up with the Jones' is a well-known phenomenon in other societies, but the Japanese, more than anybody else, 'conform in dress, conduct, style of life, and even thought to the norms of their group'.[80] This attitude towards conformity is fully exploited by sales promotion, and the payment of bonuses every year is invariably followed by a boom in the consumer durables market.

Another major feature of Japanese society is the great emphasis on hierarchy.[81] In Japan human relations are organised mainly on vertical lines, with a ranking order based on relative age, year of entry into a company or date of appointment, etc.[82] As Nakane stresses, 'without consciousness of ranking, life could not be carried on smoothly in Japan, for rank is the social norm on which Japanese life is based'.[83]

For this reason exchange of business cards is so much more important in Japan. It is this exchange which allows both parties to establish their relative ranks and adjust their behaviour towards each other accordingly.

The vertical relationship, traditionally known as the *Oyabun-Kobun* (parent-child), is based on a one-to-one relationship between two individuals, and ensures that the *Kobun* receives moral and material support from his *Oyabun* (sometimes even more than he could expect from his own parents), and in return the *Kobun* owes his allegiance to the *Oyabun* and is ready to offer his services whenever required to do so. By and large, such vertical relationships form one of the main bases of group organisation in Japan.[84] This system invariably works against an ambitious though capable young person. He has to be either content with his own position and to wait his turn in the hierarchy, or quit and form his own group. The 'group' character of Japanese society does not allow for an individual's self-gratification. Nor is there considerable scope for open dissent with his superiors. There is always a risk that this would not only hurt the feelings of a superior and undermine the harmony and order of the group but there is a possibility that a dissenter may be relegated to the position of an outcast.[85] On the other hand, the leader of a group is expected to be sensitive to the feelings of his subordinates. Superiors in Japan do not force their views on their juniors: decisions are taken only after a lengthy process of informal discussion involving subordinates, and juniors are encouraged to submit their individual views. The final decisions are taken by a small group at the top based on the 'consensus'. However, this lengthy, time-consuming process has two distinct advantages. One is educational; all members of staff become fully familiarised with a problem and are therefore in a better position to implement the solution.[86] The other advantage is that subordinates feel part of the decisionmaking process, can identify with the decisions and can therefore implement them more willingly. Sometimes the initiative may come from the junior members of a government department or a large company. The method, commonly known as *Ringi*, is described by Kahn:[87]

> . . . Junior people in a department achieve a consensus among themselves on an issue on which they think a decision should be made, and then they draft a paper on it. The department head will approve the paper. This paper will then be circulated in other departments, usually at the lower levels, with much discussion and correction ensuing. The paper may go back and forth a number of times as changes are made, and eventually a reasonable consensus

is achieved at the lower levels. The paper is then passed on to the department heads and from there to the corporate heads, who now are under serious pressure to sign and forward it to the president's office or other centralized decision-making point for final implementation.

Such 'decisionmaking from below' is very time-consuming but it creates a sense of involvement among young executives and is also a morale-booster for them.[88]

In the group-conscious vertical society of Japan, the value of the man at the top does not necessarily depend on his individual intelligence or competence to do his work but 'on his skill in charming extremely talented subordinates by his personality, his artfulness in synthesizing the group and his ability to direct all the talent at his disposal'.[89] There is always the risk that a man of outstanding personal ability may alienate his subordinates by usurping some of their functions. It is expected of a Japanese team-leader that he 'will be dependent on his men. The leader must have some weaknesses for which his men are always ready to compensate or provide support. Having established a firm relationship in this manner, the followers are always eager to understand and cooperate with the leader's ideas and actions.'[90]

Vertical ranking, the *Oyabun-Kobun* relationship and the group consciousness also pervade industrial and commercial organisations. It is not unusual to find a large business or an industrial firm to act as the *Oyabun* to a number of affiliated and subordinate companies and to treat each as 'child-company'.[91] We have already described the merits and demerits of the system in relation to subcontracting firms. Each group tries to be as self-sufficient as possible in terms of sources of raw materials, finance, transport, marketing, etc. Involvement in a number of sectors and activities means that the risks of business are widely spread. Even in a serious recession not all sectors and activities are equally affected. As a result, such conglomerates survive recessions better than specialised enterprises.

The one-to-one interpersonal relationships have their counterparts in the world of business as well, so a conglomerate (the *Zaibatsu*) keeps its 'solidarity and exclusiveness'.[92] However, in order to compete successfully in the fierce world of oligopolistic competition, every group tries to imitate the pattern of its rival. This has led to the emergence of a 'standard pattern' in every field of activity.[93] This tendency to conform is further strengthened by the Japanese attitude to *relativism*, the desire to belong to a 'select' group. The Japanese are dominated by 'a desire to be on a level similar to the other person who is supposed to be higher than oneself'.[94] Business or industrial enterprises are not immune from this obsession. To rise in the hierarchy of a particular sector is a universal ambition among such enterprises and dropping in an industrial league table is viewed as a social disgrace by both the management and the workers.[95] A major enterprise feels itself 'obliged, for reasons of prestige, to obtain a share of every new industry as it appears and to hold its own in all fields with the rivals'.[96] This motive, at least in part, explains high investment rates even in the face of existing excess capacity.

In a survey of business behaviour conducted by Kobe University, nearly 80 per cent of respondents indicated that maintenance or increase in market share was a major determinant of investment, and nearly two-thirds of this group conceded that their concern for market share originated in one's effort 'to improve one's status in the industry'.[97]

The State and Big Business

This group consciousness and the acceptance of a ranking order as the main elements in the harmonious working of a group has made it easier for the state to provide the lead and for business and industry to follow it. It is commonly accepted that one of the most important factors in Japan's rapid economic growth has been the special relationship between government and business.[98] The fact that there is a close relationship between the political leadership, the bureaucracy and the large companies cannot easily be controverted. As Yanaga suggests, the

> business community shapes the basic trends and direction of Japanese politics as well as the economy. As the largest and most dependable source of funds for political parties, big business is a *sine qua non* of success for political candidates. Business is well represented on the Cabinet, advisory councils, the Diet and the party. Moreover, through the effective use of mass media, some of which it controls, organised business exerts a powerful influence on society as a whole.[99]

Even those who do not believe that the large companies have considerable influence on political parties readily concede that: 'There can be no argument about the importance of the financial aid from business to the LDP [Liberal Democratic Party].'[100] Another reason for the businessmen's influence on political decisionmaking is their intimate relationship with the civil service. Traditionally, these officials are not only responsible for legislative programmes submitted to the Diet by the cabinet but also formulate the budget, offer administrative guidelines, dispense government contracts and allocate subsidies, loans, investments and purchases on behalf of the government.[101] With their wide administrative powers various ministries come into close contact with the industries in their own sphere. Both formal and informal contact is also maintained through the various advisory councils of the ministries. In addition there is considerable scope for social intercourse through elite clubs. On top of all this is the practice of retired civil servants (known as *amakudari*) accepting jobs with businesses. Civil servants generally retire in Japan between the ages of 48 and 55, after which the more ambitious ones enter politics and many become members of the Diet while others join public or private enterprises, banks, etc. Those who opt for political careers after their retirement need the endorsement of a political party, and they have to look to businessmen for funds. There is a natural tendency for an ambitious official to cultivate friendship with influential political as well as business leaders. This they can do by rendering services during their term of office within a ministry through their discretionary powers, of which there are many. Retired civil servants who join a business not only bring with them considerable administrative ability and experience but also intimate personal relationships with their former colleagues in the civil service.[102] This system of recruitment of former government officials to prominent positions in private enterprises has come to be criticised as a major source of political corruption, and demands are now being made for restrictions on the practice.[103]

Nevertheless, the term 'Japan Incorporated', which seems to suggest that politicians and civil servants, in league with big business, manipulate the Japanese economy in their own interests fails to catch the essence of the relationship between these three groups. Only if 'Japan Incorporated' is viewed as a 'familialistic national community' geared to the common national goal of 'washing away the sense of shame'[104] by 'catching up with the West' one comes nearer the truth. From the day Commodore Perry forced Japan to open her doors to foreigners, the goal has remained the same. The tactics after the defeat in World War II had to change. It was inconceivable, in the immediate post-war years, to wash away the sense of shame by militaristic means; therefore the only alternative left was to 'catch up with the West' in economic terms. Most developing countries have felt humiliated by the treatment

they have received at the hands of the West in the past and would like
to catch up with them. But because of the Japanese preoccupation with
relativism, they suffer from an obsession with 'catching up with the
West' and in time of 'surpassing the West'. Much of their foreign policy
and their trade and aid policies have been based on a hierarchical view of
the world.[105] While they have so far found it easier to accept the
superiority of the West, particularly the USA, they find it difficult
to operate on a level of equality with the 'Third World' countries. The
very feeling that Japan has not been accorded her 'proper station in the
world' makes the Japanese feel challenged and, as Hirschmeier stresses,
'in periods of outside challenge economic nationalism takes precedence
over the interests of the individual group. This asserted itself strongest
in the Meiji period, but is notably felt throughout the modern period
because the Japanese feel challenged by the very fact of being still
behind, of still not having attained the first place somehow due to
them.'[106]

Since the Japanese government and the business leaders think very
much alike in terms of 'familialistic national community', their
relationship 'is not that of mutually suspicious adversaries, as in the
United States, but of close collaborators'.[107] This has helped the
government in the setting up of broad objectives and in steering the
economy towards such goals. The legendary role of the Ministry of
International Trade and Industry (MITI) in guiding industrial growth
and in restructuring the Japanese industrial scene is symbolic of this:

> The Ministry of International Trade and Industry [after the war]
> decided to establish in Japan industries which require extensive
> employment of capital and technology, industries that in
> consideration of comparative cost of production should be the most
> appropriate for Japan, industries such as steel, oil refining, petro-
> chemicals, automobiles, aircraft, industrial machinery of all sorts,
> and electronics, including electronic computers. From a short-run,
> static viewpoint, encouragement of such industries would seem to
> conflict with economic rationalism. But, from a long-range viewpoint,
> these are precisely the industries where income elasticity of demand
> is high, technological progress is rapid, and labour productivity
> rises fastest . . . According to Napoleon and Clausewitz, the secret
> of a successful strategy is the concentration of fighting power on
> the main battle grounds; fortunately . . . Japn has been able to
> concentrate its scant capital in strategic industries . . .

... MITI policies have succeeded in the quarter of a century since the war in overcoming an imbalance of surplus population and scarcity of natural resources, capital and technology by bringing about economic development, mainly through encouragement of industry and promotion of exports, and in building on a cramped land area a giant economy that ranks second in the free world.[108]

The MITI not only tries to steer industries towards more advantageous activities but also assists mergers of companies in declining industries.[109] It also attempts to persuade companies in depressed sectors to form a 'depression cartel' to reduce capacity.[110] It encourages formation of consortia for the exploitation of foreign sources of raw materials and markets. In the past it has circumvented or slowed down the process of trade and capital liberalisation to protect the domestic industries, and if foreign political pressures make a change inevitable it persuades exporters to adopt a policy of 'voluntary' restraint. The MITI does not have statutory authority to do many of these things. Much of the leverage can be exerted through the pervasive practice of administrative guidance.[111] There is no obligation on the industries to comply with the desire of the MITI or of any other relevant ministry or agencies, but the industries know that such a policy may be in their own or the national interest. Besides, the civil service has wide-ranging powers to make their life difficult. For instance, it can withhold building permits, regulate raw material imports and discriminate against the company in terms of providing material incentives.

Such material incentives are many. The government may provide capacity expansion loans through financial institutions such as the Japan Development Bank, the long-term Credit Bank or the Industrial Bank of Japan. The last named is privately owned, but it is greatly influenced by the government. Government departments can also influence commercial banks to lend to a particular industry. Sometimes the government guarantees such loans or subsidises the interest. Apart from the conventional methods of tax allowance on depreciation, research and development expenditure and costs of developing foreign markets, the government directly subsidises the development of technology. For instance, out of the total computer research and development expenditure of Y116.5 billion in 1976, direct government grants to companies and associations amounted to Y18.9 billion. Another estimated Y3.4 billion was passed on to the computer manufacturers in the form of tax credits and accelerated depreciation. Another Y5.8 billion of public funds were allocated to university and government laboratories.[112] Thus almost a quarter of the computer research and development expenditure came from public funds. Similarly, for software development the government entered into a joint venture with the computer industry and provided one billion yen as equity and, apart from special tax benefits, provided Y8 billion towards research and development funds between 1970 and 1977.[113] The government has also provided financial assistance to purchasers of computers. It inspired a joint venture with equity-sharing among the seven manufacturers. The Japan Electronic Computer Corporation (JECC) was created to purchase computers from domestic producers and lease them to customers.[114] Almost a third of the finance came from the Japan Development Bank.

Nevertheless, the MITI does not always get what it wants. For instance, it did not succeed in attempts to merge the large car-manufacturers nor could it consolidate the computer industry.[115]

On the whole, the initiative of government departments or their administrative guidance works not because of the fear of sanctions or the temptation of material rewards but because there is a rapport between an industry and the relevant government department. As already pointed out, such goodwill is conscientiously cultivated by both sides in their mutual interest.

Thriftiness and Frugality

Another feature of Japanese society which is considered to have contributed significantly to rapid growth is the Japanese preference for thriftiness and frugality. As Shinohara puts it:

> What should be emphasized here is that thriftiness is a very notable characteristic of Japan, for in this country frugality and thriftiness have been esteemed as important virtues from the Tokugawa feudal age or even earlier, and such thinking continues to exist even now, particularly in the rural areas. The Confucian influence, which had been permeating the way of life of the people including the general public as well as the *Samurai* class, was a decidedly important element.[116]

How widespread[117] this traditional virtue was during the Tokugawa period is difficult to say, but the fact remains that the Japanese savings rate is considerably higher than in other countries. For instance, in 1977,

Japanese gross domestic savings was equivalent to 32 per cent of her GDP as against only 18 per cent for the USA, 21 per cent for Italy and the UK, 24 for France and 25 per cent for West Germany.[118] In 1970-2 the highest contribution of around 44 per cent of the gross savings was made by the household sector representing nearly 17 per cent[119] of the GNP and around 21 per cent of the disposable income. By world standards these savings are pretty high. The share of the corporate sector was a little more than a third. The public sector contributed just over a fifth.[120] The share of corporate savings has increased considerably in recent years. The net contribution of the corporate sector to net savings between 1951 and 1957 was only around 3.9 per cent[121] of the GNP. Such a low share reflects the traditional reliance of Japanese firms on bank lending for capital expansion. In 1972 only 18 per cent of total capitalisation came from equities. The remainder was financed by bond issue and bank loans,[122] the latter being substantially higher than the former. The recent increase in corporate savings has resulted mainly from the boom in corporate profit since 1968, but it has also been supported by various tax concessions and depreciation allowances by the government.[123] Another factor which accounts for a higher level of corporate savings is the low dividend payments, arising mainly because of the inter-corporate stockholdings. In such a situation only the dividend payment to the non-corporate stockholders leaves the corporate sector while inter-corporate dividend payments remain within the sector.[124]

Higher personal savings result not only from the 'traditional' preference for 'thrift' but also from the weaknesses of the economic and social system. Insufficiency of social security, more so for the self-employed and for those engaged in small industries and business, has always been considered as a major cause of high personal savings.[125] To this must be added the Japanese attitude to kinship. In Japan a member of the family living in a separate household is treated as an outsider. Because of the primacy of the household in Japanese society a person cannot fall back on his kin even if he is wealthy. As Nakane mentions, a 'wealthy brother normally does not help the poor brother or sister, who has set up a separate household, as long as the latter can somehow support his or her existence; by the same token the latter will not dare to ask for help until the last grain of rice has gone'.[126] It is the lack of identification with 'outsiders' which explains much of the lack of concern in Japan for the poor and the underprivileged within (such as the *buraku*) and outside Japan. Voluntary organisations in Japan often suffer from a lack of 'social recognition by the general public'.[127]

With the growing international involvement of Japan, such attitudes are changing. In a public opinion poll conducted in June 1979 it was found that 49 per cent of respondents favoured admitting the Vietnamese refugees and 67 per cent were in favour of providing economic assistance to developing countries.

In recent years the situation with regard to pensions has improved significantly. However, large numbers of senior citizens are not protected by any pension scheme at all, and nearly 7 million pensioners who are members of schemes other than employee schemes receive a sum inadequate to meet their barest needs.[128] Medical expenses are another major item for which a family has to save. Although the situation has improved after the establishment of the health care system, the patient (except those over 70 years of age) has to pay the doctor's fee and a third of the cost.[129] Medical services are now reported to be 'plagued by rising medical fees, excessive use of medicine and unnecessarily frequent inspections of the patient'.[130] Housing and education are the other two main reasons for high personal savings. Housing in Japan has been extremely unsatisfactory. Employees in the large companies are initially entitled to single persons' dormitories and later to company-owned houses. Others such as the self-employed have serious difficulties in obtaining houses, particularly in recent years when land prices have rocketed and construction costs have risen substantially. Since 1970 both companies as well as the government have been encouraging employees to buy their own houses by providing them with loans at subsidised interest rates.

Education has a high premium in most Asian societies, and more so in Japan. Even in the 1870s the literacy rate 'was considerably higher than in most of the underdeveloped countries today. It probably compared favourably even then with some contemporary European countries.'[131] Learning has traditionally been considered 'the royal road not only to the professions and to government, but also to business success as well'.[132] By and large, education is fairly democratic in Japan and entrance to even distinguished schools and to the universities is by open competition. Entrance examinations are highly competitive and generate great pressure on the examinee, and as 'the child approaches his crucial entrance examinations, the whole life of the family centres around facilitating his studies'.[133] Families are prepared to undergo considerable economic and other deprivation in order to save and see their children enter prestigious schools and universities. In addition, the cost of education has risen dramatically in recent years. A recent survey by the Federation of Electrical Workers'

Unions in 1979 indicated that the cost of education is the single major factor pushing up the cost of living for workers above the age of 40.[134]

It has been argued that the system of semi-annual bonuses may contribute towards savings, but its role cannot be significant. As we have seen earlier, the bonuses are geared to buying consumer durables and it is doubtful whether much is left after the shopping spree is over. In a survey conducted in October 1977 it was found that 33 per cent of personal savings was to provide for sudden illnesses and emergencies, another 20 per cent for education and weddings of children, 17 per cent for purchase of houses and 15 per cent for retirement.[135]

All in all, there are both economic and sociological reasons for high personal savings in Japan. Economic growth alone cannot explain fully the superiority of Japan's savings performance[136] over most industrialised countries of the world.

Japan's Relative Economic Strength

Beyond doubt the long-cherished ambition of the Japanese leadership of catching up with the West has now come to fruition. On any economic criteria Japan is an economic giant. Its share of world total output (GDP) has increased from only 3.2 per cent in 1955 to just over 10 per cent (Table 1.1) in 1978 against nearly 22 per cent for the USA and 20 per cent for the European Economic Community (EEC). It is one and a half times that of West Germany, a little over twice as much as France, three times that of the UK, and four times that of Italy. Thus in the so-called 'Free World' it is next only to the USA. If the Communist countries are included in the list Japan would be superseded by the Soviet Union by only 30 per cent. In terms of income per capita Japan is ahead of Italy and the UK while still significantly behind West Germany and the USA and marginally behind France. She is also behind Switzerland, Belgium, the Netherlands and the Scandinavian countries.

As mentioned earlier, the Japanese gross fixed capital formation around 30 per cent of GDP is considerably higher than those of the other industrialised countries of the world and exceeds German and French capital formation by as much as 40 per cent and the US, UK and Italian by nearly two thirds. Her gross fixed capital formation in transport, machinery and other equipment exceeds her trading partners by 20 to 50 per cent. In total exports and imports Japan ranks third after the USA and West Germany while it exceeds the UK and

Table 1.1: Selected Economic Indicators, 1979

	Japan	USA	France	Italy	UK	West Germany
Land area (thousand km²)	372	9,363	547	301	244	249
Population (millions)	115.9	220.6	53.5	56.9	55.8[a]	61.3
GDP[a] (at market prices) (billion US $)	973.9	2,112.4	471.6	218.3	309.2	638.9
Share in the world GNP[a] (%)	10.0	21.8	4.9	2.4	3.2	6.6
GDP[a] per capita (US $)	8,480	9,660	8,850	4,590	5,530	10,420
Gross fixed capital formation (% of GDP)	30.2	18.1	21.5	18.8	18.1	21.5
Gross fixed capital formation, transport, machinery and equipment (% of GDP)	10.9	7.3	9.1	7.8	9.2	8.9
Merchandise export fob (billion US $)	103.5	181.8	98.0	72.1	90.8	171.5
Merchandise import cif (billion US $)	110.7	207.1	106.9	77.8	102.8	157.8

a. Refers to 1978.
Sources: The World Bank *World Development Report, 1980:* OECD, *OECD Economic Surveys: Japan* (1980).

Italy substantially. As we shall see later, in terms of the share of world exports Japan accounts for 8 per cent against nearly 12 per cent each for the USA and West Germany. Expressed in terms of per capita, Japanese exports are the lowest, except the USA. The per capita export of West Germany is 2.7 times that of Japan and even the UK export per capita is 50 per cent more than that for Japan. Smaller industrialised countries such as Belgium and the Netherlands in per capita terms export five to six times as much as Japan.

Japan's relative industrial strength and weakness can be assessed from Table 1.2. The resource deficiency of Japan is clearly reflected in the fact that her coal output is a fraction of the total output of the USA and is almost a fifth of that of West Germany. The situation is much the same for natural gas, crude petroleum and iron ore. While in terms of crude petroleum and iron ore West Germany, France and Italy are only marginally better off, in natural gas they are much better endowed, though not as much as the USA or even the UK, which is a poor second to the USA in all three. In spite of this serious resource deficiency Japan has built up a huge industrial capacity. But if the industrial output is expressed in terms of per capita gross manufacturing

Table 1.2: Selected Indicators of Industrial Strengths, 1979

	Japan	USA	France	Italy	UK	West Germany
Coal[a] (million metric tons)	17.6[b]	703.8	18.6	–	122.8	86.9
Lignite and brown coal (million metric tons)	0.04[c]	38.0	2.5	1.1	–	130.6
Natural gas (billion Kcal/m³)	25.9	4,846.1	70.6	125.4[d]	357.8	173.5
Crude petroleum (million metric tons)	0.5	420.5	1.2	1.7	77.8	4.8
Iron ore[e] (million metric tons)	0.5	86.5	31.7	0.3[d]	4.3[d]	1.6
Pig iron and ferro-alloys (million metric tons)	85.7	79.0	20.3	11.6[d]	11.4	35.4
Crude steel (million metric tons)	111.7	124.3	23.4	24.4	21.5	46.0
Aluminium $(A + B)$[f] (million metric tons)	1.8	5.7	0.6	0.3	0.5	0.4
Copper (smelter and refined) (million metric tons)	1.9	2.9	0.04	–	0.1	0.5[g]
Lead $(A + B)$[f] (million metric tons)	0.2	1.2	0.2	0.04	0.2	0.3
Tin (million metric tons)	1.3	3.9	–	–	9.5[d]	3.2[d]
Zinc (million metric tons)	0.8	0.5	0.3	0.2	0.1	0.5
Cement (million metric tons)	87.8	70.5	28.8	39.7	16.1	35.5
Newsprint (million metric tons)	2.6	3.4	0.3	0.3	0.4	0.6
Synthetic rubber (million metric tons)	1.1	2.5	0.5	0.3	0.3	0.4
Sulphuric acid (million metric tons)	6.6	37.9	4.9	3.0	3.5	5.4
Caustic soda (million metric tons)	3.0	11.2	1.3[d]	1.0	–	3.4
Motor vehicles: Passenger cars (millions)	6.2	8.1	3.7	1.5[d]	1.1	3.9
Commercial vehicles (millions)	3.5	3.0	0.5	0.2[d]	0.4	0.3

a. Anthracite and bituminous coal.
b. Includes brown coal.
c. Excludes brown coal.
d. 1978.
e. With differing metal contents: USA 61%, Japan 54%, France 30%, Italy 44%, UK 26%, West Germany 32%
f. A primary, B secondary (obtained from scrap, etc.).
g. Includes smelter for 1978 and not 1979.
Source: UN, *Monthly Bulletin of Statistics*, vol. XXXIV, no.7 (July 1980).
Figures in that publication are given as monthly averages. To convert these into annual averages they have been multiplied by 12.

output, comparable levels have been reached not only by France and
West Germany but also by smaller countries like the Netherlands and
Belgium.[137] There is another similarity: the Netherlands has become
one of the largest exporters of animal products, in spite of the fact that
it is an extremely densely populated country. In the late nineteenth
century, when cheap feed grains became readily available, she decided
to develop a livestock 'processing' economy based on imported raw
materials. What the Netherlands did in the livestock sector Japan has
succeeded in doing in the manufacturing sector. The Netherlands'
record in industrial production is also quite creditable. With only
11 per cent of land area and 12 per cent of population of Japan, her
value-added in manufacturing is 11 per cent of that of Japan.[138]

The fact that comparable feats have been achieved by other
countries in no way undermines the magnitude of Japanese industrial
achievement. As shown in Table 1.2, her production of crude steel
in 1979 was only second to that of the USA and her output of steel was
a little less than the sum total of steel production in the four countries
of the EEC included in Table 1.2. In the current year Japan has
reportedly exceeded the steel output of the USA.[139] In cement Japanese
output during 1979 exceeded US production by nearly 25 per cent,
although it was only three-quarters of the total produced by the other
four countries. Newsprint production in Japan was only three-quarters
of US production but was nearly 70 per cent more than the combined
total of the four EEC countries. In synthetic rubber Japan was
considerably behind the USA as well as the total for the four European
countries. In chemicals such as sulphuric acid and caustic soda Japanese
output exceeded the individual outputs of the European countries but
was far behind that of the USA as well as the combined total of the
four EEC countries. In motor vehicles Japan had almost caught up with
the USA in 1979.[140] Thus in terms of key manufacturing industries
Japan is a major industrial giant. In total output as well as in
diversification of the industrial base she matches the performance of
the USA and individually supersedes the four EEC countries in Table 1.2.

Selected Social Indicators

Contrary to common belief, Japanese industrial achievements were not
bought at the cost of complete social neglect. Admittedly, in the early
post-war years and extending into the 1960s growth objectives were
given prominence almost at a complete neglect of environmental

considerations. The conditions of housing, roads, drainage and domestic sanitary facilities continue to be inadequate by Western standards, particularly when compared with those of the USA. But a comparison between the USA, a country rich in land and resources, and Japan is rather unfair. On the other hand, the US record in providing social amenities for their minorities and minority-dominated areas is not a creditable one. Much the same is true of housing and other social amenities in the urban slums and depressed areas in the UK or France.

Notwithstanding inadequate housing and sanitation, Japanese nutritional and health standards compare favourably with the West (Table 1.3). Average consumption of calories and proteins (animal proteins in particular) in Japan is definitely lower than that of the USA and the European countries. But it is no way deficient in terms of nutritional requirements. It is common knowledge that the richer countries in the West eat excessive amounts of food, particularly animal protein, with almost a callous disregard of the food requirements of the poorer countries, and it is a pity that Japan is indiscriminately copying Western patterns of excessive food consumption. Japan does not compare favourably with either the USA or with the European countries in terms of availability of doctors. But life-expectation at birth in Japan is the highest of the six countries considered here, as are infant mortality rates. In the field of education Japan compares favourably with the West but in terms of enrolment in higher education they are still behind the USA. In terms of consumer durables Japan seems to lag behind the USA but not necessarily the European countries. More recent surveys suggest a high proportion of families owning colour television sets (97.7 per cent), stereo receivers (56.3 per cent), cars (51.7 per cent), refrigerators (99.4 per cent) and washing machines (98.7 per cent).[141] The Japanese obsession for material things is not yet on the wane but increasing concern is being voiced against this. It is being argued that emphasis on materialism is destroying traditional values. The growing need for mothers to work is reported to have turned many children into 'latchkey kids'.[142]

An increasing number of books, magazines and newspapers are reporting that the 'Japanese family is developing along pathological lines'.[143] A number of reports of mothers killing their babies and of children killing their parents have appeared in the press. Nevertheless, on the basis of a statistical analysis of the seven indices — infanticide, parricide, family suicide, elderly suicide, child suicide, illegitimacy and divorce — commonly used to diagnose family pathology, Yuzawa Yasuhiko, Professor of Sociology at Ochanomizu University, concludes

Table 1.3: Selected Social Indicators

	Japan	USA	France	Italy	UK	West Germany
Calories per capita per day (1975-7)	2,840	3,537	3,458	3,462	3,305	3,362
Proportion of calories from vegetable sources (%)	81.3	63.3	63.0	77.5	62.2	61.2
Protein per capita per day (1975-7) (g)	86.5	106.2	102.7	98.2	91.6	85.3
Proportion of protein from vegetable sources (%)	51.6	31.5	36.0	54.4	39.0	36.1
Energy consumption per capita (1978) (kg of coal equivalent)	3,825	11,374	4,368	3,230	5,212	6,015
Population per physician (1977)	850	580	610	490	750	490
Population per nursing person (1977)	290	150	170	330	300	260
Life expectancy at birth (1978) (years)	76	73	73	73	73	72
Infant mortality rate (1978)	10	14	11	18	14	15
Number enrolled in higher education as percentage of population aged 20-24 years (1976)	29	56	24	27	19	25
Number enrolled in secondary school as percentage of age group (15-19) (1977)	93	93	83	73	82	84
Newsprint consumption per capita (1977) (kg)	20.3	41.6	11.0	3.8	25.9	19.4
Television sets per 1,000 inhabitants (1977)	239[a]	571[a]	274[b]	224	324	308
Radio receivers per 1,000 inhabitants (1976)	530	1,882[a]	330	232	706	329
Telephones per 100 inhabitants (1977)	424	744	329	285	415	374
Passenger cars per 1,000 inhabitants (1977)	173	505[b]	314	289	255[b]	326

a. 1975.
b. 1976.
Sources: FAO, *FAO Production Year Book, 1979* (1980): The World Bank, *World Development Report 1980*: UN, *Statistical Yearbook, 1978* (1979); *OECD Economic Surveys; Japan.*

that there is no real increase in the incidence of these social problems. People are more aware of them because of growing coverage by the mass media which has a tendency to sensationalise such issues. He suggests that 'the volume of coverage by these media is the decisive factor determining the general perception of whether the ailing family is or is not a social problem'.[144]

However, the fact remains that the number of people 'dropping out' of society is on the increase, as is juvenile delinquency, the use of drugs and consumption of alcohol.[145] Nevertheless, the crime rate and vandalism in Japan is much the same as in the Western European countries, although it is extremely low compared with the USA (Table 1.4). A comparison of crime rates between Japan and the USA has to be made with a great deal of caution. Japan is traditionally a homogeneous society while the USA is a heterogeneous one; in fact, US society is still in a state of flux and, in spite of its commitment to

Table 1.4: Mortality Rates Resulting from Accidents and Crimes (per 100,000 persons)

	Japan (1978)	USA (1977)	France (1976)	Italy (1975)	UK (England and Wales only) (1977)	West Germany (1978)
Motor vehicle accidents (per million persons)	10.5	22.9	23.3	21.5	11.9	23.1
Accidents caused by fires	1.4	2.9	1.5	0.7	1.3	0.9
Suicides and self-inflicted injury	17.6	13.3	15.8	5.6	8.0	22.2
Homicides and injury purposely inflicted by others (legal interventions)	1.1	9.2	0.9	1.3	0.9	1.2
Total of all types of accidents, etc.	46.4	72.2	93.0	53.8	41.3	74.5

Source: WHO, *World Health Statistics* (1979): WHO, *World Health Statistics* (1980).

'moralism' continues to be an 'unjust' society. Glorification of the 'Wild West' image and the ease with which lethal weapons can be bought and sold also accounts for a high incidence of homicide. In this sense US social behaviour is distinctly different from the parent population in Europe. The suicide rate in Japan is high; this partly reflects increasing social tension, as in the case of West Germany and France, but also because traditionally Japanese society places some degree of respectability on suicide.

Thus even a cursory look at the selected social indicators suggests that Japan does not lag far behind the West, as is often suggested. On the other hand, one has to remember that social problems and tensions emerge not so much in an expanding phase of an economy but in periods when the pace of growth is slowing down. The risk of such problems emerging in Japan certainly exists. Such risks can be further exacerbated by international reaction to Japanese success.

International Repercussions

Japan's outstanding success in catching up with the West has generated considerable international trade friction between Japan and the West. Japan is not only blamed for all Western economic ailments but also for taking undue advantage of US security arrangements without making an adequate contribution towards her own national security. This is reflected in the US slogan of 'free ride'. It is highly debatable whether the USA genuinely wishes to withdraw her armed forces from allied territories or to see Japan and other allies emerging as a major military power but it is not unusual for the USA to use this ploy to extract trade and other economic concessions from her allies. It is commonly known that this 'bargaining tool is particularly important for the United States, whose allies are concerned about potential Soviet threats, and which has fewer other means of influence over its allies than does the Soviet Union over its Eastern European partners. The United States has, accordingly, taken advantage of the Europeans' (particularly the Germans') desire for its protection and linked the issue of troop levels in Europe to trade and monetary negotiations.'[146] The Japanese military build-up has a direct economic advantage, at least in the short run, for the US armament industries, which in the post-Vietnam era had to face severe contraction in demand. The success of the USA in extracting economic and trade concessions from Japan in recent years has also led the EEC, itself a highly protected group of countries, to some hard bargaining with Japan.

Our main concern in this book is with these international issues confronting Japan but domestic and international issues are not mutually exclusive. It is highly likely that Japanese efforts to meet Western demands will hurt her domestic industries. If this creates excessive unemployment, the national 'consensus', on which the stability and the growth of the Japanese economy and society depends, may itself be threatened.

On the other hand, if the Japanese leadership does not accede to Western 'demands' the 'West', particularly the USA, may not hesitate to use the political and economic leverage that she possesses as being a main source of food and raw materials as well as the single largest buyer of Japanese products. As happened in the inter-war years this may threaten the very existence of a liberal Japan and create a favourable environment for the rebirth of militarism. Japan has been living with a sense of being unfairly discriminated against since the 'unequal treaties' of 1858. She has not forgotten her humiliation at the Versailles Conference, when the Japanese request to include 'racial equality' as a basic principle of the League of Nations Covenant was refused by the West. Then came the refusal of the US Senate to ratify the Versailles Conference decision to award the German rights in China to Japan. More recently (in the 1950s) the European countries invoked GATT Article 35 to refuse the most-favoured-nation treatment. Growing pressures for trade liberalisation recreates in the minds of the Japanese leadership the memories of past injustices and exacerbates their sense of suspicion towards the West. Such a fear was expressed by Healey, a member of the British Cabinet, as early as 1971. He argued that due to increasing pressures from the US, the single largest market for Japanese exports, Japan would be forced to diversify her market, and it is possible that a significant part of the displaced products would be redirected towards the EEC. Such a move would certainly be opposed in Europe. He concluded that:

> Apart from the increased risks of a world trade war which would result, it is difficult to imagine that a Japan thus twice rebuffed by the Western world would not turn inwards and rely once more on its military power for both political and commercial influence.[147]

Japan's outstanding industrial success is in this sense more a liability than an asset. It has made Japan increasingly dependent on the US and her 'allies' or 'client' states such as Canada, Australia and Brazil. Almost the entire Japanese grain and oilseeds import comes from the USA, Canada and Australia alone; more than half of the iron ore and iron scraps and nearly 90 per cent of coal and coke come from the above four countries (Table 1.5). Therefore Japan's economic future depends very much on the good will of the USA. Under the circumstances, Japan

Table 1.5: Japanese Import Dependence on the USA and her Allies, 1978 (%)

Items	Japan's share in world imports	Share of countries in Japan's imports				Total of four countries
		USA	Canada	Australia	Brazil	
Wheat (unmilled)	11.6	58.9	22.1	19.0	–	100
Barley (unmilled)	11.0	5.1	52.6	42.4	–	100
Maize (unmilled)	21.2	81.3	–	–	–	81.3
Sugar	12.7	–	–	24.4	–	–
Animal feed stuffs	5.3	45.8	19.9	4.22	–	71.2
Oilseeds, nuts and kernels	20.4	75.6	17.1	–	–	–
Wood (rough)	55.4	22.6	–	–	–	–
Cotton	23.4	35.4	–	–	–	–
Iron ore	40.5	–	–	45.9	18.2	–
Iron and steel scrap	16.3	83.3	–	5.4	–	–
Non-ferrous metal ore	27.1	–	9.0	28.3	–	–
Coal, coke, etc.	30.0	17.0	21.0	48.2	–	–

may find it difficult to resist US pressure or to pursue an independent foreign policy.

Japan's success may be a liability in another sense. After all, the Japanese leadership harbours 'superpower' ambitions as any other major world power, and the vision of the twenty-first century as the Japanese era — the *pax-Japonica* — excites many in Japan. Given their hierarchic view of the world and of *relativism*, it is not unthinkable that they might try to achieve that end. Some Japanese intellectuals are already openly arguing that unless Japan has a military power commensurate with her economic power she cannot be taken seriously by other world powers. It is further argued that if she cannot defend the sea-lanes, the very lifeline of Japan, as a 'processor' of imported raw material she will be at risk. According to this line of thinking, a strong defence capability becomes a precondition of the economic viability of Japan. Some have gone as far as arguing that without a major defence capability Japan cannot be considered even a sovereign state. Such a latent tendency in Japanese society to become 'number one', at least within the so-called 'Free World', is being actively aided and abetted by some American scholars. If Japan seriously decides to become a major military power it has all the ingredients; it is a disciplined and proud nation and it has the economic resources as well as the industrial and technical capability. However, a serious decision to move in this direction is bound to have its repercussions on the USSR, which is already nervous about increasing a security axis between Washington, Peking and Tokyo. The question is not whether such an axis exists, but whether it is perceived as such. This, together with Chinese bellicosity, at least partly explains the Soviet military build-up in the Far East. Coming at a time when the Japanese see the US role declining in the Far East, an increased defence build-up by the USSR provides the 'hawks' in Japan with a credibility they did not possess before.

It is for the same reason that the 'Soviet threat' has been grossly exaggerated in the press and the media in recent months, aided and abetted by the military establishment in Japan. Big business in Japan, particularly the military-industrial complex (though not as large as in the USA), sees in increased military expenditure (and possibly exports of arms, which continue to be illegal) an additional major source of augmenting profits which may be pruned as a result of increasing foreign competition at home and abroad. They have already been asking the government to move in this direction. With their influence with the ruling party and the civil service they may even succeed. If foreign pressures on trade and economic liberalisation results in a substantial increase in unemployment and social distress the labour movement and the left-wing political parties could not sustain their opposition to Japan's becoming a major military power. Thus both because of foreign as well as domestic pressures the economic and defence arguments in Japan have become intertwined. An economically powerful Japan is poised to take decisions regarding her future options which may turn out to be irrevocable not only for Japan but also for the world. It is in this context that this book analyses the nature of economic pressures from the West on Japan and its economic, social and political consequences. It also traces how such foreign pressures, together with the perception of the changing role of the USA in the world and the increasing 'threat' of the USSR are gradually pushing Japanese society away from 'pacifism' to which they had committed themselves after the defeat in the Pacific War.

The first four chapters of this book are mainly economic in nature. The next two chapters examine the nature of the military threat to Japan and the changing attitudes in Japan towards militarisation. The final chapter contains some speculative remarks on the prospect of Japan achieving her objectives as 'number one' of the twenty-first century without walking the slippery slope of militarisation.

Notes

1. E.A. Ackerman, *Japanese Natural Resources*, p.528: quoted in S. Tsuru, *Essays on Economic Development*, p.182.
2. F. Dyson, *Disturbing the Universe*, p.41.
3. Ibid.
4. H. Patrick and H. Rosovsky (eds.), *Asia's New Giant: How the Japanese Economy Works*, p.9.
5. UN Economic Commission for Asia and the Far East (ECAFE), Department of Economic Affairs, *Economic Survey of Asia and the Far East, 1948*, p.34.
6. Tsuru, *Economic Development*, p.160.
7. Patrick and Rosovsky (eds.), *Asia's New Giant*, p.9.
8. Quoted in Tsuru, *Economic Development*, pp.176-7.
9. K. Sheridan, 'A Review of the Japanese National Economic Plans: 1956-1986' (mimeo), p.1.
10. Tsuru, *Economic Development*, p.233.
11. W.W. Lockwood, *The Economic Development of Japan*, p.339.
12. R.E. Caves and M. Uekusa, *Industrial Organisation in Japan*, p.9.
13. Ibid., p.10: see also J. Hirschmeier and T. Yui, *The Development of Japanese Business, 1600-1973*, Ch.4: and K. Noda, 'Postwar Japanese Executives' in R. Komiya (ed.), *Postwar Economic Growth in Japan*, pp.231-5.
14. Caves and Uekusa, *Industrial Organisation*, p.62.
15. E.O. Reischauer, *The Japanese*, p.259.
16. C. Yanaga, *Japan since Perry*, p.654.

17. ECAFE, *Economic Survey of Asia and the Far East, 1950*, pp.233-7.
18. Ibid., p.244.
19. Ibid., p.248.
20. Ibid., p.251.
21. Ibid.
22. ECAFE, *Economic Survey of Asia and the Far East, 1948*, pp.96-7.
23. Ibid., p.102.
24. Ibid., p.103.
25. Tsuru, *Economic Development*, p.224.
26. Ibid., pp.224-5.
27. Ibid., p.161.
28. Ibid., p.185.
29. L. Krause and S. Sekiguchi, 'Japan and the World Economy' in Patrick and Rosovsky (eds.), *Asia's New Giant*, p.419.
30. GATT, *International Trade, 1964*, p.1, table 1.
31. World Bank, *World Development Report, 1980*, p.100.
32. Tsuru, *Economic Development*, p.230.
33. Krause and Sekiguchi, *Asia's New Giant*, p.434.
34. R.W. Van Alstyne, *The United States and the East Asia*, p.168.
35. M. Shinohara, *Structural Change in Japan's Economic Development*, p.16.
36. Z. Matsumura, 'Economic Growth and Foreign Exchange Reserves' in J. Yao (ed.), *Monetary Factors in Japanese Economic Growth*, p.130.
37. J.K. Emmerson, *Arms, Yen and Power: The Japanese Dilemma*, pp.138-9.
38. Ibid., pp.313-14.
39. W.J. Sebald and C.N. Spinks, *Japan: Prospects, Options and Opportunities*, pp.71-2.
40. Krause and Sekiguchi, 'Japan and the World Economy', p.414.
41. R.Z. Aliber, 'U.S.-Japanese Economic Relationships: Economic Structure and Policy in the 1960's, 1970's and 1980's' in M.A. Kaplan and K. Mushakoji (eds.), *Japan, America and the Future World Order*, p.227.
42. Ibid.
43. H. Patrick and H. Rosovsky, 'Japan's Economic Performance: An Overview' in Patrick and Rosovsky (eds.), *Asia's New Giant*, p.45.
44. R. Dore, *British Factory — Japanese Factory: The Origins of National Diversity in Industrial Relations*, p.297.
45. Ibid.
46. Ibid.
47. Ibid., p.298.
48. C. Nakane, *Japanese Society*, p.3.
49. Ibid.
50. Reischauer, *The Japanese*, p.186.
51. For details about the differences in the two countries see Dore, *British Factory — Japanese Factory*, Chs.4-7.
52. Nakane, *Japanese Society*, pp.14-15.
53. M. Tsuda, 'Japanese Wage Structure and its Significance for International Comparison', *British Journal of Industrial Relations*, vol. III, no.2 (1965): see also Dore, *British Factory — Japanese Factory*, Chs. 2 and 3.
54. Tsuda, 'Japanese Wage Structure', p.194.
55. Ibid.
56. W. Galenson and K. Odaka, 'The Japanese Labour Market' in Patrick and Rosovsky (eds.), *Asia's New Giant*, pp.614-15.
57. Reischauer, *The Japanese*, p.185.
58. S. Crawcour, 'The Japanese Employment System', *Journal of Japanese Studies*, vol.4, no.2 (1978), p.245.
59. Ibid., p.227.

60. Ibid., p.228.
61. Ibid., p.229: see also Lockwood, *Economic Development*, p.557.
62. Lockwood, ibid., p.30.
63. Ibid., p.558.
64. Ibid., pp.234-5.
65. H. Befu, 'The Group Model of Japanese Society and an Alternative', *Rice University Studies*, vol.66, no.1 (1980), p.173.
66. Ibid.
67. Crawcour, 'The Japanese Employment System', p.238.
68. Ibid.
69. J. Pechman and K. Kaizuka, 'Taxation' in Patrick and Rosovsky (eds.), *Asia's New Giant*, p.330.
70. Ibid.
71. Caves and Uekusa, *Industrial Organisation*, p.512.
72. Befu, 'The Group Model of Japanese Society', p.172.
73. Joint Struggle Committee for the People's Spring Struggle (ed.), *White Paper on the 1980 Spring Struggle, Sohyo News*, no.358, 15 March 1980, pp.29-30.
74. S. Watanabe, 'Technological Linkages between Formal and Informal Sectors of Manufacturing Industries', mimeographed ILO Working Paper, p.45.
75. Caves and Uekusa, *Industrial Organisation*, pp.511-12.
76. Watanabe, 'Technological Linkages', p.49.
77. M. Bronfenbrenner, 'Japan's Galbraithian Economy', *The Public Interest*, no.21 (1970), p.152.
78. In the case of government employees it may be three times.
79. Galenson and Odaka, 'The Japanese Labour Market', pp.607-8.
80. Reischauer, *The Japanese*, p.127.
81. Ibid., p.157.
82. Much of the description which follows is based on Nakane, *Japanese Society*, Chs. 2 and 3. We are aware of the criticisms of Nakane's 'model' of the Japanese society. (For such criticisms see, for instance, Befu, 'The Group Model': see also R. Mouer and Y. Sugimoto, 'Some Questions Concerning Commonly Accepted Stereotypes of Japanese Society', *Australia-Japan Economic Relations Research Project: Research Paper No.64*.) However, we feel that if Nakane's description is taken not as the ideal type but as a broad approximation she is not too far wrong in her assessment.
83. Nakane, *Japanese Society*, p.33.
84. Ibid., p.42.
85. Ibid., p.37.
86. Reischauer, *The Japanese*, p.188.
87. H. Kahn, *The Emerging Japanese Superstate*, p.44.
88. E.F. Vogel, *Japan as Number One*, p.145.
89. Nakane, *Japanese Society*, p.74.
90. Ibid., pp.68-9.
91. Ibid., pp.96-7.
92. Ibid., p.102.
93. Ibid., p.103. Nakane illustrates this fact with a number of examples. She mentions that the coverage, the content and the layouts are surprisingly similar in each of the three largest daily newspapers in Japan (p.103).
94. Ibid., p.155.
95. A. Boltho, *Japan: An Economic Survey*, p.82.
96. G.C. Allen, *Japan's Economic Expansion*, p.192.
97. Boltho, *Japan*, p.83.
98. Reischauer, *The Japanese*, p.183.
99. C. Yanaga, *Big Business in Japan*, pp.34-5.
100. P.T. Trezise and Y. Suzuki, 'Politics, Government and Economic Growth

in Japan' in Patrick and Rosovsky (eds.), *Asia's New Giant*, p.767.
    101. K. Fukumoto, *Kanryo*, pp.149-238, referred to in Yanaga, *Big Business*, p.104.
    102. Yanaga, ibid., pp.110-12.
    103. T. Tachibana, 'What Must Be Done?' *Japan Echo*, vol. III, no.4 (1976), p.75. Currently a retired civil servant cannot join a private enterprise within two years of retirement, but this rule is often circumvented.
    104. The term 'washing away the shame' of a country in regard to foreign relations was used in a memorandum on the foreign relations of Japan drawn up by the Japanese Foreign Office in 1869.
    105. This has been reflected in the past in various major policy documents. See, for instance, Kahn, *The Emerging Japanese Superstate*, p.33.
    106. J. Hirschmeier, 'The Japanese Spirit of Enterprise, 1867-1970', *The Business History Review*, vol. XLIV, no.1 (1970), p.15.
    107. Reischauer, *The Japanese*, p.191.
    108. OECD, *The Industrial Policy of Japan*, pp.15-17.
    109. Vogel, *Japan as Number One*, p.71.
    110. Ibid.
    111. I.C. Magaziner and T.M. Hout, *Japanese Industrial Policy*, p.34.
    112. Ibid., pp.82-3.
    113. Ibid., p.83.
    114. Ibid., p.85.
    115. Ibid., p.38.
    116. Shinohara, *Structural Change*, p.66.
    117. Japanese philosophers often complained of the extravagance of the rich. One such example is quoted below from Kyuso Muro, a Chu Hsi philosopher (1658-1734):

> From what I have heard about the recent state of the capital, the provinces are full of avaricious officials, and the towns are full of money-grubbers. Many of them, while they seem outwardly to obey the law and be above bribery, work privately for profit and love luxury . . . From what I hear of their intercourse with one another, they strive for sumptuousness in their banquets, they vie with one another in the elegance of songs and dances, and spend immense sums in a day . . . When they see a man who is frugal and honest they ridicule him as rustic and unaccustomed to the ways of the world. (Quoted in R. Tsunoda *et al.*, *Sources of Japanese Tradition*, Vol. I, pp.431-2.)

    118. The World Bank, *World Development Report, 1980*, Annex, pp.118-19, table 5.
    119. H.C. Wallich and M.I. Wallich, 'Banking and Finance' in Patrick and Rosovsky (eds.), *Asia's New Giant*, pp.256-7, tables 4-1 and 4-2.
    120. Ibid., tables 4-1 and 4-2.
    121. K. Kurihara, *The Growth Potential of the Japanese Economy*, p.29, table 12.
    122. Wallich and Wallich, 'Banking and Finance', p.267.
    123. Ibid., p.262.
    124. Ibid., p.263.
    125. Shinohara, *Structural Change*, p.58.
    126. Nakane, *Japanese Society*, p.6.
    127. Ibid., p.62.
    128. *Sohyo News*, 15 March 1980, p.68.
    129. Vogel, *Japan as Number One*, p.187.
    130. *Sohyo News*, 15 March 1980, p.51.
    131. R.P. Dore, *Education in Tokugawa Japan*, p.291.
    132. Ibid., p.293.
    133. Reischauer, *The Japanese*, p.172.

134. *Sohyo News*, 15 March 1980, p.45.

135. US — Japan Trade Council, *Report No. 7*, 15 Feb. 1980, p.16.

136. K. Odaka, 'An Analysis of the Personal Consumption Expenditure in Japan, 1892-1967' quoted in Wallich and Wallich, 'Banking and Finance', p.259.

137. According to the World Bank gross manufacturing output per capita in 1975 in the Netherlands was $2,391 against $2,561 for Japan. (*World Development Report, 1980*, p.121.)

138. Estimates based on the *World Development Report, 1980*, p.121.

139. P. Hazelhurst, 'Economic Miracle Based on Hard Work, Superior Skills and Ability to Adapt', *The Times*, 21 July 1980.

140. Recent reports suggest that in terms of total car output Japan has now superseded the USA.

141. US-Japan Trade Council, *Report No. 7*, p.19.

142. Ibid., p.6.

143. Y. Yasuhiko, 'Analyzing Trends in Family Pathology', *Japan Echo*, vol. VII, no.3, p.77.

144. Ibid., p.85.

145. US-Japan Trade Council, *Report No. 7*, p.6.

146. R.O. Keohane and J.S. Nye, *Power and Interdependence*, p.28.

147. D. Healey, 'The Japanese Threat', *Sunday Times*, 3 October 1971.

2 THE NATURE AND COMPOSITION OF JAPANESE FOREIGN TRADE

The Relative Importance of Japanese Foreign Trade

For almost two decades Japan has not only been the envy of the world but has also aroused significant hostility in the West from governments and manufacturers because of her rapid rate of economic growth and her export performance. Admittedly, in terms of the rate of growth of exports, Japan has done very well; starting from a narrow base, particularly after World War II, her performance has been quite outstanding. But in terms of various indicators such as exports as a proportion of GNP of world exports, or of the total exports of the industrialised countries, her share is considerably lower than that of other developed nations. For instance, Japanese exports account for only 10 per cent of her GNP as against 16.8 per cent for France and between 22 and 23 per cent for Italy, West Germany and the UK. Among the six major industrialised countries in the non-Communist world, only in the USA are exports less significant as a percentage of GNP than in Japan. In view of the size and geographical diversity and richness of the USA this is not surprising.

Similarly, Japan's share in world exports, though higher than those of France, Italy and the UK is significantly lower than those of the USA and West Germany. In fact, the Japanese share is only 60 per cent of that of West Germany, 10 per cent as against 16.3 per cent for West Germany and 17.2 per cent for the USA (Table 2.1).

Table 2.1: The Relative Importance of Exports in Selected Countries, 1979 (%)

Countries	Share of GNP	Share of world exports	Share of total exports of industrial countries
Japan	10.0[a]	6.8	9.7
USA	7.8	12.1	17.2
France	16.8[a]	6.7	9.5
Italy	22.3	4.8	6.8
UK	23.2[a]	6.0	8.6
West Germany	22.6	11.4	16.3

a. 1978.
Based on: IMF, *International Financial Statistics*, vol. XXXIII, no.7 (July 1980).

In per capita terms, in 1979 Japan exported only about $883 worth of goods as against $2,802 for West Germany, $1,890 for France, $1,631 for the UK and $1,269 for Italy. Only the USA at $826 had a lower figure of per capita exports than Japan (Table 2.2). Therefore there does not seem to be any real justification for the West's view of Japanese exports as a threat to employment.

Table 2.2: Per Capita Exports and Imports of Selected Countries, 1979 (in US $)

Countries	Exports	Imports	Ratio between imports and exports (imports ÷ exports)
Japan	882.7	947.7	1.07
USA	826.0	994.7	1.20
France	1,889.8	2,008.4	1.06
Italy	1,269.2	1,369.9	1.07
UK	1,630.5	1,844.3	1.13
West Germany	2,802.2	2,603.7	0.93
EEC	2,220.6	2,324.3	1.05

Calculated on the basis of mid-1979 population totals and dollar values of 1979 exports and imports reported in IMF, *International Financial Statistics*, vol. XXXIII, no.7 (July 1980).

It is true that the ratio of Japanese imports per unit of exports is much lower than those of the USA and the UK but it is very close to France and Italy as well as the EEC as a whole. Apart from the fact that a low import/export ratio may reflect higher efficiency in the use of raw materials and intermediate products, it is also true that Japan and West Germany are the two most developed countries with the poorest natural resources. In fact, West Germany is somewhat better placed than Japan (Table 2.3). Both countries are totally dependent on imported oil. However, as seen earlier, West Germany has an abundant domestic supply of coal, whereas Japan has to import a little over three-quarters of its coal. Similarly, in natural gas reserves, West Germany is relatively better off. In iron ore the situation of the two countries is similar but in lumber Japan is far more dependent on imports than West Germany. The latter is also far more self-sufficient in food. While domestic grain production in West Germany was around 380 kg per person in 1978, in Japan it was only 140 kg.[1] Similarly, meat production per capita in Japan was only 21 kg against 72 kg for West Germany.[2]

Table 2.3: Import Dependence of Selected Countries (%)

Items	Japan (1976)	USA (1976)	West Germany (1976)	France (1974)	UK (1974)	Italy (1974)
Wheat	96.3	0.1	24.1	–	32.2	20.7
Maize	99.9	–	97.0	–	100.0	45.0
Soybeans	97.0	–	100.0	–	–	–
Beef	23.4	4.8	14.7	–	17.1	32.0
Cotton	100.0	1.3	100.0	100.0	100.0	99.6
Wool	100.0	28.6	100.0	82.0	53.2	82.4
Lumber	66.5	0.2	10.0	3.1	77.6	43.9
Iron ore	99.4	36.5	95.4	8.8	80.3	97.9
Copper	93.3	24.6	99.1	99.9	100.0	99.7
Lead	66.0	12.0	85.4	88.2	98.5	88.9
Zinc	67.8	24.4	84.2	95.3	98.9	61.6
Bauxite	100.0	87.2	100.0	–	100.0	91.0
Tin	99.8	100.0	88.5	98.2	80.8	100.0
Nickel	99.3	100.0	99.1	100.0	100.0	100.0
Coal	77.6	0.2	3.5	37.2	–	93.5
Crude oil	99.7	39.4	95.0	99.1	99.9[a]	99.2
Natural gas	72.3	4.6	59.6	–	–	–

a. Since the development of North Sea oil, the UK's dependence has been considerably reduced, and it is now self-sufficient in crude oil.
Sources: JETRO, *White Paper on International Trade: Japan 1976*, p.10, table 5, for France, UK and Italy: US Government General Accounting Office, *United States-Japan Trade: Issues and Problems*, p.12, table 4, for Japan, USA and West Germany.

Although Japan's balance of trade and her international reserves have attracted a great deal of attention and criticism in the West, they have been no stronger than those of West Germany. A summary of the balance of trade situations of the various countries is given in Table 2.4.

It is clear that in all the seven years between 1973 and 1979 both Japan and West Germany had positive trade balances. Except in 1978, when the Japanese trade surplus was marginally greater than that of West Germany, Japan's surpluses were considerably less than the corresponding totals for West Germany. Even in 1979, when the Japanese balance had dropped from an all-time high of $25.3 billion to only $1.9 billion, the German balance stood at $13.2 billion.

Much the same can be said about the balance on current account, except that in the three years when Japan had a surplus on current

Table 2.4: Trade Balance^a of Selected Countries (in billion US $)

Countries	1973	1974	1975	1976	1977	1978	1979
Japan	3.7	1.4	4.9	9.8	17.1	25.3	1.9
USA	1.0	−5.3	9.1	−9.3	−30.9	−33.8	−29.5
France	0.7	−4.3	1.0	−4.6	−2.7	0.7	−1.6
Italy	−3.7	−8.5	−1.2	−4.2	−0.1	2.9	−
UK	−5.9	−12.0	−6.8	−6.4	−3.4	−2.3	−6.3
West Germany	14.8	20.7	15.9	15.1	18.3	23.4	13.2

a. Merchantile exports minus imports, both fob.
Source: IMF, *International Financial Statistics*, vol. XXXIII, no. 7 (July 1980).

Table 2.5a: Current Account Balance^a of Selected Countries (in billion US $)

Countries	1973	1974	1975	1976	1977	1978	1979
Japan	−0.1	−4.7	−0.7	3.7	10.9	17.6	−8.3
USA	7.1	2.1	18.3	4.5	−14.1	−13.6	−0.2
France	−0.6	−5.9	0	−5.9	−3.0	3.8	1.6
Italy	−2.2	−8.0	−0.6	−2.9	2.5	6.4	−
UK	−2.6	−8.0	−3.9	−2.1	−0.2	1.9	−4.9
West Germany	4.6	10.1	3.9	3.5	3.9	8.8	−8.5

a. Includes goods, services and private transfers.

Table 2.5b: Balance on Services^a (in billion US $)

Countries	1973	1974	1975	1976	1977	1978	1979
Japan	−3.5	−5.8	−5.3	−5.7	−5.9	−7.0	−9.1
USA	10.3	14.9	14.1	19.1	21.9	25.7	35.4
France	0.8	1.0	1.6	1.2	2.6	6.4	7.1
Italy	2.0	1.0	1.2	2.0	3.4	5.0	−
UK	4.4	5.1	4.1	5.8	5.2	7.9	6.5
West Germany	−4.6	−4.6	−5.1	−4.6	−7.1	−6.3	−11.2

a. 'Other goods, services and Income' in the IMF classification.
Source: IMF, *International Financial Statistics*, vol. XXXIII, no. 7 (July 1980).

account, she had greater surpluses than those for West Germany
(Table 2.5a).

The position of the international reserves as well as the gold reserves
indicate similar stories. West German international reserves have
consistently remained healthier than the Japanese (Table 2.6a).
Admittedly, the position of Japanese reserves in 1978 was the strongest
of the five countries other than West Germany, but even then Japanese
reserves were only two-thirds of West German reserves. However, in
1979, the Japanese reserves fell from $32.4 billion to only $19.5
billion while the West German reserves rose to $52.6 billion. It may
also be noted that Japanese gold reserves, though comparable with those
of the UK are considerably lower than those of the other four countries
(Table 2.6b).

Table 2.6a: International Reserves[a] *in Selected Countries (in billion US $)*

Countries	1973	1974	1975	1976	1977	1978	1979
Japan	11.4	12.6	12.0	15.8	22.3	32.4	19.5
USA	2.7	4.2	4.6	7.2	7.6	7.0	7.8
France	4.3	4.5	8.5	5.6	5.9	9.3	17.6
Italy	3.0	3.4	1.4	3.3	8.1	11.1	18.2
UK	5.6	6.0	4.6	3.4	20.1	16.0	19.7
West Germany	28.2	27.4	26.2	30.0	34.7	48.5	52.6

a. Total reserves minus gold.

Table 2.6b: National Gold Reserves in Selected Countries (in million troy ounces)

Countries	1973	1974	1975	1976	1977	1978	1979
Japan	21.1	21.1	21.1	21.1	21.6	24.0	24.2
USA	276.0	276.0	274.7	274.7	277.6	276.4	264.6
France	100.9	100.9	100.9	101.0	101.7	102.0	81.9
Italy	82.5	82.5	82.5	82.5	82.9	83.1	66.7
UK	21.0	21.0	21.0	21.0	22.2	22.8	18.3
West Germany	117.6	117.6	117.6	117.6	118.3	118.6	95.3

Source: IMF, *International Financial Statistics*, vol. XXXIII, no. 7 (July 1980).

Thus on almost all criteria — total and per capita exports, surplus on balance of trade or on current balance as well as reserves — the Japanese performance was poorer than that of West Germany. What can explain the West's fury over Japanese export performance? As we shall see later, after 1971 Japan, though under pressure from the West, was opening up its economy to foreigners fairly rapidly. Therefore 'closeness' of the economy cannot be a justifiable excuse for 'Japan-bashing'. One has to look for both non-economic as well as economic reasons for these views. Non-economic explanations are speculative but do not lack credibility. One of the main reasons for these persistent complaints was the image of Japan as a highly successful country. Unfortunately, Japan became the victim of her own propaganda (and that of her well-meaning friends who were bent on proving Japan to be number one in everything). By its pronouncements and actions Japan started to believe (and make the world believe) that it had not only come of age but was also an economic 'superpower'. The West Germans, even if they had similar feelings, were not so vocal. It can also be surmised that because of the Eurocentric thinking of the West, Japan's power continues to be suspect. Increasing industrialisation in the East has always been considered a threat to the West[3] and, naturally, Japan's rapidly expanding industries which challenge their Western counterparts in their domestic markets could not be viewed otherwise. Similar attitudes are evident regarding the newly-industrialising countries such as Taiwan, Korea and Singapore. This is clearly reflected in titles like 'A Recurring Trade Crisis with Japan to be Repeated by the "New Japans"'[4] or 'Anticipating Disruptive Imports' in official publications.[5]

However, the main reason for the West's alarm over Japanese exports lies in the *direction* of her exports (which, though fast-changing, has been largely centred on the USA) as well as on the *commodity concentration* (i.e. dependence on a small number of items). The latter, even though rational on economic or technological grounds, often hurts the importing countries in sensitive areas and thereby creates political problems.

To understand the nature of and the justification for the West's grievances it is important to analyse the direction and composition of Japanese trade. This is what we shall attempt to do in the remaining part of this chapter.

The Direction of Japanese Foreign Trade

Exports

Japan's exports in 1979 totalled $103 billion (fob).[6] Out of this total nearly $48.8 billion went to the developed countries and $46.9 billion to the developing countries. The remaining $7.4 billion worth of exports was destined for the Communist countries (Table 2.7). Between 1974 and 1979 the share of Japanese exports in the developed world marginally declined from 47.6 per cent to 47.3 per cent, while the share of exports to developing countries as well as to Communist countries increased marginally. Thus the developing countries' markets are nearly as important to Japan as those of the developed countries. On a regional basis, North America still constituted the largest single market, buying 27.3 per cent of Japanese exports, closely followed by the South-east Asian developing countries, which bought 25.3 per cent. The share of Western Europe in Japanese exports has remained almost constant at 16 per cent. The share of the EEC increased from 10.8 per cent to 12.3 per cent during the same period. While the EEC has raised so much fuss about increasing imports from Japan, her imports from Japan are less than half those of South-east Asia and a little more than those of

Table 2.7: Japan's Exports by Regions (totals in billion US $)

Regions	1974		1979	
	Total	Percentage share	Total	Percentage share
Developed countries	26.4	47.6	48.8	47.3
North America	14.4	25.9	28.1	27.3
Western Europe	8.6	15.5	16.4	15.9
EEC	6.0	10.8	12.7	12.3
Australia, New Zealand	2.5	4.5	3.2	3.1
South Africa	1.0	1.7	1.0	1.0
Developing countries	25.2	45.4	46.9	45.5
Latin America	5.1	9.1	6.6	6.4
South-east Asia[a]	12.7	22.9	26.1	25.3
Middle East and North Africa	3.7	6.6	10.7	10.4
Sub-Saharan Africa	3.5	6.4	3.1	3.0
Communist countries	3.9	7.1	7.4	7.2

a. Includes South Asia.
Based on the Ministry of Finance figures, quoted in US-Japan Trade Council, *Yearbook of US-Japan Economic Relations, 1978* (1979), p.124, table 25: US-Japan Trade Council, *Yearbook of US-Japan Economic Relations, 1979* (1980), p.119, table 24.

the Middle East and North Africa. The relative importance of the
different countries as importers of Japanese goods is shown in Table 2.8.
The fifteen countries listed account for two-thirds of Japanese exports.

*Table 2.8: Japan's Exports by Countries, 1979 (totals in billion US $,
share in percentages)*

Countries	Total	Share of total	Rank
USA	26.4	25.6	1
South Korea	6.3	6.0	2
Taiwan	4.3	4.2	3
West Germany	4.3	4.2	4
Saudi Arabia	3.8	3.7	5
China	3.7	3.6	6
Hong Kong	3.4	3.3	7
UK	3.1	3.0	8
Australia	2.6	2.5	9
USSR	2.5	2.4	10
Singapore	2.7	2.6	11
Indonesia	2.1	2.0	12
Canada	1.7	1.7	13
Thailand	1.7	1.7	14
The Netherlands	1.7	1.7	15

Based on US-Japan Trade Council, *Yearbook, 1979*, p.17, table 24.

Obviously, the USA, with a quarter of Japanese exports, is by far the
largest importer. Next is South Korea, with about 6 per cent. Of the
European countries, only West Germany and the UK appear among the
first ten importers from Japan. However, the entire imports of the EEC
from Japan are significantly less than the sum total of Japanese exports
to South Korea, Taiwan and Hong Kong. Therefore, while there may
be a genuine reason for the grievances of the USA against Japan, EEC
complaints, at least on grounds of total imports from Japan, are difficult
to understand.

Commodity Composition of Exports

The commodity composition of Japanese exports is summarised in
Table 2.9. Machinery and transport equipment constituted about
46 per cent of Japanese exports, closely followed by manufactured
goods, which accounted for nearly a third of exports in 1974. As we

Table 2.9: Commodity Composition of Japanese Exports (total in billion US $; share in percentages in total)

Commodity groups	1974		1979	
	Total	Share (%)	Total	Share (%)
Food and live animals	0.8	1.5	1.1	1.0
Beverages and tobacco	0	0.1	0.1	0.1
Crude materials (excl. fuels)	1.1	2.0	1.2	1.1
Mineral fuels	0.2	0.4	0.4	0.4
Animal and vegetable oils and fats	0.1	0.2	0.1	0.1
Chemicals	4.1	7.3	6.1	5.9
Manufactured goods, classified mainly by materials	18.7	33.7	26.1	25.4
Machinery and transport equipment	25.3	45.5	55.3	53.7
Miscellaneous manufactured goods	4.4	7.9	11.6	11.2
Unclassified	0.8	1.5	1.1	1.1

Based on US-Japan Trade Council, *Yearbook, 1979*, pp.119-20, table 24. The figures for some groups in this table are different to those reported in JETRO, *White Paper On International Trade, 1979*. Such differences arise as a result of differences in classification. For instance in the *White Paper* 'precision instruments' are included under 'machinery and equipment', whereas in the above table they are listed under 'miscellaneous manufactured goods'.

shall see later, because of increasing trade protectionism in the West and increasing competition from the developing countries, coupled with the increasing sophistication of Japanese manufacturing, an increased ability to move into high value-added per worker branches of production and an increasing willingness to allow labour-intensive branches to decline, the relative importance of manufactured consumer goods, particularly textiles, iron and steel products, etc. has declined significantly. The group share came down from 33.7 per cent in 1974 to only 25.4 per cent in 1979. There was some fall in the share of chemicals as well. Against this, the share of machinery and transport equipment as a group increased from 45.5 per cent to 53.7 per cent between 1974 and 1979. Similarly, miscellaneous goods such as scientific, medical and optical instruments, watches and clocks, tape recorders and record players improved their share.

Among manufactured items, metal and fibre goods are the most important and have created a major international controversy. Iron and steel products, constituting nearly three-quarters of Japanese metal goods exports, are by far the most important group.[7] In 1978 these consisted of steel pipes and tubes (19.3 per cent), light plates (13.8 per cent), hoop steel (9.2 per cent), bars and shaped steel (8.1 per cent), heavy plates (6.4 per cent) and other iron and steel items (17.0 per cent). The remaining goods in this group consist of metal manufactured items and non-ferrous metals.

Nearly 26 per cent of iron and steel exports were destined for South-east Asia; North America and the Communist bloc countries each imported around 21 per cent; almost a quarter was shared between West Asia (11.7 per cent), Central and South America (8.2 per cent) and Africa (4.6 per cent). The share of Western Europe was a mere 4.2 per cent and Oceania's (Australia, New Zealand and Pacific Islands) only 2.2 per cent. In terms of value, the EEC's iron and steel imports from Japan were significantly less than those of Singapore.

The share of textiles in Japanese exports has been declining rapidly. Between 1974 and 1978 it came down from 7.3 per cent to only 5.0 per cent. Woven fabrics, primarily of synthetic fibres, constitute slightly more than half of the textile exports, secondary textile products such as apparel account for nearly a fifth and textile raw materials, such as synthetic yarns, threads and fibres, between them account for just over a quarter. In terms of destination the South-east Asian markets are the largest importers of Japanese textiles, accounting for nearly 36 per cent of exports; the share of North America is around 16.7 per cent, closely followed by West Asia with 15.9 per cent. Africa and Central and South America import around 11 per cent and the Communist bloc 8.5 per cent. Western Europe's share is only 6.9 per cent. Japan's textile exports to the EEC in 1978 were less than half of her exports to Hong Kong during the same year.

As seen earlier, Japanese chemical goods have not fared well during the last few years. Their share in total exports declined from 7.3 per cent in 1974 to only 5.2 per cent in 1978. Two most important items in this group are organic compounds and man-made plastics, which between them constitute nearly two-thirds of the chemical exports. South-east Asia is by far the largest market, taking about half (48.4 per cent) of total exports. Next come the Communist bloc countries with 14.5 per cent, closely followed by 12.3 per cent for North America and only 11.7 per cent for Western Europe. The EEC imports of Japanese chemicals in 1978 were lower than those of Taiwan.

Contrary to the experience with exports of textiles, metals and chemicals, the share of Japanese machinery and equipment rose from nearly 50 per cent to 64 per cent of total exports.[8] Among this group, transport machinery had the biggest share with 43.9 per cent, which represented a slight decline from the previous year. The share of electrical machinery remained almost constant around 26 per cent. General machinery, which in 1978 accounted for nearly 23 per cent, also showed some decline but precision machinery recorded a slight increase. North America, with her 30.7 per cent share, continued to be by far the largest market for Japanese machinery exports. South-east Asia with her 19.4 per cent became the second largest market, overtaking Western Europe with 18.1 per cent. West Asia took nearly 9.3 per cent. Central and South America and Africa between them bought around 7.6 per cent and another 7 per cent was split almost equally between the Communist bloc countries and Oceania. The share of the EEC was 13.5 per cent, just over two-thirds of the totals for South-east Asia (Table 2.10).

It seems, therefore, that while in terms of total exports the USA leads South-east Asia by a small margin, this lead is not always maintained by individual commodity groups. South-east Asia's share in Japanese exports exceeds that of the USA for foodstuffs, raw materials and fuels, and textiles. The same is true with chemicals, metal and metal products. It is mainly in the cases of machinery and equipment, including transport equipment and precision instruments, that the USA has a significant lead. She also has an edge over South-east Asia in non-metallic mineral products and light industrial goods, but this lead is rather small. Against this the EEC buys only a small proportion of Japanese exports. It is only in the case of precision instruments that the EEC buys just over a quarter of Japanese exports; in light industrial products its share is only 18 per cent, for machinery and equipment only 13 per cent and even for transport equipment only 12 per cent. In most cases, with the sole exception of precision instruments, the EEC buys significantly less than South-east Asia. As seen before, its overall share of Japanese exports is less than half of South-east Asia.

Imports

Japan's total imports in 1979 amounted to around $110.7 billion, out of which nearly $43.0 billion, i.e. about 39 per cent, was from the developed countries and around 62.2 billion, or nearly 56 per cent, came from developing countries (Table 2.11). As a result of Japan's heavy dependence on imported fuel, the Middle East and North Africa had the largest share, with around 27 per cent. The second largest share was that of South and South-east Asia, followed closely by North

Table 2.10: The Relative Importance of the USA, South-east Asia and the EEC for Selected Japanese Exports, 1978 (in billion US $, shares in percentages)

	Total	USA		South-east Asia		EEC	
		Total	Percentage share	Total	Percentage share	Total	Percentage share
Foodstuffs	1.1	0.2	21.0	0.3	26.7	0.1	8.6
Raw materials and fuels	0.9	0.1	8.0	0.5	51.7	0.1a	5.8
Light industrial products	11.1	2.3	21.0	3.3	29.5	1.3	11.4
Textiles	4.9	0.7	14.6	1.8	36.1	0.3	5.8
Non-metallic products	1.4	0.4	29.0	0.4	26.1	0.1b	3.6
Other light industrial products	4.9	1.2	25.2	1.2	23.8	0.9	18.2
Chemicals	5.1	0.6	11.6	2.5	48.4	0.5	9.4
Metal and metal products	16.0	3.5	21.9	4.2	26.3	0.1	3.7
Iron and steel	11.9	2.4	20.1	3.1	26.2	0.3	2.4
Machinery and equipment	62.5	18.0	28.7	12.1	19.4	8.4	13.5
General machinery	14.2	2.7	19.0	4.5	31.5	1.2	8.5
Electrical machinery	16.2	4.7	29.2	3.6	22.1	2.7	12.8
Transport equipment	27.4	9.1	33.0	3.3	12.0	3.3	11.9
Motor vehicles (excl. parts)	15.5	7.0	45.3	1.6	10.1	1.8	11.6
Ships and boats	7.2	0.2	2.9	0.9	12.3	0.8	11.0
Precision instruments	4.7	1.5	31.5	0.8	16.7	1.2	26.2
Total exports	97.5	24.9	25.5	23.1	23.7	11.1	11.4

a. West Germany and Belgium and Luxemburg only.   b. West Germany only.
Based on JETRO, *White Paper on International Trade*, 1979.

Table 2.11: Japan's Imports by Region (totals in billion US $, cif, shares in percentages)

	1974		1979	
	Total	Percentage share	Total	Percentage share
Developed countries	25.8	41.5	43.0	38.9
North America	15.4	24.7	24.5	22.2
Western Europe	5.2	8.4	10.1	9.1
EEC	4.0	6.4	7.6	6.9
Australia, New Zealand	4.4	7.1	7.1	6.4
South Africa	0.8	1.2	1.3	1.2
Developing countries	33.2	53.4	62.2	56.2
Latin America	2.7	3.5	4.5	4.1
South-east Asia[a]	12.5	20.1	26.2	23.7
Middle East and North Africa	15.9	25.6	29.4	26.6
Sub-Saharan Africa	1.6	2.5	1.6	1.5
Communist countries	3.1	5.1	5.4	4.9

a. Includes South Asia.
Source: US-Japan Trade Council, *Yearbook, 1978*, p.125, table 25: US-Japan Trade Council, *Yearbook, 1979*, p.118, table 25.

America. Once again this was mainly because of Japan's dependence on imported food and raw materials. In spite of significant increases in oil prices, the share of the Middle East and North Africa increased only slightly betwen 1974 and 1979, while the share of North America declined from 24.7 per cent in 1974 to 22.2 per cent in 1979. During the same period other developed countries of Western Europe, including the EEC, increased their share slightly. Among the developing regions, the shares of South-east Asia, Latin America and the Middle East and North Africa increased at the expense of sub-Saharan Africa.

Even in the case of Japanese imports, the USA is by far Japan's largest supplier, providing nearly 18 per cent of her imports (Table 2.12). The second in rank is Saudi Arabia, with nearly 11 per cent. Indonesia account for 8 per cent, and Australia around 6 per cent. Kuwait, Iran and Canada each supply around 4 per cent. The share of the remaining eight countries varies between 1.5 per cent for the UK and 3.3 per cent for the United Arab Emirates. It is important to note that in the first

Table 2.12: Japan's Imports by Countries, 1979 (totals in billion US $, cif, shares in percentages)

Countries	Total	Share of total	Rank
USA	20.4	18.5	1
Saudi Arabia	12.1	11.0	2
Indonesia	8.8	7.9	3
Australia	6.3	5.7	4
Kuwait	4.4	4.0	5
Iran	4.3	3.9	6
Canada	4.1	3.7	7
United Arab Emirates	3.6	3.3	8
South Korea	3.4	3.0	9
Malaysia	3.3	3.0	10
China	3.0	2.7	11
West Germany	2.6	2.3	12
Taiwan	2.5	2.2	13
USSR	1.9	1.7	14
UK	1.7	1.5	15

Based on US-Japan Trade Council, *Yearbook, 1979*, p.118, table 25.

ten countries at least five (Saudi Arabia, Indonesia, Kuwait, Iran and the United Arab Emirates) are oil-producing countries; the USA, Canada and Australia, though developed industrialised countries, are large producers of primary products. Among the developed exporters of manufactured goods only West Germany and the UK have any significant share, their combined totals being 3.9 per cent. South Korea and Taiwan, with their combined total of 5.3 per cent, represent the newly emerging industrialised nations.

The Commodity Composition of Imports

Mineral fuels were much the most important category of Japanese imports in 1979. Their share was 40.9 per cent, followed by 19.7 per cent for crude materials (Table 2.13). The share of food and live animals came to 12.5 per cent.

The share of various groups in Japanese imports does not seem to have changed much between 1974 and 1978 except that the share of food, crude materials and machinery and transport equipment declined

Table 2.13: Commodity Composition of Japanese Imports (total in billion US $, share in percentages)

	1974		1979	
	Total	Share	Total	Share
Food and live animals	7.8	12.5	13.7	12.4
Beverages and tobacco	0.4	0.6	0.7	0.7
Crude materials (excluding fuels)	14.1	22.8	21.8	19.8
Mineral fuels	24.9	40.1	45.3	40.9
Chemicals	2.7	4.3	5.2	4.7
Manufactured goods classified mainly by materials	5.2	8.3	9.4	8.5
Machinery and transport equipment	4.3	6.9	7.3	6.6
Miscellaneous manufactured goods	2.4	3.9	5.2	4.7
Unclassified[a]	0.4	0.7	2.0	1.8

a. Includes animal and vegetable oils and fats
Source: US-Japan Trade Council, *Yearbook, 1978*, pp.128-9, table 28: and US-Japan Trade Council, *Yearbook, 1979*, pp.121-2, table 27.

Table 2.14: Share of Manufactured Goods[a] in the Import of Selected Countries, 1977 (in billion US $, share in percentages)

Countries	Total import of manufactured goods	Share of manufactured goods in total imports
Japan	14.7	20.8
USA	76.6	51.8
France	40.7	57.9
Italy	21.0	45.0
UK	37.8	59.3
West Germany	57.4	57.0

a. Manufactured goods refers to chemicals, machinery, transport equipment, and other manufactured goods except mineral fuel products, processed foods, fats, oils, fire-arms and ammunition.
Source: US General Accounting Office, *United States-Japan Trade: Issues and Problems*, p.13, table 5.

somewhat and those of chemicals and miscellaneous manufactured goods increased marginally. Mineral fuels and crude materials remained the dominant groups while the share of manufactured goods (including machinery and transport equipment) remained low at around 21 per cent in 1977 (Table 2.14). This figure rose slightly to 24.5 per cent in 1979 (Table 2.13).

This has been one of the main bones of contention between the USA and the EEC on one side and Japan on the other. It has been argued by the West that Japan continues to maintain artificial barriers to keep out foreign manufactured goods. There is some validity in this argument, though such barriers have been of diminishing importance since 1971 and particularly since 1974. As we shall see later, both tariff and non-tariff barriers in Japan are either lower than or comparable to those of the West, particularly the EEC.

Moreover, it should be stressed that this emphasis on the low share of manufactured goods in Japanese imports is not a particularly justifiable one. After all, the conventional theory and practice of international trade – largely developed in the West – did not require a balance of import and export of each commodity group, nor was it concerned with bilateral export and import balance of one country (or region) versus the other, but relied instead on some sort of global balance. Viewed from that angle, while it is true that the share of manufactured goods in Japanese imports is low, the share of primary products in total imports in Japan is nearly 79 per cent, almost twice as much as in West Germany and the UK (Table 2.15). However, in

Table 2.15: Import of Primary Products[a] by Selected Countries, 1977

Country	Total import of primary products (billion US $)	Per capita imports of primary products ($)	Share of primary products in country's total imports (%)
Japan	55.6	483.8	78.8
USA	66.5	299.8	45.0
France	29.5	553.5	42.0
Italy	25.5	449.6	54.6
UK	25.7	460.6	40.4
West Germany	41.1	670.6	40.8

a. Primary products include foodstuffs, raw materials and fuels.

terms of per capita imports of primary products Japanese imports are much less than those of West Germany, though substantially larger than those of the USA. On the other hand, Japan imports considerably more primary products from the USA than does West Germany (Table 2.16). Of the total US exports to Japan, 61 per cent consist of primary products against only 29 per cent for West Germany. In much the same way, as we shall see later, even though Japan does have a favourable

Table 2.16: US Exports of Primary Products to Japan and West Germany, 1978 (as a percentage of total US exports to a particular country)

Items	Japan	West Germany
Food and live animals	23.6	12.3
Beverages and tobacco	2.1	1.7
Crude materials except fuels	28.9	13.8
Mineral fuels	6.4	1.3
Total	61.0	29.1

Source: GAO, *United States-Japan Trade*, p.14, table 6.

balance of trade in manufactured goods with the EEC, she runs a considerable deficit on invisible earnings.

Some Sensitive Export Items

The ten most important categories of Japanese exports are given in Table 2.17. By far the most important item is cars, followed by steel universals, plates and sheets, and cargo ships. Other items include scientific, medical and optical instruments; steel tubes, pipes and fittings; assembled trucks and buses; radios; woven fabrics; power-generating machinery and motor cycles and parts. Among other sensitive items are television sets, tape recorders, etc., but their share in Japanese exports is less than 2 per cent each.

Out of the ten items, steel universals, plates and sheets showed a considerable decline in their share from 7.5 per cent to 4.7 per cent. This was mainly the result of the introduction of the US trigger price mechanism in 1977 and a similar minimum price system in the EEC. Steel tubes, pipes and fittings marginally improved their share. Woven fabrics were the other items whose share declined, primarily as a result of a more restrictive multi-fibre agreement (MFA). Other items retained their competitiveness and increased their share in spite of the appreciation of the yen and the world recession. However, to understand the real nature of Western criticism one has to look into some of these categories in a more detailed fashion. Here three main groups, road vehicles, telecommunication equipment and iron and steel, are selected for a detailed discussion.

Table 2.17: Japan's Ten Largest Export Items, 1978 (in billion US $, share in percentages)

	1974		1979	
	Total	Share	Total	Share
Cars	3.5	6.3	12.0	11.6
Universals, plates and sheets (steel)	4.2	7.5	5.2	5.0
Tubes, pipes and fittings (steel)	1.9	3.3	3.9	3.8
Scientific, medical and official instruments	1.3	2.4	3.9	3.8
Assembled trucks and buses	0.9	1.7	3.1	3.0
Woven fabrics	2.0	3.5	2.7	2.7
Radios	1.4	2.4	2.5	2.4
Organic chemicals	1.4	2.6	2.2	2.1
Motor cycles and parts	1.5	2.7	2.2	2.1
Audio and video tape recorders, etc.	0.7	1.3	2.1	2.0

Source: US-Japan Trade Council, *Yearbook, 1978*, pp.126-7, table 27: and US-Japan Trade Council, *Yearbook, 1979*, pp.119-20, table 26.

Road Vehicles[9]

It is well known that this is one of the most sensitive groups of export items in Japanese trade relationships with the West. In 1979 this group as a whole constituted (in value terms) around 16.5 per cent of Japanese exports (of which passenger cars were nearly 70 per cent). Japan's share in total world exports of road vehicles in 1978 was only 20 per cent against 21 per cent for West Germany, 14.2 per cent for the USA and 10.1 per cent for Canada. The combined total for the EEC was 48.4 per cent.[10] Therefore Japan was neither the largest exporter nor had an abnormally high share compared with either the USA or the EEC. However, its share of US imports was around 37 per cent as against only 20 per cent for the EEC as a whole, although the largest exporter to the USA was Canada, with 40.2 per cent of total exports to the USA. As far as the EEC is concerned, in 1978 Japan supplied only 8.2 per cent of total EEC imports. To put it in perspective, West German exports of road vehicles to Belgium and Luxembourg alone exceeds the total Japanese exports to the whole of the EEC.

Therefore, the Community's complaint about Japanese cars is largely a reflection of increasing protectionist trends in the member countries. After all, the economic union of these countries was motivated, to a considerable extent, by the aim of creating a highly protected economic unit. This is further reflected in the attitudes of

individual countries with chronic economic ailments like the UK which
in the past survived, to a considerable extent, by shifting the incidence
of her economic inefficiency to her colonies by various methods,
including direct and indirect controls to slow down the industrialisation
in the colonies, manipulation of their exchange rates and arrangements
such as Imperial Preference. Japan supplied only 16 per cent (in value
terms) of UK imports of road vehicles in 1978, as against 33 per cent
from West Germany and 17 per cent from France.[11] When Japan agreed
in 1976 to limit her share of the UK market to below 10 per cent
(the current agreed figure is 11 per cent[12]), the share of domestic cars
declined (instead of increasing); the slack was taken up by other
European cars. Similarly, the share of Japanese cars in French road
vehicle imports is 5.6 per cent (value terms) against 40.2 per cent for
West Germany. Yet France has, through a policy of 'administrative
guidance to importers', kept Japanese car sales severely restricted. On
the occasion of the opening of the Paris motor show, President d'Estaing
said that Japanese cars would not be allowed to take more than 3 per
cent of the French car market.[13] In Italy also entry of Japanese cars
is severely restricted.[14] In West Germany, where domestic quality cars
can compete favourably with Japanese imports, until recently both the
industry and the government were opposed to introducing any artificial
restrictions on car imports. In 1975 Japan accounted for only 1.7 per
cent of the West German car market. Even in 1979 this figure was as
low as 5.6 per cent.[15] However, in the first half of 1980 this share went
up to 8.7 per cent. The West German car industry has 'called for joint
action between German manufacturers, the Government and the trade
unions to control the rise in Japanese imports'.[16] The West German
government has so far opposed such protectionist moves but has tended
to favour 'self-discipline' by the Japanese.[17]

Both the Japanese government and the car manufacturers are worried
about the growing mood of protectionism in the EEC, and would like to
meet EEC demands for 'self-restraint' or for production of Japanese cars
in Europe, but their main worry is about US criticism, as the USA
continues to be the single largest market for Japanese road vehicles.
During 1979, sales from Japan totalled 1.8 million cars and 0.47 million
light pick-up trucks, representing an increase over 1978 of 30.5 per cent
and 39.0 per cent respectively.[18] In 1979 Japanese car imports
represented approximately 22 per cent of the total US sales of new
cars against only 17.7 per cent in 1978. This share is expected to have
reached 25 per cent this year.[19] Against this in 1979 the USA sold
only 16,700 cars in the Japanese market. This 'enormous bilateral

imbalance in auto sales' is the main bone of contention between the two countries. According to US car manufacturers such an imbalance is caused by the highly 'protected' nature of the Japanese domestic market. It must be remembered that in the 1950s and 1960s the expansion of Japanese car production was highly subsidised by official measures and the domestic market was protected by extremely high tariff rates. However, formal import restrictions in Japan have been greatly relaxed in recent years.[20] In 1978 tariffs on cars in Japan had zero rating against tariffs of 3 per cent in the USA and 11 per cent in the EEC.[21] On the other hand, the commodity and the road taxes in Japan militate against imported large cars. The commodity tax in Japan is levied on the basis of three factors: wheel-base, width and the size of engine. The smaller car (with an engine capacity of 2,000 cc, a width of less than 1700 mm and a wheel-base of less than 2700 mm) is taxed at 15 per cent; others are taxed at 20 per cent.[22] On domestic manufactured goods the tax is levied at the factory price, while on imported cars it is on the cif price. Similarly, the biannual road tax favours the small against the larger and heavier cars.

Japanese safety and environmental standards are more rigorous than in the USA and the modifications required for imported cars in 1979 added anything between \$110 and \$535 to the price of American compact and sub-compact cars.[23] Similarly, the extensive documentation for insurance together with strict inspection of *each* car added another \$200 per car.[24] Importers also contend that the Japanese distribution system is one of the major hindrances to expansion of their trade. This complaint is made by importers of other products as well, a point that we shall discuss in greater detail later. There is some justification behind some of these complaints of foreign importers but it is conceded by official US sources that much of the problem arises from the nature of the product itself. As the recent Government Accounting Office report underlined, much can be done 'to improve opportunities for foreign manufactures in the Japanese market. Test procedures can be streamlined, minor standards that do not affect safety can be dropped, and road motor tax increases by size of car can be made proportional to the increased gasoline required rather than greater [size]. However, even if all these changes were to be made, the economics of land and energy would dictate that the mass market in Japan is for small cars alone.'[25]

It is mainly this reluctance by US manufacturers to produce small and energy-efficient cars that has helped Japanese cars in the US market.[26] This point has not only been stressed by Toshio Nakamura,[27] the managing director of the Japan Automobile Manufacturers

Association (JAMA), but also by some leading US experts. For
instance, William Niskanen, Jr, until recently director of economics of
the Ford Motor Company, stresses that 'the increase in import sales over
the past two years accounts for only one-eighth of the drop in domestic-
make sales. Thus, most of the industry's decline is more correctly
attributable to the recession and to structural changes in the industry
resulting from higher gasoline prices. For Ford, "bad product decisions"
compounded this.'[28] Niskanen had advised against Ford's active
publicity and lobbying campaign for government controls on Japanese
cars. The closest ally of the Ford Motor Company in this venture has
been the United Auto Workers Union (UAW). Both the UAW and
the Ford Motor Company filed their petitions to the US International
Trade Commission (ITC), requesting a temporary remedy against
Japanese imports on the grounds that they were causing serious injury
to the US motor industry.[29] General Motors and Chrysler, the two
other major car-manufacturers, continue to support 'voluntary
restraint'.[30] After five months' deliberation, on 10 November 1980
the ITC rejected the claims of Ford and of the UAW that Japanese
imports had 'seriously damaged' the domestic car industry.[31] The
controversy is still continuing. In a press conference on 15 November
1980 Richard Cooper, the then Under-Secretary of State of Economic
Affairs, asserted that the Japan-US car trade issue has not been settled
yet from a political viewpoint despite the recent ITC decision.[32]
Senator Howard Metzenbaum introduced legislation to cut total
imports of cars and trucks to 30 per cent below the 1979 level, with
a sliding scale for subsequent years.[33] Another proposal, introduced
by Senator Donald Riegle, aims to cut imports of Japanese cars and
trucks by 0.5 million below the 1979 level.[34] Yet another proposal by
Congressman John Seiberling calls for limiting imports of foreign cars
at the 1976 level of 1.7 million for the next three years.[35] Several other
similar proposals have been passed or are being considered by the US
Congress.[36]

Another aspect of US (and to some extent EEC) pressures on
Japanese car producers is their attempts to persuade them to locate
production in the USA and in EEC countries. In response to these
pressures, Japanese car-manufacturers are now slowly moving into the
USA. Early in 1980 Honda Giken decided to produce small passenger
cars in the state of Ohio. They aim at producing 15,000 cars a month
and production is scheduled to start in 1982.[37] Similarly, Nissan Motors
decided to start small truck production in the USA with a monthly
capacity of 10,000 small trucks a month.[38] In mid-July 1980 Toyota

Motors and the Ford Motor Company entered into an agreement for co-production of small passenger cars.[39] Production is to start by 1982; the rate of local procurement of parts will be around 75 per cent.[40] So far, such appeasement of the USA by Japanese car producers has not reduced official or unofficial criticism.

Telecommunication Equipment[41]

Japan's share in world exports of telecommunication equipment stood at nearly 31 per cent in 1978, and was valued at $6.6 billion. Next in importance came West Germany with 13.4 per cent and the USA with 11.8 per cent of world exports. The combined share of the EEC was 37.5 per cent. Japan supplied nearly 46.3 per cent of US imports but only around 18.9 per cent of the EEC's imports.[42]

Complaints about Japanese electronics had already started in the EEC member countries in the early 1970s. As early as 1972 the *Financial Times* wrote about the UK market:

> Concern is perhaps the greatest in the consumer electronic
> field. Imports of record players rose 126 per cent last year and
> imports of radios and transistors doubled. The colour television
> set market in Britain is still rapidly growing and Japanese imports
> are as yet relatively small, but the speed of increase is alarming.[43]

It also reported that Britain regarded 'these sectors — ball bearings, polyester fibre and TV sets — as of primary importance where Japanese action to curb unbridled upsurges in shipments will be regarded as the acid test of her good intentions'.[44] Japan agreed on a voluntary restraint.

Similarly, as early as 1968, the Imports Committee of the Tube Division of the US Electronic Industries brought a complaint before the US Treasury that Japanese colour and black and white television sets were being imported and sold at less than fair value (LTFV).[45] In 1970 the Treasury announced that this was the case. The US Tariff Commission (now the International Trade Commission) voted unanimously in March 1971 that these sales were damaging domestic industries. The Treasury was now entitled to impose anti-dumping duties. Pending the determination of appropriate duties on each specific model, importers of Japanese television sets were required to post entry bonds against dumping liability in addition to import duties. The initial rate of 9 per cent of (fob) value was increased to 20 per cent in 1977.[46] When, after a protracted process, the US Treasury announced

in March 1978 that a total of $46 million duty on pre-July 1973 sales
was to be paid by the importers of Japanese sets retroactively to 1970,
this assessment was challenged by almost all the 120 importers involved.
The payment deadline for pre-July 1973 assessment was extended three
times. Only a small proportion has so far been paid and the dispute
continues. Zenith, a leading US colour television manufacturer which
controls nearly a fifth of the US market,[47] has repeatedly attempted
to challenge Japanese competition through recourse to court and
administrative procedures. It recently lost its countervailing duty suit
in the Supreme Court, but cases relating to the implementation of the
Treasury's anti-dumping decision of 1971 and anti-trust violations are
still pending.[48] As far as the US domestic market for television sets is
concerned, Japan entered into an orderly marketing arrangement (OMA)
on colour television sets with the US government which restricts the
entry of assembled sets and specified sub-assemblies at 1.75 million
units a year for a period of three years.[49] Between July 1978 and
June 1979 only 1.15 million Japanese sets were imported into the USA.
Japan's share of the US imported colour television set market has fallen
from 81.4 per cent in 1976 to only 33.8 per cent in 1978.[50] Some of
this cutback has been offset by an increase in the sales of sets
produced by Japanese electronic companies from their US plants.
But part of the decline is the result of increasing competition from
Taiwan, Korea and Canada. The USA has now concluded orderly
marketing arrangements with Taiwan and Korea.

Japanese imports of telecommunication equipment continues to be
low. In 1978 it was only about 1.4 per cent (in value terms) of total
world imports. Some of the main complaints of US producers of
television sets such as Zenith against the Japanese domestic market
relates to the 'approval systems for product acceptance, the
distribution system, the commodity tax and the availability of foreign
exchange allocations'.[51] Among the other complaints some relate to
'design specifications, quality control and safety standards'.[52] These
are considered to be more stringent than those imposed by the US
government. Some of these allegations have been made by other foreign
industries interested in entering the Japanese market, and they have
some justification. But the fact remains that the West, as we shall see
later, has similar tariff and non-tariff barriers, yet Japanese products
succeed in their domestic markets, while many products originating
in the West do not make much headway in Japan's domestic markets.
As far as the television set market is concerned, some experts[53] stress that
in the early stages of its development it was less well protected than the

markets for textiles, steel or cars, and the failure of US industries to penetrate the Japanese market was essentially a story of missed opportunities.

Steel

Steel exports has been another sensitive area of Japan's economic relations with the West, although here again there are major differences between the USA and the EEC. This group of exports consists of a large number of finished as well as intermediate products and a discussion of all such items is rather difficult. So a specific group of products (universals, plates and sheets, etc.) is selected because this group is the second most important export item after cars. Japan's share in world exports (in value terms) of this group was 29.3 per cent in 1978,[54] the USA being the most important market. US imports from Japan amounted to 32.5 per cent of total US imports and represented nearly 23.8 per cent of Japanese exports. So far as the EEC was concerned, Japanese exports accounted for only 4.1 per cent of the former's imports.

The US steel industry, particularly since the oil crisis of 1973 and the related recession, has been suffering from excess capacity and sluggish and unprofitable price levels.[55] This has led to widespread redundancies and unemployment. However, although the recovery of the economy in 1977 meant that steel demand in the US market increased significantly, the major beneficiaries of this increased demand were the foreign exporters of steel to the US market. This led to the accusation by the US steel interests that the increase in imports resulted from the unfair trade practices of the major steel-exporting countries, particularly the EEC.[56] In 1977 at least nineteen steel-dumping petitions were brought before the US Treasury. It must be remembered that 'voluntary' restraints were already applicable to EEC and Japanese shipments to the US market between 1969 and 1974, but these were not sufficient to prevent the decline of the US steel industry. With a view to regulating imports in December 1977 the US Treasury announced the 'trigger price mechanism' (TPM), which in 1978 covered nearly 90 per cent of US steel purchases.[57] The trigger prices were based upon Japanese production costs for all steel production. Allowance was made for variations in specifications, quality, importation costs, etc. The trigger price was then taken as a basis for determining whether a certain product was being sold at LTFV. In cases where it was considered that sales were LTFV, the Treasury could take what is termed 'fast-track' anti-dumping action.

The introduction of the trigger price mechanism has resulted in a contraction of shipments from Japan by nearly 17 per cent in 1978 while there was a 9.2 per cent rise in imports from the EEC.[58] Imports from other countries such as Canada, South Korea, Spain, South Africa, Poland, Brazil and Argentina also increased.[59] During 1979 most steel imports to the USA remained subject to TPM and the base price was revised upwards by nearly 7 per cent in the first quarter and lowered by 1.4 per cent in the third quarter.[60] In response to the US President's refusal to increase the base price further for the April-June (1980) quarter, the US Steel Corporation, the largest steel-maker in the country, filed anti-dumping suits against seven EEC countries on 21 March 1980.[61] The Carter Administration retaliated by suspending the TPM. After a protracted negotiation between the Administration and the US steel industry, a new aid package for the industry was announced by the President on 30 September 1980.[62] The US Steel Corporation agreed to withdraw dumping complaints and the Administration agreed to reinstate the TPM and to raise the base rate by 12 per cent over the rates prevailing at the time of suspension in March 1980. The US steel industry was promised that the government would go slow with enforcing clean air and water-quality standards required by the Environmental Protection Agency, and that it would receive a more generous depreciation allowance on investment tax credits as well as access to additional unemployment insurance proposed by the Carter administration.

Japan's Trade Balance with Selected Regions

It is clear from Table 2.18 that between 1974 and 1978, when Japan emerged with a significant trade surplus, her major trading partners such as the USA and Western Europe increased their deficits with Japan substantially. This came at a time when the world had been passing through the most serious recession since World War II. The recession, which started in late 1974, lasted for almost six quarters and resulted in a significant decline in mining and industrial production in the developed countries. As a result, there was a considerable increase in unemployment; in 1975, with the exception of Canada, Italy and Japan, unemployment rates reached their highest level since 1955.[63] In the last quarter of 1975 and the first quarter of 1976 there were signs of a business upturn, but the trend halted in the second quarter of 1976. However, as a result of attempts by the developed countries to

Table 2.18: Japan's Trade Balance with Selected Regions or Countries (in billion US $)

Countries or regions	1974			1978			1979		
	Exports[a]	Imports[b]	Surplus or deficit	Exports[a]	Imports[b]	Surplus or deficit	Exports[a]	Imports[b]	Surplus or deficit
Total developed	26.4	25.8	0.6	45.7	33.1	12.6	48.8	43.0	5.7
USA	12.8	12.7	0.1	24.9	14.8	10.1	26.4	20.4	6.0
Canada	1.6	2.7	-1.1	1.9	3.2	-1.3	1.7	4.1	-2.4
Western Europe	8.6	5.2	3.4	14.8	8.1	6.7	16.4	10.1	6.3
UK	1.5	0.9	0.7	2.3	1.4	1.0	3.1	1.7	1.4
France	0.7	0.6	0.2	1.1	0.8	0.4	1.4	1.1	0.3
West Germany	1.5	1.5	0.1	3.7	2.0	1.7	4.3	2.6	1.7
EEC	6.0	4.0	2.0	11.1	6.1	5.0	12.7	7.6	5.1
Australia	2.0	4.0	-2.0	2.7	5.3	-2.6	2.6	6.3	-3.7
New Zealand	0.5	0.4	0.1	0.4	0.6	-0.2	0.6	0.8	-0.2
South Africa	1.0	0.8	0.2	1.0	1.0	-0.1	1.0	1.3	-0.3
Total developing	25.2	33.2	-8.0	45.2	42.4	2.9	46.9	62.2	-15.3
Latin America	5.1	2.7	2.4	6.6	3.1	3.6	6.6	4.5	2.0
South-east Asia[c]	12.7	12.5	0.2	23.1	17.3	5.7	26.1	26.2	-0.1
Middle East and North Africa	3.7	15.9	-12.2	10.8	20.8	-10.0	10.7	29.4	-18.6
Total Communist block	3.9	3.1	0.8	6.7	3.9	2.2	7.4	5.4	2.0
PRC	2.0	1.3	0.7	3.1	2.0	1.0	3.7	3.0	0.7
USSR	1.1	1.4	-0.3	2.5	1.4	1.1	2.5	1.9	0.6
Total	55.6	62.1	-6.6	97.5	79.2	18.2	103.0	110.7	-7.6

a. Exports fob.   b. Imports cif.   c. Includes South Asia.
Source: US-Japan Trade Council, *Yearbook, 1978*, pp.124-5, tables 25 & 26; US-Japan Trade Council, *Yearbook, 1979*, pp. 117-18, tables 24 &25.
Note: The surplus and deficit figures do not always match the difference between exports and imports, and are the result of rounding off.

push up their growth rates, there was some recovery in the last quarter of 1976, continuing into 1977. But the situation continued to be one of sluggish growth. In fact, the major feature of the 1978 world economic scene was the continuance of the slow rate of recovery from the 1974-5 recession.

In 1979 the world continued to be plagued by a slow rate of economic growth, estimated at nearly 3 per cent. According to IMF estimates, the real GNP growth in fourteen industrialised countries was around 3.5 per cent against 4 per cent in 1978.[64] However, the pattern of growth among these countries remained uneven; there was a slowdown in the USA, France, the UK and Canada, while there was some rise in that of West Germany, Italy and Japan. Nevertheless, the volume of world trade in 1979 increased by 6 or 7 per cent.[65] For the industrial countries the value of exports rose by nearly 20 per cent while imports rose by 28 per cent. A substantial part of this increase was caused by an inflationary rise in prices, particularly of primary products and oil. As a result, the trade deficit of industrialised countries *vis-à-vis* the rest of the world increased from only $45 billion in 1978 to $105 billion in 1979.[66]

During the same period (i.e. 1976-8) Japan managed to keep economic growth reasonably high (between 5 and 6 per cent) and the rate of inflation and unemployment within manageable proportions. Her trade balance against the world increased to $18.2 billion in 1978 against a deficit of $6.6 billion in 1974. In 1978 her trade surplus against the USA stood at $10.1 billion and nearly $5.0 billion against the EEC (Table 2.18). Her international reserves had jumped to $32.4 billion in 1978 against only $12.6 billion in 1974 (Table 2.6a).

Thus Japan's relative economic success, which has long been a cause for envy in many developed countries, once again became the basis for an increased clamour for protectionism in the West, and often unjustifiable demands for unilateral accommodation from Japan. One of the most unfortunate recent trends has been to insist on balance in the trade of individual commodity groups, or a bilateral balance of trade between individual (or a group of) countries rather than a global balance. The Japanese authorities rightly argue that Japanese people and companies spend a considerable sum abroad in travel, insurance, etc. According to the IMF estimates in 1978, Japan had a deficit of $7.0 billion dollars in services which rose to $9.1 billion in 1979 (Table 2.5b). There is no doubt that much of this goes to the West, particularly to the USA, France and the UK. In addition, a significant part of her deficit with the Middle East and North America also ends up in the US banks and the Eurodollar market, so in any trade friction, it is extremely unfair to focus on the trade balance alone.

As we shall see later, Japanese government and business have tried by various means to reduce their trade surplus with their major trading partners. In 1979 their trade surplus with the USA was reduced by almost half; with all developed countries it was only 45 per cent of the surplus in 1978. For the world as a whole, the Japanese surplus of nearly $18.2 billion in 1978 was converted into a deficit of $7.6 billion (Table 2.18). The current account in 1979 also showed a significant deficit, estimated by the IMF at $8.3 billion.[67] A substantial deficit for 1980 is anticipated.[68] Yet criticism of Japan by her trading partners continues unabated.

Notes

1. US National Foreign Assessment Centre, *Handbook of Economics Statistics, 1979*, Table 1. The corresponding figures for the USA were 1,220 kg, France 820 kg, Italy 300 kg, UK 310 kg, and the average for the EEC was 440 kg.
2. The average for the EEC was 72 kg; for the USA it was 113 kg.
3. For an excellent study of such attitudes, see G.E. Hubbard, *Eastern Industrialization and its Effects on the West*.
4. US Subcommittee on Trade, *Task Force Report, On United States-Japan Trade* (1979), p.50.
5. US Joint Economic Committee, *Anticipating Disruptive Imports* (1978).
6. US-Japan Trade Council, *Yearbook of US-Japan Economic Relations, 1979*, p.119.
7. All the statistical information in this section is based on JETRO, *White Paper on International Trade, 1979*.
8. This figure is somewhat higher than in Table 2.9. For reasons see the explanation to the table.
9. This group includes cars, assembled trucks and buses, trucks and bus chassis and engines, road vehicle parts, motorcycles and parts.
10. This information, unless otherwise specified, is based on UN *Yearbook of International Trade Statistics, 1978*, vol. 2, pp.1148-9.
11. Ibid., pp.1148-9.
12. *Financial Times*, 11 Sept. 1980. Such gentlemen's agreements are reached between the Japanese Automobile Manufacturers' Association (JAMA) and the UK Society of Motor Manufacturers and Traders (SMMT).
13. P. Lewis, 'Europe Car Makers Assail Japan Imports', *New York Times*, 4 Oct. 1980.
14. A. Field, 'Pressure for More Overseas Plants', *Financial Times*, 29 Oct. 1980.
15. *Financial Times*, 11 July 1980.
16. *Financial Times*, 25 July 1980.
17. Ibid.
18. K.D. Nanto, 'Automobiles Imported from Japan', Issue Brief Number 1B 80030, Congressional Research Service, US Library of Congres, 1980, p. CRS-1.
19. C. Higashi, 'U.S. Foreign Policy and Auto Wars', *Look Japan*, 10 April 1980.

20. GAO, *United States-Japan Trade: Issues and Problems*, p.43.
21. Ibid., p.44.
22. Nanto, 'Automobiles Imported from Japan', p. CRS-2.
23. Ibid., p. CRS-2.
24. Ibid.
25. GAO, *United States-Japan Trade*, p.57.
26. Ibid., pp.38-9.
27. Interview with Toshio Nakamura in *Look Japan*, 10 May 1980, p.2.
28. R.L. Simison, 'Ford Fires an Economist', *Wall Street Journal*, 30 July 1980.
29. *Financial Times*, 6 Aug. 1980.
30. *Wall Street Journal*, 17 Sept. 1980: also *Financial Times*, 6 Aug. 1980.
31. *The Economist*, 15 Nov. 1980.
32. *The Japan Times Weekly*, 22 Nov. 1980.
33. *The Economist*, 15 Nov. 1980, p.77.
34. Ibid.
35. *The Japan Times Weekly*, 22 Nov. 1980, p.1.
36. Some of those restricting imports as listed in Nanto, 'Automobiles Imported from Japan' are as follows: H.R. 6645 (Mottl *et al.*) introduced 12 Feb. 1980; H.R. 6718 (Traxler *et al.*) introduced 5 March 1980; H.R. 7803 (Gaydos) introduced 23 July 1980; H.J. Res. 580 (Heftel *et al.*) introduced 30 June 1980.
37. *Nihon Keizai*, 11 Jan. 1980.
38. *Nihon Keizai*, 23 Jan. 1980.
39. *Tokyo Shimbun*, 11 July 1980.
40. *Nikkan Kogyo*, 17 July 1980.
41. This group consists of television sets, radios, microphones, loudspeakers and amplifiers and transceivers.
42. UN, *Yearbook of International Trade Statistics, 1978*, vol.2, p.1138.
43. C. Jones, 'Trade: Britain Presses her Case with Japan', *Financial Times*, 4 Sept. 1972.
44. Ibid.
45. US-Japan Trade Council, *Yearbook of US-Japan Economic Relations*, 1978, pp.63-4.
46. Ibid., p.64.
47. J. Wyles, 'The Japanese Onslaught on American TV Makers', *Financial Times*, 18 Oct. 1977.
48. GAO, *United States-Japan Trade*, p.86.
49. US-Japan Trade Council, *Yearbook, 1979*, p.70.
50. Ibid.
51. GAO, *United States-Japan Trade*, p.90.
52. Ibid., p.91.
53. J.C. Abegglen and W.V. Rapp, 'The Competitive Impact of Japanese Growth' in J.B. Cohen (ed.), *Pacific Partnership: United States-Japan*, pp.40-1.
54. UN, *Yearbook of International Trade Statistics, 1978*, vol.2, p.1076.
55. US-Japan Trade Council, *Yearbook, 1978*, p.65.
56. Ibid., p.65.
57. Ibid., p.66.
58. Ibid., p.67.
59. Ibid., p.67.
60. US-Japan Trade Council, *Yearbook 1979*, p.69.
61. *The Economist*, 29 March 1980, p.105.
62. *New York Times*, 1 Oct. 1980.
63. JETRO, *White Paper on International Trade: Japan 1976*, p.2.
64. US-Japan Trade Council, *Yearbook, 1979*, p.29.
65. The IMF estimates suggest 6 per cent and those of GATT 7 per cent (see

US-Japan Trade Council, *Yearbook, 1979*, p.30).

66. IBID., p.30 (based on export fob and imports cif).

67. During the 1979 fiscal year (1 April-30 March) the deficit was reported at $13.9 billion (see C. Smith, 'Fears of a Nightmare Deficit Vanish', *Financial Times*, 3 Dec. 1980).

68. Ibid.

3 THE NATURE OF THE WEST'S CRITICISM OF JAPAN

In spite of much evidence of the superiority of Japanese industrial and managerial efficiency, labour relations and her active salesmanship based on a considerable knowledge of foreign markets, US and EEC business interests and politicians continue to regard Japanese 'unfair' trading practices as the main cause of the increasing trade imbalance between Japan on the one hand and the USA and the EEC on the other. At least four sets of 'unfair' practices are highlighted:[1]

(1) Explicit Japanese barriers to imports (tariffs, quotas and procurement policies);
(2) Non-tariff practices that both promote exports and limit imports;
(3) The Japanese distribution system which allegedly limits imports;
(4) The restrictions on foreign banks operating in the Japanese market.

Tariffs, Quotas and Procurement

During her post-war reconstruction years in the 1950s Japan enjoyed some immunity from foreign criticism of her restrictive trade policies. The USA came to see an economically stable Japan as a bulwark against Communism and, as a result, assisted the economic development of Japan through direct and indirect financial aid (e.g. war-related purchases at the time of the Korean war) and an easy, almost unlimited access to the US market. However, by the mid-1950s voices were being raised against Japanese imports, and the US government enforced a 'voluntary' quota on Japanese textiles, later to be subsumed under GATT's cotton textile and multi-fibre agreements.[2]

As Japan became increasingly competitive in the 1960s the USA started pressurising her to accept 'voluntary' restraints on exports in other products, particularly steel. By this time the EEC, which itself had developed into a highly protected market, began to exert similar pressures on Japan (and on the developing countries). Because of these increasing pressures, Japan started dismantling – though slowly – her quantitative restrictions on imports and modifying her methods of stimulating exports.[3] The pace of liberalisation was significantly accelerated after 1970, so that now, as we shall see later, Japan is no more restrictive than the West, an assessment shared by the IMF and by GATT.[4] For example, so far as tariffs are concerned, Japanese levels average 3.7 per cent on mining and manufactured products compared with 6 per cent for the US and 6.4 per cent for the EEC.[5] As late as 1975 the nominal tariff averaged around 15 per cent against 7 to 8 per cent in the USA and the EEC (Table 3.1).

Table 3.1: The Ratio between the Effective and the Nominal Rate of Protective Tariff (%)

Country	(A) Nominal	(B) Effective	B/A Ratio
Japan	14.8	19.3	130
USA (estimate 1)	7.4	15.4	208
USA (estimate 2)	7.5	14.3	191
EEC	8.3	14.4	173
Canada	11.0	20.7	188
All non-US countries	10.3	18.0	175

Source: USITC, *Protection in Major Trading Countries* (1975), quoted in D. Lal, *Market Access for Semi-manufactures from Developing Countries*, p.10, table 111(A).

Non-tariff Barriers

Much the same is probably true of non-tariff barriers, for example, quotas and voluntary restrictions. For instance, the USA imposes import quotas on the following commodity groups:[6] (1) cotton, certain cotton waste and products, most dairy products, and peanuts; (2) certain fish and certain potatoes; (3) sugar; (4) certain types of meat, and (5) stainless steel and alloy steel tool products. Under the provisions of the GATT Arrangement Regarding International Trade in Textiles, as well as bilateral textile agreements, the USA sets the levels of import quotas for various trading partners. At least twelve bilateral agreements and one memorandum of understanding restrict the imports of fresh, frozen or chilled beef, veal, mutton and goat's meat.[7] Similar bilateral agreements effectively restrict the imports of a number of manufactured products such as shoes, television sets and, in particular, steel.[8] At the end of 1978 over 80 items of steel were subject to control. Similarly, almost 80 per cent of US imports of textiles and clothing are subject to quantitative restrictions.[9]

The EEC has also concluded bilateral agreements with major steel-exporting countries, restricting their quantity of exports to the EEC. Their quantitative restrictions on cotton textiles are more stringent. Some of these are imposed under the Multifibre Arrangement (MFA). Similar arrangements have been made with countries not participating in the MFA.[10] Imports of most products covered by the Common Agricultural Policy of the EEC are subject to variable import levies.

Against this the 'available information indicates that Japan has introduced relatively few import restrictions'.[11] The products which came to be affected by quantitative restrictions during the period 1974-7 include bovine meat, thrown silk and silk fabrics and a small number of other products.[12] Of the commodities on which these restrictions continue to operate 22 out of 27 are agricultural commodities. Their number in 1969 was as high as 90.[13]

Undoubtedly there is considerable scope for further liberalisation of import restrictions on agricultural products in Japan. It can be argued that the continuation of such import restrictions has considerable domestic social costs. As Yujiro Hayami has argued, in the case of beef alone:

> Obviously, domestic consumers are the major beneficiaries from the trade liberalization program: their gain in the form of the increase in consumers' surplus will amount to 300 to 400 billion yen (about 1.5 to 2 billion US dollars) per year. Net social benefit from the liberalization plan also will be very large, ranging from 150 to 250 billion yen.[14]

A recent study has shown that the Japanese government's intervention in food markets resulted in 1975/76 consumption losses of 32 billion yen for dairy products, 17 billion for rice, 415 million for soybean and 59 million for poultry.[15]

These studies are obviously based on some highly restrictive assumptions, and the estimates are highly conjectural. But the fact remains that trade barriers often distort the optimal allocation of national and world resources, and therefore liberalisation of trade barriers in Japan may add to the welfare of the Japanese people together with the world at large. But the same argument applies for trade barriers in the USA and the EEC. It is rather hypocritical of the West to demand liberalisation in Japan while they themselves keep on raising their trade barriers. It is not difficult to find instances of a double standard. Let us look at the following statements of the *Task Force Report* relating to the cigarette manufacturing and tanning industries:

> The United States has a cigarette manufacturing industry that is competitive throughout the world. Japanese insistence on importing leaf tobacco and conducting the manufacturing in Japan is a blatant and unacceptable form of protectionism.[16]

Again,

> The American tanners must compete with Japanese tanners who are buying U.S. hides. At current yen/dollar relations, the U.S. market is very attractive and Japan is the largest purchaser of U.S. hides. Yet U.S. tanners are denied access to the Japanese market by an incredibly restrictive quota.[17]

The irony of the situation is that the richer countries of the West have done precisely what they expect Japan not to do to their own products. Tariff schedules in the West are so constituted that raw materials not available in their countries are generally admitted duty-free or at very low rates. Tariff rates tend to increase with the level of processing, with moderate tariffs on semi-manufactured goods and higher tariffs on finished products. As a result of the escalation of the nominal tariff structure by stages of processing there is a considerable difference between the nominal and effective rates of tariff in developed countries, Japan being no exception. In fact, according to an estimate by the US International Trade Commission, the absolute rates of both nominal and effective protection in 1975 were significantly higher in Japan than in the USA and the EEC. However, as Lal points out, the effective rate of protection given in Table 3.1 is now probably an overestimate. Since Japan made unilateral cuts in tariffs after the completion of the Kennedy Round it is possible that the correct average effective tariff in Japan has dropped significantly.[18] Moreover, the differential between nominal and effective rates of protection is lowest in Japan (Table 3.1).

The escalation of tariff rates on semi-manufactured and finished products has been clearly brought out in a study prepared by the World Bank for the Tokyo Round of multilateral trade negotiations (MTN). It shows that in the EEC the average tariff on dutiable raw material in 1973 was around 3.4 per cent as against 9.6 per cent on semi-manufactured products. In the USA the respective rates were 6.1 and 9 per cent, while in Japan they were 9.3 and 9.9 per cent.[19] Thus in the EEC the tariffs on semi-manufactured products were nearly three times those on raw materials. In the USA tariffs on semi-manufactured products were almost 50 per cent more while the differential in Japan was only 6 per cent, even though the rate of tariff on semi-manufactured products was much the same as in the EEC and the USA. However, as stated earlier, because of the unilateral reduction in tariffs the Japanese tariff levels on semi-manufactured products are now probably significantly lower than in the EEC and the USA.

It seems, therefore, that in protecting their agriculture as well as discriminating between the import of raw materials and finished and semi-finished products Japan has adopted policies similar to those commonly practised by the West. Most of the richer countries of the West, particularly the USA and the EEC, have used government procurement policies, administrative and technical regulations, including those relating to quality control, health standards, measurement and packing specifications etc. for the explicit or implicit purpose of restricting imports, particularly from the developing countries. Japanese policies in this respect are much the same as those adopted by the West. It has been estimated that over half of the non-tariff barriers (NTBs) in Japan and the USA are due to various health, sanitary and special licencing regulations such as quarantine regulations for pets etc. France uses special import charges and quantitative import restrictions to restrict entry. In the USA quantitative restrictions and voluntary export restraints are fairly common.[20]

Seen in this perspective, the outcry in the West against Japanese import restriction does not have much justification. We shall now examine the nature and justification of some of the grievances in greater detail.

One of the most common Western complaints relates to Japanese product standards. The *Task Force Report* complained that 'As a rule, Japanese agencies do not accept the results of tests conducted outside of Japan when those agencies are considering applications for approval for sale of particular products in Japan. To repeat the tests in Japan is extra cost to American firms and can result in enormous time delays.'[21] It is suggested that, contrary to the Japanese practice, US official agencies are generally willing to accept foreign companies' self-certification or a foreign laboratory's test.[22] The Japanese government has already introduced significant changes for electrical appliance testing.[23] Such standards in Japan are often set by joint committees formed by Japanese industries and the government. In the past it was alleged that foreign companies were often 'taken by surprise' because of sudden changes in such regulations. To meet this grievance the Japanese government has gone out of its way to allow qualified technical representatives of US industries to join these technical committees. The Japanese government has also decided to produce an official English language translation of the electrical standards.[24]

The other common complaint concerns the MITI's 'administrative guidance'. The US *Task Force Report* mentions several cases, one of them diammonium phosphate (DAP), a chemical largely imported from the USA for use in the manufacture of a chemical fertiliser as a substitute for rock phosphate. The US argument is that because of the rising costs of energy it pays to use DAP rather than rock phosphate. Under the circumstances, the MITI guidelines to limit imports of DAP at 20 per cent of the demand was unfair and discriminatory towards the US DAP industry. The reason for the MITI guidelines (which were not mandatory in any case) to any neutral observer would seem perfectly justified. The Japanese fertiliser industry has a significant fixed investment in rock-processing facilities which have been operating at less than 50 per cent capacity. US industries in their negotiations with foreign countries have often insisted that they would buy their raw materials from their own subsidiaries even though it has often been more expensive than the domestically available raw materials.[25] In any case, as the MITI claimed, the 'guidelines' were flexible and the DAP already being imported into Japan since 1978 was in fact 35 per cent of the total supply,[26] nearly twice as much as the 'guidelines' had suggested.

Another case that the *Task Force Report* pointed out related to a hepatitis-testing reagent manufactured by an American firm. The report complained that a 'buy Japanese' bias has limited imports from the US companies. In spite of the technical superiority of the product the manufacturers have failed to persuade the Japanese Red Cross to use this product. Nor have the manufacturers been able to obtain approval for reimbursement under a national health insurance plan. The report also referred to the case of dialysis filters produced by another US firm which has suffered a decline in its demand because of the change in the method of reimbursement by the Japanese Ministry of Health and Welfare (MHW) in early 1978. In both cases the Japanese government has been pressurised into giving in.[27]

One of the most publicised issues between the two countries has been the government's 'buy Japanese' procurement policies. In Japan, as in other countries, government procurement is a highly decentralised process which gives a great deal of autonomy to the lower levels of the official hierarchy. The US argument is that procurement in Japan is

carried out through thousands of individual bureau offices which solicit
bids through the 'old school tie' network. In many cases this is based on
oral, informal or vague standards and 'extra-legal administrative
guidance'.[28]

Once again this grievance seems strange coming from the USA when
a similar system prevails there. According to Malcolm Crawford

> Government procurement is another major non-tariff barrier. Here
> the US Federal Government is probably a little cleaner than Britain,
> France or Japan. Defence spending in or near the US is virtually
> closed to foreign suppliers, but other centralized federal purchasing
> departments use only a 6% margin of preference (generally)[29] for the
> American product under the Buy American Act. State and local
> government preferences tend to be more arbitrary, though, and
> there is much more in the way of implicit 'Buy American' clauses
> in the private sector than there is in Europe. Insurance companies,
> for instance, tend to insist on testing arrangements provided by
> domestic industries, and these often imply buying the domestic
> equipment as well.[30]

Under the Tokyo Round of the Multilateral Trade Negotiations (MTN)
it has been agreed that the participating countries would discontinue
preferential treatment for domestic products and domestic suppliers in
government procurement. The code governing procurement came into
effect in January 1981. But the scope of the code is still under dispute.
In fact, the US Trade Agreements Act of 1979 provides for several
exclusions from the operation of the code, such as small business and
minority business programmes, certain Defence Department purchases,
state and local government preferences and various transportation
programmes.[31]

Government procurement is one more instance where the Japanese
government has given way to somewhat unfair US pressure. In 1978
the Japanese government announced 'unilateral efforts' to open their
government procurement to foreign bidding.[32] The Nippon Telephone
and Telegraph Public Corporation's (NTT) claim that since it was a
semi-government organisation it was not bound by recent procurement
regulation changes, continues to be contested by the US government
under pressure from the US telecommunication industry. It has been
argued by US interests that

> the Japanese are using their protected home market to improve their

telecommunications technology while exporting as much as they can as fast as they can into the open American market. Since telecommunications is one of the industries 'of the future', this type of one-sided and unfair trade competition is particularly serious. There is growing concern that in telecommunications the United States may be facing job-displacing import competition while items which the United States makes competitively are denied access to export markets.[33]

The Japanese case is based on similar considerations. Manufacturers argue that the 'open door policy' will have serious adverse consequences particularly for medium- and small-scale enterprises. It is suggested that 'the so-called "NTT Family" which consists of the companies delivering their products to NTT, has about 200 members.[34] With the exception of four big companies (Japan Electric, Fujitsu, Hitachi, and Oki Electric Industry) almost all of these members are medium and small enterprises, whose products are purchased almost exclusively by NTT. They will be affected seriously.'[35] The related labour unions such as the National Telecommunications Workers Union (*Zendentsu*) and the National Federation of Electric Machinery Workers Union (*Denki Roren*) are alarmed that the 'employment situation, which is already reaching serious proportions, will worsen even further'.[36] Other arguments relate to technical matters. It is argued by the Japanese that if equipment produced by different manufacturers is mixed together within the same system, the functioning of the system as a whole will decline, leading to a deterioration of service and an increase in maintenance expenses.[37] *Nikkan Kogyo* wrote that the opening up of the telecommunications industry was reminiscent of the 'British tragedy'. According to that newspaper, at the end of the 1960s when an open bidding system was adopted in Britain the delivery of switching systems was greatly delayed,[38] which resulted in a decline in the quality of telephone services. The Japanese telecommunications industry is also concerned that it will have to share its know-how with foreign suppliers. This concern was recently voiced by the chairman of the Communications Machine Industry Association:

If the open bidding system is adopted, the biggest weakness lies at the stage where the specifications are prepared. Although specifications can be mentioned sweepingly, the contents are complex. Tens of check items concerning materials, structure, and inspection are arranged, and minute figures fill the space between lines compactly. Moreover, the specifications contain not only numerical figures but also nuances which do not appear between the lines. They are technological know-how.[39]

There is concern in the industry that 'some of the technology worked out with difficulty will be easily handed over to various foreign countries'.[40] There is an increasing fear among Japanese manufacturers that the US government is conniving with the US telecommunications and computer industries, who have been attempting to obtain Japanese technology but so far without success. *Mainichi* recently wrote:

. . . the Japanese manufacturers fear, above all, that NTT's superb technology, which was a hidden motive power for the rapid growth of production of communications apparatuses and computers in Japan, may become known to their American rivals. As a matter of fact, IBM, a giant in the world of computer production, strongly requested the release of the patent rights held by NTT several years ago. This request, however, did not realize, because it was strongly opposed by NTT. Among the Japanese manufacturers of communications apparatuses and computers, therefore, there is the persistent view that the request for the opening of the door by NTT represents the request of IBM and other American manufacturers of communications apparatuses for the release of NTT's up-to-date technology. So it is possible to think that the present problem is not a problem for NTT alone, but a race between Japan and the US for leadership in the field of communications and data processing, where fierce struggles among enterprises of the advanced countries are expected to occur hereafter.[41]

It must be remembered that the NTT was right in pointing out that most of the EEC nations and northern European countries maintain the negotiated formula even for the procurement of materials and goods by government-affiliated enterprises.[42] In the US itself, American Telephone & Telegraph Company (ATT), which is a private enterprise, purchases about 80 per cent of the material it needs from its subsidiary Western Electric (WE), and the remaining 20 per cent is purchased under negotiated contracts rather than through open tenders.[43]

It can also be argued that both the NTT fears about reduced efficiency and loss of technological 'secrets' have some validity. So far, under the so-called 'negotiated formula' the NTT issues orders mainly to those enterprises which have, in co-operation with the NTT, invested considerable sums in research and development expenditure. The enterprises which have not done so have to pay charges for technological guidance — which amounts to a charge on the accummulated know-how — to the enterprises which co-operated in the joint development of technology.[44] NTT prescribes very rigid specifications; it investigates enterprises' production processes, methods of purchasing materials and quality control as well as the training of their employees. When defective items are discovered, the supplier is punished by suspension of existing or new orders. The NTT has a significant influence over its subcontractors in much the same way as other major Japanese industries maintain rigorous control over theirs. The NTT calculates the supply price on a cost-plus basis which takes into account cost of materials, working efficiency, etc. It is unlikely that the NTT could have the same kind of quality control over products supplied from foreign sources. If the rejection rates were high, manufacturers from the West would question the NTT's motives and pressurise their governments to intervene on their behalf. It is interesting to see that the 'vanguards' of free enterprise and *laissez-faire* run to the state to protect (or support) them, through the political process, against their competitors.

This is not a new phenomenon. It is exactly what British industry did in the nineteenth century to prevent industrialisation in British colonies. It is well known that with the emergence of the cotton-textile industry in India the petitioning by the Manchester Chamber of Commerce to the British parliament to obtain official action for slowing down Indian industrialisation was not unusual.[45]

The way that the US handles these complaints, as if they were national issues of some magnitude, has continually irritated the Japanese. This is clear from a recent *Japan Times* editorial on the NTT affair. The newspaper was rather critical of the NTT's 'buy Japanese' policies but on the whole it expressed a deep sense of exasperation at the particular issue being blown out of proportion. It wondered whether the 'particular issue is worth the hue and cry raised about it'.[46] Although it felt satisfaction over the Strauss-Ushiba agreement[47] of certain principles for future negotiations over government procurement, it stressed:

In spite of the temporary return of peace or the prospect for orderly negotiations over the NTT issue ahead, the present accord does not necessarily mean that Japan and the US will never again run into abrasive trade issues in the future. New problems rather will inevitably crop up in both new and familiar fields of the

Japan-US trade.

Lying at the root of the Japan-US trade disequilibrium are not only trade barriers in Japan, real or imagined, but the decline in productivity and competitiveness on the part of US industry. The problems of productivity and export performance are of a structural nature, and for this reason cannot be expected to disappear overnight.

Even when the scope of the NTT's procurement open to foreign bidding is expanded to a major extent, American electronics and computer manufacturers would not always be successful bidders. Although US producers of communication equipment are often credited with a technological lead over their Japanese counterparts, such facts as pricing, product reliability, the date of delivery, and post-sales services are equally decisive in final decisions on the awarding of contracts.

All in all, the bilateral trade disequilibrium with the U.S. will be likely to persist for a long time to come . . .

After protracted negotiation the Japanese and US governments reached an agreement in December 1980.[48] Japan agreed to open NTT contracts to foreigners in three stages. Materials and equipment that are not related directly to NTT's telecommunications system will be procured by competitive bidding from both domestic and foreign suppliers. The total value of such purchases is estimated at $1.5 billion per annum. Those standardised items which the NTT needs for its telecommunications system will continue to be bought from selected suppliers. For highly sophisticated mainframe equipment, like switchboards, the NTT will invite leading Japanese and foreign producers to participate in joint research and development.[49]

This agreement is not going to bring the US-Japan trade friction to an end. In this context the point made by the *Japan Times* about the need for structural change in the US economy — and for that matter in most Western economies — is a vital one. Increasing protectionism, at best, gives them a breathing space. In so far as it means inaction on the structural front, no amount of accommodation by the Japanese is going to help them out of their malaise. Increasing trade restrictions at home and pressurising Japan politically to give more and more concessions will in the end be self-defeating. This process will not only further delay the domestic structural changes required within these countries but also hurt world trade and consequently world economic expansion. We will take up some of these points in some detail later.

Non-tariff Export Promotion

Foreign competitors have frequently accused the Japanese government of artificially stimulating exports.[50] The main attack is on government export promotion and market expansion programmes, official export financing and tax policies. 'Western' trade interests have argued that such programmes, by increasing the competitiveness of Japanese exports, have hampered the export prospects of US and EEC products. It is true that the Japanese export stimulation programmes are well organised but, on the other hand, they are not the only countries with such programmes. All the major competitors (the USA, West Germany, the UK, France, Italy and Canada) have similar programmes. In fact, the UK, France and Italy have more rigorous programmes than those of Japan.

Export Promotion

Most countries have basic informational services as well as marketing assistance programmes such as trade fairs, centres, missions and visitors' programmes. Some also have domestic programmes to encourage and assist potential exporters.[51] The British government have 'the largest and the most intensive promotional program'.[52] They maintain a subsidised computer data system on export opportunities and also provide a full range of export services such as overseas trade intelligence, trade fairs and foreign export publicity together with subsidised programmes for the encouragement of market research. Official efforts are directed towards the sales of British invisible exports (e.g. financial and engineering services, insurance, professional consultancies). French government programmes offer a substantial range of services and are as intensive as the British, but they concentrate mainly on the small- and medium-sized firms, which is not necessarily the case with British programmes, which provide benefits mainly to large concerns.[53] The US export promotion programme, one of the largest in terms of costs and expenditure, gives particular emphasis to marketing intelligence and overseas promotion activities through trade fairs and centres. In order to encourage export awareness the USA maintains 43 field offices within the country to service potential exporters. This programme is considered to be one of the strongest in the world. Only the Dutch and West German export programmes are relatively modest. Their official efforts are largely confined to providing basic economic intelligence to their exporters. They do, however, subsidise their chambers of commerce to run and expand their export promotion activities.[54]

According to estimates of the US Congressional Research Service the UK has the largest gross outlay on official export promotion (Table 3.2).

Table 3.2: Export Promotion Expenditure in Selected Countries, 1976

Countries	Total value of exports (million US $)	Government promotion spending (million US $)	Relative promotion intensity (spending per $1,000 of exports)
Japan	67,710	60.7	0.9
UK	46,042	95.7	2.1
Italy	36,170	59.8	1.7
France	56,607	80.7	1.4
USA	114,887	64.4	0.6
The Netherlands	40,592	18.7	0.5
Canada	39,028	14.5	0.4
West Germany	103,560	15.5	0.2
Switzerland	14,938	1.8	0.1

Source: Congressional Research Service, *Export Stimulation Programs* (1978), p. CRS 18.

This is closely followed by France; the third largest outlay is by the USA; in terms of total expenditure Japan ranks fourth. She has been spending substantially less than the UK, France and the USA, the three most vocal critics of Japanese official export promotion efforts. A more meaningful comparison is to express total export promotion outlays in terms of total exports (column 4, Table 3.2), which is defined as the relative promotion intensity. It is clear that Japanese efforts are certainly more intense than the USA but they are much less than those of the UK, France and Italy. In terms of promotional expenditure per $1,000 of exports the UK government spends more than twice as much as the Japanese, France 80 per cent more and Italy 50 per cent more.

Even in terms of overseas manpower availability, the UK and France are better provided than Japan. For instance, France maintains about 190 Foreign Ministry commercial offices and 1,100 other overseas French staff in addition to some 500 local employees at 229 foreign posts. The UK employs an extensive network of 396 commercial offices plus over 1,100 support staff at 196 foreign posts. Against this Japan maintains only 275 Foreign Ministry commercial offices at 146 foreign posts and 275 JETRO professionals at 76 foreign posts.[55]

Thus both in terms of financial resources and of personnel the UK and French programmes are much larger than those of the Japanese.

Export Financing

As in the case of export promotion, most advanced countries have some system of official assistance to private financing of exports, and this takes various forms. Sometimes the government operates as a 'lender of last resort' and provides credits at rates cheaper than what is available on the market and for longer terms if private lending institutions are not forthcoming. In addition, it may decide to offer guarantees or insurance and thereby reduce the risks of private lenders or investors. Sometimes the government may provide the credit as well as the guarantees required for promoting a sale.[56] According to the US Congressional Research Service, France has the most concessional export financial system. Apart from encouraging the private banks to make special medium-term fixed rate loans to exporters the government provides direct credits up to 85 per cent of the value of export contracts on long-term loans (over seven years).[57] In the case of exports to developing countries, foreign aid credit (up to 50 per cent of the value of the contract) is available to exporters to enable them to extend longer term loans (up to 25 years) at very low rates (3 per cent) of interest.[58] Capital goods exports are supported by cheap insurance cover. Exporters are also provided with highly subsidised insurance protection against inflation or exchange rate fluctuations.[59] The British government assists exports through refinancing and interest subsidies. They also provide comprehensive export insurance and loan guarantees covering most short-term contracts as well as medium- and long-term contracts with regard to capital goods and construction services.[60] Exporters are also given some coverage by inflation-indemnity insurance. In the USA export financing is available in the form of long-term credits at near-commercial rates for nearly 42 per cent of the contract value of large capital equipment and services. Some insurance against political risk is also provided.[61] In Japan direct credit up to half the contract value for medium- and long-term export is provided at near-market rates. The government also provides export credit insurance and guarantees for private bank loans at relatively low cost.[62] They also provide exchange risk insurance for Japanese exporters. A summary of the comparative official export financing programmes is given in Table 3.3.

It appears that on the criteria of both total outstanding credits and credit authorisation Japan has been spending significantly less than the

Table 3.3: Export Financing Programmes in Selected Countries, 1976 (in million US $)

Item	Japan	Canada	France	Italy	UK	West Germany	USA
Total outstanding	656	3,077	1,799	1,862	6,393	KFW^a 1,334	15,415
Net 1976 increase or decrease	NA	550	–114	–711	–24	KFW 54	91 direct −93 re-fin.
Credit authorisation	3,266	718	1,395	1,451	1,152	KFW 1,135	2,285 direct (2,098)
(Disbursement)	(2,263)	(504)	(NA)	(264)	(2,256)	KFW (392)	1,204 re-fin. (101)
Credit disbursements as share of capital goods exports	9.8%	4.2%	NA	3.3%	15.8%	1.3%	5.7% direct 0.3% re-fin.
Total outstanding insurance (Net 1976 increase)	51,949 (13,849)	886 (70)	24,477 (8,987)	9,376 (371)	31,556 (2,529)	27,762 (7,882)	10,100 (330)
Share of exports benefiting from official programmes	49%	5%	39%	9%	45%	10%	8%

a. KFW is an official agency. In addition low-cost export capital is provided by AKA, which is a consortium of private banks.
Source: Congressional Research Service, *Export Stimulation Programs* (1978), p. CRS 47.

UK, France and the USA. It is only with respect to outstanding insurance or insurance authorisation that Japan seems to provide better financial support. On the other hand, nearly half of Japanese exports benefit from official programmes, whereas the proportion is as low as 8 per cent for the USA. However, the shares for the UK at 45 per cent and France at 39 per cent are not far behind that of Japan.

Two other measures of export financing — the share of credit supplied by official and semi-official sources and the cost of borrowing — can be important elements in export competitiveness. On both these criteria Japanese official supports are not very different to those of its competitors. Official sources cover only about half of Japanese export credits both for medium- and long-term as against anything between 60 and 85 per cent for other countries (Table 3.4). Only in the case of long-term export credits do USA official sources provide a little less (i.e. an average of 42 per cent). So far as the effective cost to borrowers is concerned the Japanese rates come out much the same as her competitors. It can therefore be concluded that the Japanese government does not provide subsidised credit to her exporters on a more lavish scale than most of her competitors. British and French governments do much more.

Table 3.4: Relative Rates for Official Export Credit Programmes in Selected Countries (%)

Countries	Most common rate		Percentage of contract officially supported		Effective cost of funds to borrowers	
	Medium-term	Long-term	Medium-term	Long-term	Medium-term	Long-term
Japan	7.0	7.5	50	50	8.3	8.6
Canada	–	8.5	–	60	–	9.2
France	–	–	60	60	8.0	8.2
Germany	5.6	8.0	80	45	8.1	8.6
Italy	8.5	8.5	85	85	9.0	9.0
UK	7.5	8.0	85	85	8.7	8.9
USA	8.0	8.4	85	42	9.2	8.3

Source: Congressional Research Service, *Export Stimulation Programs* (1978), p. CRS 59.

Tax Policies

There are two common methods of export promotion through tax incentives. One consists of rebates to indirect taxes, the second of deferring tax on earnings from exports. The practice adopted by most countries is to rebate export earning against indirect taxes and to impose a comparable tax on imports.[63] This method does not contravene GATT regulations since the practice does not discriminate between foreign and locally produced goods.[64]

The GATT rule was recently challenged in the US courts. Under the provisions of the Trade Act of 1974, the Zenith Radio Corporation requested the US Treasury to impose countervailing duties on Japanese electronic imports, which benefited from the Japanese government's policy of granting rebates from indirect taxes. The US Customs gave the judgement in favour of Zenith but this decision was set aside by the US Court of Customs and Patent Appeals. Later, the US Supreme Court upheld the view that the rebate on the Japanese commodity tax was not a bounty or subsidy.[65]

GATT rules do not permit rebate on direct tax. In practice, however, some partial exemption is allowed. Many European countries do not tax − or do not tax within the current tax year - incomes earned by their subsidiaries incorporated overseas. For instance, it is alleged that the French government allows exporters to arrange their intra-company transfers in such a way that most of the profits accrue to a subsidiary in a low-tax country. Most other countries, including the USA, have the same provision for deferral or exemption of taxes on foreign earnings or the possibility of transferring profits to a sales subsidiary.[66]

Since 1972 the US government has allowed tax-deferral from federal income tax on one half of export profits. This benefit is provided under the Domestic International Sales Corporations (DISC) provision of the tax code to companies forming a DISC. The legality of this provision was challenged in the GATT by the Dutch, French and Belgian governments. The USA government brought a countercharge against the three countries that their practice of allowing export profits to escape taxation by the use of exempt foreign sales subsidiaries was against GATT provisions. The GATT decision went against both groups, which indicated that all four countries were violating GATT rules with regard to direct taxes.[67] Although there is some provision for a deferral of taxes on export profits in Japan, they are more limited than in the USA and some of the EEC countries; certainly Japan has not been found to be violating GATT regulations.

Dumping

Another issue related to export promotion is the question of dumping. The GATT provides 'that importing countries may take compensating action against trading partners found to be dumping goods in their markets or expanding sales through subsidization of their exports. The importing country may impose antidumping duties whenever and to the extent that the sale of imported goods takes place in the importing country's market at less than its "normal value" and results in material injury to the domestic industry'.[68]

Both the USA and the EEC have had frequent recourse to these GATT provisions. For instance, during 1971-7 the US International Trade Commission considered 57 'escape clause' cases which, if proved genuine might have led to the imposition of higher customs tariffs or import quotas, including orderly marketing agreements and voluntary export restraint agreements.[69] Within the same period 140 cases were investigated under the anti-dumping provisions.[70] Not all these cases led to the imposition of higher customs tariffs or import quotas but it certainly amounted to harassment and annoyance of the parties concerned. As to the 57 'escape clause' cases, in only four cases[71] were further import restrictions imposed. In 26 cases the findings of the US International Trade Commission were negative. In the remaining 27 cases the International Trade Commission recommendations were drastically modified by the US President. He decided either not to impose higher import duties or to soften the hardships on the affected industries and their workers by providing adjustment assistance.[72] Similarly, out of 140 anti-dumping cases investigated, positive findings were made in only 41 cases, of which only 17 involved Japanese products.[73] Out of the 30 cases involving Japanes companies investigated or decided during 1978 during the Antidumping Act of 1921, the Trade Act of 1974 ('escape clause') and the Tariff Act of 1930 (relating to countervailing and unfair practices) only in six cases did the Department of Treasury find that the allegations of less than fair value (LTFV) sales were partially or wholly true.[74] However, only in three cases (carbon steel plates, steel wires strand and impression fabric) did the International Trade Commission (ITC) decide that the Japanese LTFV sales were injuring or likely to harm domestic industries. Out of the six 'escape clause' investigations during 1978 the ITC found only four (citizen band (CB) transceivers, industrial fasteners, stainless steel table flatware and bicycle tyres and tubes) to be causing substantial injury to domestic industries and recommended impositions of higher import duties for five years. The US President rejected the imposition of higher duties on steel flatware and bicycle tyres and tubes. He also rejected initially the raising of import duty on industrial fasteners, but under increasing pressure from Congress he agreed to raise the import duties on steel bolts, nuts and large screws as well as on CB transceivers. But in all these cases the President decided on a smaller rise and for shorter periods than the ITC had recommended.[75] More recently, in a case brought before the ITC by the UAW and Ford Motor Company, the Commission ruled that the perilous state of the US motor industry was caused by the energy crisis and the changing demands of the consumers and not by Japanese car imports.[76] It seems, therefore, that many of the dumping cases brought against the Japanese firms did not have much substance.

Thus it is clear that both in terms of import restrictions, i.e. tariffs, quotas and procurement, and export promotion and export incentives the Japanese situation is not very different to those of the USA and the EEC. On any count the EEC has become a more protected region, while its export promotion, particularly in France and the UK, is certainly more intensive than that of Japan. So the reasons for the relative success of Japanese exports and the relative failure of these countries to make any substantial gains in the Japanese market has to be found more in the inability of these countries to bring about significant increases in productivity and in their slowness in bringing about structural changes rather than in Japanese import restrictions and export promotion. But before we discuss the nature and significance of such factors it may be useful to look into some of the allegations directed at the Japanese distribution system.

The Japanese Distribution System

It is frequently alleged that one of the chief non-tariff barriers to increased trade with Japan is the Japanese distribution system. It has been suggested that it is 'the closeness of the links between manufacturers, wholesalers and customers in the Japanese distribution system which makes entry by foreign firms a time-consuming and expensive business'.[77] This comment by a British parliamentarian is typical of foreign criticism of the Japanese distribution system. Japanese government sources admit 'that distribution is a field where modernisation is lagging behind, various stages of distribution are complicated and distribution routes involve multiple levels of wholesaling'.[78] An official report by the MITI, covering six main product areas — cars, golf clubs, cigarette lighters, wine, whisky and chocolate — has conceded that because of the complexity of the distribution system and the high margins charged by dealers, the difference between the retail and the cif price for imported goods was substantially higher in Japan than in her competitors.[79] For instance, imported cars in Japan sell at nearly 2 to 2.4 times the cif price. This differential is only 1.3 to 1.4 times in the USA. However, the situation in France was close to that in Japan. For golf clubs the cif price in Japan was only 40 per cent of retail prices. In France it was only 35 per cent. In fact, the distribution cost of Japanese home-made golf clubs was still higher. For cigarette lighters the Japanese retail price was 7.5 times higher than the cif price, a ratio similar to that of the USA. In the case of a particular (unnamed) brand of whisky the retail price in Japan was 10 times the cif price, but it was not much different in France. With wine and chocolate the Japanese differential between cif and retail prices was the highest.

It is also acknowledged in official circles that in the case of products such as cars, electrical household appliances and pianos the market is highly oligopolistic and their distribution channels are governed by a chain of close business affiliations. As a result it is difficult for a foreign business to get its product into the distribution network of a rival Japanese firm. On the other hand, there are large numbers of foreign firms, even British (British Oxygen Company, British Engineers Ltd, Cadbury, Davy International, EMI, etc.),[80] who have achieved significant success. It is important to note the term 'British' because the questionable export performance of British industries *vis-à-vis* other competitors is legendary. The complaints against British goods (unreliability, old-fashioned, disregard of consumers' preferences, delay in delivery, etc.) commonly heard in overseas markets today were not uncommon in the 1890s. Except for very expensive luxuries like Rolls Royce cars, British goods could not easily compete with German and US products even in colonial markets.[81] Much the same situation exists today. Most British successes in the Japanese market have been 'largely confined to specialities and high-quality goods. Mass-produced articles are notably absent from the list.'[82] It is often forgotten by foreign exporters that the Japanese consumer is rather discerning and attaches overwhelming importance to reliability in delivery dates, spare parts and servicing. It is reported that 'Toyota regards a customer as lost if he is not delivered the exact model of his choice — colour, styling, accessories — within ten days of his order'.[83]

As we shall see later, the Japanese government and large companies in their anxiety to avert unwarranted import restrictions on their products in the West have gone out of their way to run seminars, organise trade fairs and provide information to foreign companies on how to sell their products in the Japanese market.[84]

One of the leading organisations in this field is the JETRO, whose mandate was to assist Japanese export promotion. JETRO has done so much to assist foreign businessmen in expanding their exports to the Japanese market that it has been nicknamed JITRO by the Japanese, the Japanese Import Trade Organisation.[85] Besides, some large companies have, in fact, set up a separate division to handle imports of Western goods into Japan. One of the best examples is the Sony Trading Corporation, which came to naught because of the unreliability of British products. Some time ago Sony Trading signed a contract to import British gas heaters. Reportedly,[86] when the heaters arrived at Yokohama docks too many of them were defective; the pilot lights blew out in the Japanese northerly gales. As a result the entire consignment was dumped into the Pacific and an investment of half a million dollars had to be written off. Much the same happened to Heathkit, not because of technical problems but because of high costs. Sony found that after paying the costs of transport, insurance, etc. together with distributions costs, it was too expensive to sell, but Heathkit would not allow a larger discount, nor would they permit Sony to produce and market the parts in Japan as a joint venture. Sony had to incur a loss on this transaction as well.[87]

More recently, the Tokyo Metropolitan Consumers' Centre tests on imported women's wear, including those from Europe, found many defective in spite of the high-quality image. Tests were conducted on them for labelling, sewing, colour-fastness and shrinkage.[88] Similar reports are heard with regard to imported cars. A Tokyo-based car-importing firm, which has been importing cars since 1915, 'recognises that it has a problem with the generally poorer quality of imported cars . . . Even more of a stumbling block is technical quality. Foreign cars are estimated . . . to average 30 per cent more time in garage workshops every year than comparable Japanese models.'[89]

The Japanese rightly stress the fact that 'the distribution system and trading practice in a country' are 'formed through [sic] the historical progress of its society, economy and culture. Without a proper understanding of this process, no attempt to enter the market will succeed. The key to success would be "when in Rome do as the Romans do".'[90]

Unfortunately, the attitude of the West is too Eurocentric to understand, let alone make genuine efforts to learn about (and from) other countries, cultures and civilisations.[91] As a European civil servant has recently stressed:

The Europeans have consistently regarded themselves as teachers and the Japanese as imitators or learners . . . They had a 'mission civilisatrice' as the French put it. That attitude has persisted right to our own day, as the following comment made by a well-known European expert on Japan in 1978 illustrates: 'When it comes to evaluating the attitude of the Japanese toward any new technology, one could compare them to eager pupils looking up at us, their teachers'.

Japan was never a European colony, but the attitudes of colonial and imperial superiority towards an 'Oriental' people have been slow to die.

Because Europeans felt they had nothing to learn from Japan, they have consistently underestimated the country, failed to learn from it or form timely images of it, and therefore they have frequently been caught by surprise.[92]

The Americans have shown similar tendencies. Their businesses try to exert political pressures on the government through various lobbies rather than learn about the people and their culture, and make genuine efforts to enter the Japanese market. Some of these points were highlighted in a paper presented to the US-Japan Task Force by Kabun Muto, a member of the Japanese Diet:

There are a variety of differences between American enterprises and Japanese enterprises in so far as export efforts are concerned. For example, first there is a difference in the number of trading offices and employees of each in the other's country. In 1977 American enterprises had 162 trading offices in Japan with a total of 1901 employees. In contrast, Japanese concerns had some 764 such offices in the United States employing 20,884 workers, approximately 11 times the American level. Second, Japanese exporters have done thorough research on the language, way of life, and other facets of the United States as part of their efforts to promote their exports. Again in contrast, study by American exporters of the language and way of life in Japan falls far short of the necessary level, and there are even some exporters who are ignorant of the FOB, CIF, and other trading prerequisites essential to setting export prices.

Third, Japanese exporters prepare pamphlets and other materials in English for use in the United States, in this and other ways making continuous efforts to achieve exports [sic]. Here, too there is a difference, as almost all American exporters use promotional materials in their own language and break off their export efforts after only a few attempts.[93]

The *Task Force Report* admitted the validity of many of these criticisms.[94] An independent report quoted in the report also echoes the feelings of Kabun Muto. The report prepared by the Boston Consulting Group for the US government's Under-secretary of the Treasury stressed that:

> The more important relic of Japan's obdurately protectionist past, in terms of consequences for present trade flows, is found in the attitudes of the United States and European business community and some government officials towards Japan. Most American companies and most senior United States businessmen have had direct experience with Japan. Their experience has been with a closed market into which direct investment was possible only under the most onerous conditions and into which technology could be sold only under rigid scrutiny.
>
> The experience has been at best frustrating for most companies, and at its worst given rise to dangerous competitors in the domestic market. *The West has been slow to perceive the recent rapid changes in this distant and ill-understood society; many views and attitudes that are no longer valid are still tenaciously held.*[95] (Italics mine)

In view of these remarks, while one must not underestimate the difficulties of entry into the Japanese distribution network, one wonders whether a genuine effort has been made in this direction. In the West, particularly in those countries which had extensive colonial markets, businesses never really learnt to compete in foreign markets. Colonial history is full of examples of how governments, directly or indirectly, featherbedded inefficient domestic industries to enable them to survive and 'compete' in colonial markets. In the somewhat changed contemporary international scene, when industries find themselves unable to compete in foreign markets they use their political leverage with their government to obtain concessions by foreign governments.

Discrimination against Overseas Banks

The *Task Force Report* also complained that while Japanese banks have been allowed to operate freely in the US market, foreign banks face discriminatory restriction in the Japanese market. Foreign banks cannot finance trade between Japan and other countries and as a result the trade gap between Japan and the West widens. The report gave the following examples of such restrictions:

(1) Exclusion from the Tokyo Clearing House and Bank wire transfer system. Foreign banks must clear promissory notes and fund transfers through a Japanese city bank [i.e. a money market bank] that is a Clearing House member;

(2) Prohibitions on funding by issuing term debentures or certificates of deposit, while the Bank of Tokyo, which has an international orientation similar to that of foreign banks in Japan, is permitted to issue term debentures and certificates of deposit. Major Japanese money market banks with a more domestic orientation are not permitted to issue CDs, but of course have access to yen funding through a large number of branches and their deposits;

(3) Foreign banks are usually restricted to one branch and subject to guidance against soliciting deposits from the public, etc.;

(4) Foreign banks are restricted in establishing consumer finance operations;

(5) Foreign banks are prohibited from acquiring Japanese financial institutions.[96]

These feelings were echoed by the Senate Report on the International Banking Act of 1978. Some of the points raised by the *Task Force Report* were open to question and the Japanese Ministry of Foreign Affairs came out with a point-by-point rebuttal.[97] It contended that the Bank of America, the Citibank, the Chase Manhattan Bank and the Hongkong-Shanghai Bank were participating directly in the clearing of bills. There was also a provision for their participation in the all-bank data communications if they joined the Domestic Exchange Operation Organisation. The Ministry pointed out that the right to issue debentures in Japan was restricted to only three long-term credit banks and one specialised foreign exchange bank. No other Japanese banks have these rights so the question of discrimination does not arise. As to the CDs, i.e. the negotiable certificate of time deposits, there was currently no such system in Japan but arrangements were being made to create such a system in the near future, and when this is established such facilities will be available to foreign banks as well. The Ministry suggested that, contrary to the contention of the *Task Force Report*, at least thirteen of the sixty-one foreign banks had several branches. There are no restrictions on their establishing consumer finance operations. As to the report's allegation that foreign banks are prohibited from acquiring Japanese financial institutions, the Ministry's rebuttal contended that such restrictions, in accordance with the Anti-Monopoly Law, were imposed on national as well as foreign banks. They could not acquire more than 5 per cent of the stock of domestic financial concerns. However, foreign banks are required by law (Foreign Investment Law) to obtain the prior permission of the Ministry of Finance, which is given automatically if the financial institution concerned gives its consent.

Thus many of the allegations made in the report, and commonly believed in the West, even if valid in the past, are now invalid. Some, of the remaining grievances such as those relating to the Japanese distribution system are inherent to the Japanese culture and cannot be changed overnight. It does provide domestic industries with some advantages over imported goods, but this is not the only explanation for the lack of competitiveness of foreign manufacturers. If this were the case, Japanese exports would not be able to compete so effectively in the domestic markets of the West.

Notes

1. R. Ahern, 'Japan-U.S. Trade Imbalance' Issue Brief No. IB 78025', Congressional Research Service, US Library of Congress, p. CRS-5; for the fourth grievance see *Task Force Report*, pp.26-7

2. L.B. Krause and S. Sekiguchi, 'Japan and the World Economy', in H. Patrick and H. Rosovsky (eds.), *Asia's New Giant*, p.453: also Aliber, in Kaplan and Mushakoji (eds.), *Japan, America and the Future World Order*, p.227. See also G.C. Allen, *How Japan Competes: An Assessment of International Trading Practices with Special Reference to 'Dumping'*, p.23.

3. Ibid., p.24.

4. H. Ohta, 'Recent US-Japan Economic Relations: A Japanese View', *US-Japan Trade Council Report 13*, p.2.

5. Ibid.

6. IMF, *Annual Report On Exchange Arrangements and Exchange Restrictions, 1979*, p.431.

7. Ibid., p.431.

8. Ibid., p.432. Steel imports into the USA are now subject to the 'trigger price mechanism' which came into effect in February 1978. The 'trigger price' is calculated on the basis of the cost of production in Japan. If the import prices are below the 'trigger price' the US authorities initiate investigations to determine whether dumping has taken place (for details see page 62).

9. IMF, *Annual Report, 1979*, p.9.

10. Ibid., p.8.

11. IMF, *The Rise in Protectionism*, p.34.

12. Ibid., p.34.

13. Ibid., p.34.

14. Y. Hayami, 'Trade Benefits to All: A Design of the Beef Import Liberalization in Japan'. Quoted in *Task Force Report*, p.38n.

15. M.D. Bale and B.L. Greenshields, *Japan: Production and Imports of Food – An Analysis of the Welfare Cost of Protection*, USDA, Foreign Agricultural Economic Report no. 141 (1979), p.11.

16. *Task Force Report*, p.41.

17. Ibid.

18. D. Lal, *Market Access for Semi-Manufactures from Developing Countries*, p.11.

19. Ibid., p.12, table V.

20. Ibid., pp.16-17: see also V. Roningen and A. Yeats, 'Nontariff Distortions of International Trade: Some Preliminary Empirical Evidence', *Weltwirtschaftliches Archiv*, No. 4 (1976).

21. *Task Force Report*, p.21.

22. Ibid. On the other hand, the US government imposed many restrictions on food imports, 'both for health reasons and overt protection' (see M. Crawford, 'So What's New about Fortress America?', *Sunday Times*, 5 Sept. 1971). Crawford stresses how blatant the US standard regulations are. According to him: 'Standards are, perhaps, the fuzziest area in the non-tariff field. More often than not they can be justified, even where they tend to protect the domestic industry. But the US has some fairly blatant ones, such as the condition that pressure vessels must bear the stamp of the American Society of Mechanical Engineers.'

23. US-Japan Trade Council, *Yearbook of US-Japan Economic Relations, 1979*, pp.58-9.

24. *Task Force Report*, p.21.

25. For instance, a deal between the government of India and one of the leading US corporations for the production of chemical fertiliser failed because the corporation was insisting that they would buy feedstock from foreign sources, even though India had its own surplus feedstock.

26. *Task Force Report*, p.23.

27. Such pressures are being exerted through the 'Trade Study Group' (TSG) and 'Trade Facilitation Committee' (TFC) operating since August and September 1977. These groups are supposedly formats for 'Japanese and Americans to work together in a non-confrontational atmosphere to identify perceived trade barriers, define the facts in each case, and see what mutual steps can be taken to remove the trade irritant'. (*Task Force Report*, p.19). The 'TSG is a combination of government and business officials from both countries that is primarily a fact-gathering/analyzing informal problem resolution group' (ibid., p.20). 'The TFC is a formal intergovernmental organization composed only of government officials. The U.S. Government's participation . . . is supported by extensive staff work of the Department of Commerce in Washington' (ibid., p.20). It is stressed by the *Task Force Report* that 'The TFC's job is literally to "facilitate" the growth of Japan's imports . . . In addition to its efforts to identify and eliminate trade barriers, the TFC helps with various import promotion/buying mission activities' (p.20).

28. *Task Force Report*, p.31.

29. However, this margin is 12 per cent when jobs in depressed areas are at stake and up to 50 per cent on defence contracts; defence includes such items as boots, sailors' bell-bottom trousers and airmen's goggles (see *The Economist* 26 Oct. 1974).

30. Crawford, 'So What's New . . .?' It must be remembered that public procurement is a major bone of contention between the EEC and the US government. The Europeans complain that most of the contracts in the USA are awarded by the states and not by the federal government, and that the states treat European tenders shabbily (see *The Economist*, 26 Oct. 1974).

31. US-Japan Trade Council, *Yearbook, 1979*, pp.59-60.

32. *Task Force Report*, p.31.

33. Ibid., p.33.
34. However, if the original and subcontracting manufacturers are included, the number of companies concerned amounts to 2,000 to 3,000 (*Nikkan Kogyo*, 24 April 1979).
35. *Nihon Kogyo*, 21 Feb 1979.
36. Ibid. *Denki Roren* estimates that nearly 100,000 workers will lose their jobs (*Nihon Keizai*, 3 March 1979).
37. *Mainichi*, 2 May 1979.
38. *Nikkan Kogyo*, 24 April 1979.
39. Ibid.
40. Ibid.
41. *Mainichi*, 2 May 1979.
42. *Asahi*, 4 April 1979.
43. *Nihon Keizai*, 16 May 1980.
44. Ibid.
45. R.P. Dutt, *India Today*, p.125.
46. *The Japan Times*, 5 June 1979.
47. This was the agreement signed between Robert Strauss, the US President's special Representative for Trade Negotiations, and Nobuhiko Ushiba, the Japanese Minister for External Economic Affairs on 13 January 1978.
48. *The Japan Times Weekly*, 6 Dec. 1980, p.1.
49. Ibid.
50. Ahearn, 'Japan-U.S. Trade Imbalance', p.6.
51. U.S. Congressional Research Service, *Export Stimulation Programs in the Major Industrial Countries: The United States and Eight Major Competitors*, 1978, prepared for the Committee on International Relations, U.S. House of Representatives, U.S. Library of Congress, p. CRS-8.
52. Ibid., p. CRS-11.
53. Ibid., pp. CRS 9-11.
54. Ibid., p. CRS 16.
55. Ibid., pp. CRS 19-20. The Japan External Trade Organisation (JETRO) is a semi-autonomous government agency entrusted with export promotion programmes under the general supervision of the Ministry of International Trade and Industry (MITI).
56. US Congressional Research Service, *Export-Stimulation Programs* (1978), p. CRS 40.
57. Ibid., p. CRS 44.
58. Ibid., p. CRS 45.
59. Ibid., p. CRS 45.
60. Ibid., p. CRS 46-8.
61. Ibid., p. CRS 52.
62. Ibid., p. CRS 46.
63. Ibid., p. CRS 68.
64. Ibid., p. CRS 69.
65. Ibid., p. CRS 71. See also *Washington Post*, 21 June 1978, and U.S.-Japan Trade Council, *Yearbook of US-Japan Economic Relations, 1978*, p.63. A similar case was brought by the United States Steel Corporation against the EEC countries regarding the practice of rebating value-added-tax. While the Zenith case was still going on this case was withdrawn when the US government introduced the system of price-triggers.
66. US Congressional Research Service, *Export Stimulation Programs*, (1978), p. CRS 76.
67. Ibid., pp. CRS 76-7.
68. IMF, *The Rise in Protectionism*, pp.5-6.
69. Ibid., p.27.

70. Ibid., p.27.

71. The cases referred to ball-bearings (1973), steel (1976), footwear (1977) and colour television sets (1977).

72. IMF, *The Rise in Protectionism*, p.27.

73. Ibid., pp.27-30.

74. US-Japan Trade Council, *Yearbook, 1978*, p.62. The items concerned were carbon steel plate, welded stainless steel pipe and tubing, steel wire strand for prestressed concrete, motor cycles, impression fabric of man-made fibre and sorbates (p.62).

75. Ibid., p.62.

76. I. Hargreaves, 'Luckless Detroit Still Hopes to Stem Japanese Tide', *Financial Times*, 12 Nov. 1980.

77. M. Meacher, 'Peculiar Japanese Distribution Attitude Forms Non-tariff Barrier', *The Japan Economic Journal* (Supplement), 11 April 1978, p.26.

78. MITI, *Japanese Markets: The Myth and the Reality*, p.5.

79. C. Smith, 'Japan Admits High Imports Mark-up', *Financial Times*, 2 Dec. 1977.

80. For a long list see Allen, *How Japan Competes*, p.40.

81. *British Parliamentary Report*, 1897, Cmnd. 8449.

82. Allen, *How Japan Competes*, pp.40-1. Marks and Spencer is a recent exception. (See B. Appleyard, 'Understanding the Japanese Market', *The Times*, 22 Dec. 1980.)

83. *Financial Times*, 10 Oct. 1972.

84. One recent example of such an effort is the establishment of the Manufactured Imports Promotion Organisation (MIPRO), which is headed by the President of *Keidanren* and is subsidised by the government. It will provide assistance to foreign countries in exporting to Japan. Mention ought to be made also of the *World Import Mart*, launched as a joint venture by the two biggest trading companies, Mitsui and Mitsubishi, and the largest department store, the Mitsukoshi, for the wholesaling and retailing of imported goods. See S. Oba, 'Anglo-Japanese Trade – Some Practical Aspects', *The Japan Economic Journal* (Supplement), 11 April 1978.

85. K. Kentaro, 'Imports Into Japan Rising Fast', *The Japan Times*, 24 April 1979.

86. *Sunday Times*, 16 Oct. 1977.

87. Ibid.

88. *The Japan Times Weekly*, 20 Oct. 1979, p.11.

89. G. Merritt, 'Why Japan's Car Barrier is so Difficult to Breach', *Financial Times*, 7 Nov. 1980.

90. H. Arakawa, 'Japanese Distribution Channels are Flexible and Changing' in *The Japan Economic Journal* (Supplement), 11 April 1978.

91. It has recently been pointed out by the MITI how foreign manufacturers disregard the cultural biases of Japanese consumers. Two examples were mentioned. One was the case of dinner sets. Japanese dinner sets normally come in sets of five, but Western suppliers still continue to supply sets of six, which are disliked by Japanese customers. The second related to measurements. Many Western manufacturers continue to use inches and feet instead of the metric system, which is now internationally used (see *Nihon Keizai*, 19 April 1979). It is interesting to note that similar complaints were being made against British manufacturers in colonial markets in the 1880s (see *British Parliamentary Report*, 1897, Cmnd. 8449).

92. E. Wilkinson, 'It's Back to School for Europeans: Subject is Japan', *The Japan Times Weekly*, 1 Sept. 1979, p.5.

93. Quoted in *Task Force Report*, p.42.

94. Ibid., p.42.

95. Ibid., p.42n.
96. Ibid., p.26.
97. *Nihon Keizai*, 18 March 1979.

4 ECONOMIC AND SOCIAL CONSEQUENCES OF TRADE LIBERALISATION IN JAPAN

We have already mentioned that Japan has made significant efforts towards opening up its economy and liberalising its policies towards imports. In this chapter an attempt will be made to summarise the measures undertaken by the Japanese government and business to reduce the balance of payments surplus, and how these measures have affected various industries and the employment situation in those industries. Some of these measures have been adopted in connection with bilateral negotiations with various countries, particularly the USA, the major trading partner of Japan; others have been adopted in the course of multilateral trade negotiations (MTN); and some, particularly the attempts by Japanese businesses to import and distribute foreign goods, are more or less voluntary in nature. In addition, some reduction of the balance of payments surplus has resulted from the appreciation of the yen following the decision by the Japanese government to have a floating exchange rate.

Multilateral Trade Negotiations

The latest round of multilateral trade negotiations, popularly known as the 'Tokyo Round', was formally opened at a meeting in Japan in September 1973. On this occasion the ministers of the GATT member nations called for an early conclusion of the trade negotiations for tariff reductions and the possible elimination of non-tariff barriers (NTB). The pace of these negotiations was so protracted that they came to be described as 'trench warfare'.[1] Much of the delay was caused by US inability to obtain a negotiating mandate from Congress; then came the Presidential election in 1975 and it was only in March 1976 that President Carter appointed a special US trade negotiator. For obvious reasons, the negotiations were largely dominated by the USA, the EEC and Japan. One of the reasons is that this group of countries together account for 50 per cent of world trade. On the other hand, because of the nature of GATT, which was originally a 'rich men's club', the USA and the European countries have more than their fair share of political and economic power as in other international organisations such as the International Monetary Fund and the World

Bank. Although the USA and the EEC attempted to extract concessions from each other, much of the protracted negotiations, from the arrival of the US special negotiator in Geneva in March 1976 until their completion in April 1979, often degenerated into 'Japan-bashing' by the USA and the EEC.

Though not one of the major achievements of the Tokyo Round, significant reductions in tariffs were made. Unlike the Kennedy Round (1964-9) which agreed upon an across-the-board cut in tariffs, the Tokyo Round opted for a more complicated method of 'harmonisation' which in effect meant that the countries having relatively high rates had to reduce tariffs more drastically than others.

Under this scheme of harmonisation it was agreed that during the eight years following 1980 Japan would reduce its standard tariffs on industrial products by nearly 50 per cent,[2] the USA by 31 per cent and the EEC by 27 per cent.[3] The package also contained eight international codes on non-tariff barriers (NTBs) and three arrangements on trade in agricultural products.[4] The codes relate to export subsidies and countervailing duties on subsidised imports, anti-dumping measures, government procurement, product standards, customs valuation, import licensing, trade in civil aircraft and a framework of rules on preferential treatment of exports of developing countries.[5] The arrangements on trade in agricultural products consisted of guidelines for trade in dairy products and meat and the establishment of consultative machinery on agricultural trade. A summary of these non-tariff agreements, given in the *White Paper on International Trade 1979*, is reproduced in Chart 1.

Chart 1. Summary of the Non-tariff Agreements

Code		Outline
1.	Subsidies and counter-vailing duties	*Spelling out the procedures provided in GATT (procedures governing the invocation of countervailing duties, consultation and dispute processing procedures). *Specific clarification of export subsidies (subsidies for secondary products are prohibited by GATT). *Avoidance of the effects of domestic subsidies impeding upon the free flow of trade.

Code	Outline
2. Amending the code for the prevention of dumping	*Implementation of the execution procedures provided by GATT.
3. Government procurement	*Discontinuation of preferential treatment for domestic products and application of principles of nondiscrimination to both products and suppliers in cases of procurement by government and government-related agencies. *Full disclosure of laws and regulations, procedures and trade practices. *Prior publication of the terms and conditions of individual cases of public tenders.
4. Standards (specifications and standards)	*International standardisation of specifications and standards and full disclosure of domestic procedures. *Application of specifications and standards to foreign products.
5. Licensing (import license procedures)	*Simplification of procedures. *Publication of regulations governing import licensing.
6. Customs valuation	*Elimination of arbitrary valuation systems and standardisation of standards and procedures for customs valuation.
7. Civil aircraft	*Abolition of duties on civil aircraft and parts. *Restraints on government intervention in the import of civil aircraft. *Sanctioning of government subsidising of industries but avoidance of adverse effects on trade.
8. Improvement of trade framework	*Preferential treatment for developing countries. *Publication of measures relating to trade taken for balance-of-payments purposes.

Code	Outline
8. Improvement of trade framework (cont.)	*Protectionist measures for developmental purposes. *Provision of general dispute solving procedures.
9. International arrangements concerning dairy products and meat	*Exchange of information concerning products covered by the arrangements. *Institution of a council to analyse supply and demand outlook and seek resolution of market imbalance.
10. Framework of consultation on agricultural problems	*Recommend the establishment of a framework for the promotion of further cooperation in the field of agriculture.

Source: JETRO, *White Paper on International Trade 1979*, p.23, table 1-20.

The MITI welcomed the signing of the agreement and hoped that this would inhibit growing protectionist moves in the EEC and the USA.[6] In view of the Japanese experience in the course of the Tokyo Round negotiations, such optimism was rather premature. The pressures from the USA for further concessions, particularly on government procurement and the import of agricultural products, has continued. The EEC has already, even during the course of the negotiations, shown a considerable degree of scepticism about Japanese motives. This was clearly reflected in the EEC's withdrawal, just before the signing of the agreement, of their initial offer to remove import restrictions on 33 of a total of 64 Japanese imports.[7] The EEC cited the following as the main reasons for such action.[8]

(1) The Community's dissatisfaction with Japanese offers of liberalising trade, particularly its tariff-cuts, which were considered to be inadequate;
(2) Dissatisfaction with measures to be taken by Japan in response to the removal of EEC discrimination against Japanese imports; and
(3) The failure of the new trade package to incorporate a code on safeguards (emergency import controls).

It is difficult to understand why the EEC should include the third item (the non-inclusion of selective safeguards) as a grievance against Japan.

Major opposition to this came from the developing countries. Initially both the USA and Japan had reservations about this item, but by the time of signing they had moderated their views. However, because of the consistent opposition of the developing countries in particular, the question of selective imposition of emergency import controls could not be finalised and it was decided to continue negotiating. It is important to remember that Article 19 of the present GATT rules permit the imposition of such safeguards to protect domestic industries only on a non-discriminatory basis, but in recent years such safeguards have often been used by the EEC and the USA either against Japan or the developing countries. Therefore, there was an attempt, in the course of negotiations, to revise Article 19 so as to allow for a selective imposition of such safeguards. The EEC argued that they had the right to impose quantitative restrictions first and to consult the exporting country or countries later.[9] This view was initially strongly challenged by the USA (the stand was subsequently moderated)[10] as well as by developing countries such as Hong Kong and South Korea. Japan initially had serious reservations on the revision of Article 19, but later showed some willingness to accommodate. It is surmised that such a provision may ultimately be an advantage to Japan in keeping out competitive imports from developing countries (Korea, Hong Kong, etc.).[11]

The initialling of the Tokyo Round of the MTN has not reduced the pressures from the USA and the EEC on Japan. It is still not certain whether the EEC will act to restrain internal subsidies that adversely affect international trade. Nor is it certain that they will open their government procurement to international competition. Admittedly, they have done so between member states (which had to happen anyway if the economic union was to have any meaning) but, even with respect to intra-Community procurement, some major sectors of industry (among them telecommunications and data processing equipment) have been excluded.[12]

Unfortunately, the Japanese are most likely to lose from the continuing momentum of trade protectionism. It is unlikely that this trend will be reversed even with the reduction (or even elimination) of the Japanese trade surplus.

Bilateral Concessions by Japan

As stated earlier, with a view to warding off unilateral import controls by the West the Japanese government and business have taken several steps to expand imports of goods produced in the West. These steps include[13] (1) the dispatch of import promotion missions to the USA, UK, Ireland, Belgium, The Netherlands and Thailand; (2) the reception of US export development missions to Japan, headed by the US Secretary of Commerce; (3) dealing with complaints through the US-Japan Trade Facilitation Committee; (4) holding seminars on exports to Japan in major US cities; (5) the establishment of MIPRO (Manufactured Imports Promotion Organisation); and (6) the establishment of the World Import Mart.

Details of the above import promotion measures recently adopted by Japan as reported in the *White Paper on International Trade 1979* are reproduced in Chart 2.

Chart 2: Import Promotion Measures Recently Adopted

Item	Contents
1. Advancement of the date of implementation of tariff cuts (4 March 1978)	*Tariff cuts on 125 items (average 23%), such as computer mainframes and automative vehicles, well ahead of the conclusion of the Tokyo Round negotiations.
2. Liberalisation of imports and expansion of import quotas	*Partial liberalisation of residual quantitative import restrictions. Liberalisation of the parts of 12 items such as anthracite (April 1978). *Expansion of import quotas on beef, oranges and fruit juice.
3. Simplification of import procedures (1977-8)	*Revision of standard methods of settlement concerning imports (permission unnecessary for advance payment within one year, deferred payment within one year, and settlements within six months). *Abolition of the prior permission system for consignment deals.
4. Simplification of the inspection system concerning imports	*Establishment of a commissioned testing system for foreign electrical appliances (1 April 1979).

Item	Contents
5. Dispatches of import promotion missions	*Since 1973, 11 missions have been dispatched. 1978 – USA, etc., 1979 – UK and Ireland (February-March), Thailand (March), Belgium, The Netherlands (April-early May).
6. Expansion and reinforcement of permanent exhibitions of imported products (4 October 1978)	*Exhibition of foreign production by the foundation of MIPRO (Manufactured Imports Promotion Organisation). (Government assistance).
7. Making full use of JETRO (Japan External Trade Organisation)	*Holding seminars in the USA and and EEC nations to promote imports to Japan.
8. Emergency import measures	*Enhancement of emergency imports such as uranium ore and oil for storage by tankers.
9. Exhibits and sales of US products by a cruising trade-fair boat	*With the cooperation of the US Commerce Department, both the government and private sector will jointly organise a cruise of the *Shin Sakura-maru*, which will call at 13 ports throughout Japan, and exhibit and sell US products abroad. The trip is scheduled to last 51 days, starting on 21 October.

Source: JETRO, *White Paper on International Trade*, p.49, table 11-26.

Admittedly, it will be some time before some of the measures detailed in Chart 2 show significant results, but these do indicate a Japanese willingness to accommodate her trading partners. This becomes clearer if one looks at the details of some of these measures.

Liberalisation of Imports and Expansion of Import Quota

Under the terms of the Strauss-Ushiba communiqué the Japanese government eliminated import quotas on eleven agricultural and fishery products and one mineral product. Subsequently, as a result of the MTN negotiation it also agreed to expand the quotas for beef, oranges and orange and grapefruit juice. It is estimated that the relaxation of the quotas for these three products will generate nearly $200 million in additional US exports by 1983.[14]

The increase in the quotas for individual commodities was quite substantial. For instance, in 1977 the quota on fresh oranges was only 15,000 tons. As a result of the Strauss-Ushiba agreement the quota for fresh oranges was increased to 45,000 tons in 1978. By the fiscal year 1983 this quota will be increased to 83,000 tons. The quota for orange juice will increase from 600 tons in 1977 to 6,500 tons in 1983 and that for grapefruit juice from 400 tons to 6,000 tons. Under the agreement the quota for high-quality beef was increased from 6,800 tons in 1977 to 16,800 tons in 1978 and it planned to increase to 30,800 tons by 1983.[15] Under US pressure the Japanese government also lifted its ban on TBZ, a fungicide used for citrus fruits; the US government had claimed that the ban on TBZ was a non-tariff barrier. The Japanese government also accepted US fungicide procedure to protect against certain cherry pests, as a result of which US growers exported nearly $2 million worth of extra cherries within a year.[16]

Emergency Imports

The idea of emergency imports was adopted in 1977, and by November 1978 nearly $2.2 billion worth of these imports had already been procured. This consisted of $1.1 billion of advance payments to the USA for future deliveries of enriched uranium and uranium ore; $414 million for imports of crude oil by the Japan National Oil Corporation for stockpiling in empty tankers; $293 million for buying back Japanese ships from foreign owners; $166 million for imports of iron-ore pellets by steel companies for stockpiling; and $130 million for imports of commercial aircraft to be leased to foreign airlines.[17] Contracts were also signed for aircraft purchases by Japan Airlines as well as for advanced medical equipment for hospitals affiliated to a number of universities.[18]

Such emergency imports were financed by the Export-Import Bank of Japan under a special foreign currency loan programme. Loans were given at concessional rates and the foreign exchange for this programme was made available by the government.[19] In addition to raising the resources of the Export-Import Bank in this way, the Bank of Japan increased the ceiling on yen loans to the foreign exchange banks, which were thus enabled to buy additional dollars from the government's Foreign Exchange Fund Special Account for lending to importers.[20]

Simplification of Import Procedures

Between 1977 and 1978 the government eliminated by stages the system of prior approval for imports on consignment. Advance payment for imports, which was prohibited mainly to guard against currency speculation, is now permitted if the payment is made within one year of the import application. The payment period for import delivery has now been increased from four to six months after customs clearance. In addition the period of deferred payments on the import of capital goods, consumer goods and goods bought on consignment has been extended to one year, thus bringing the Japanese system closer to those of the other developed countries.[21]

Trade Missions

It has been mentioned above that the Japanese government and businesses sent missions abroad to import foreign goods. The scale of some of these missions has been rather impressive. For instance, in March 1978 a 92-member Japanese mission visited seventeen US cities and within two weeks met 1,600 US businessmen, exporters and potential exporters of various commodities (e.g machinery, processed food, fashion and leisure goods). It is estimated that the mission generated $1.9 billion in export sales. The US Department of Commerce conceded that without this mission at least $600 million worth of exports would have been lost.[22]

Several other specialised trade missions, such as the food importers mission which visited Japan in October 1978, generated further demand for US goods.

Marketing Assistance

JETRO's efforts in this direction have already been referred to above. In recent years JETRO has produced new surveys for commodities (e.g. sporting goods, home electric appliances, cosmetics, do-it-yourself

goods, interior decorations, apparel and kitchenware) which are
potentially important for exporters from other countries. Such surveys
contain information on supply and demand trends, the distribution
network, marketing margins, price trends, marketability, etc.[23]

Measures to Curb Exports

In addition to the various measures outlined above for promoting
imports, the Japanese government undertook direct measures to curb
exports. In April 1978 the MITI announced a set of guidelines for
voluntary restraints on the export of steel, cars, television sets and
ships.[24] It also decided to monitor the shipment of motor cycles,
copiers, cameras, watches and other similar 'sensitive' products.

Revaluation of the Yen and Related Issues

In Western eyes one way of reducing the competitiveness of Japanese
exports is the appreciation of the yen. The pegged exchange rate of the
yen at Y360 to a US dollar, imposed by the US in April 1949, became
anachronistic by the middle of the 1960s with Japan's increasing trade
surplus. It was increasingly felt internationally that the yen was
undervalued. This feeling was further strengthened when in the early
1970s the Canadian dollar, the Deutschmark, the Dutch guilder and
the Swiss franc appreciated. The Japanese government was somewhat
reluctant to revalue in spite of the fact that some Japanese experts
had shown that the economy would only be marginally hurt,
particularly if the 'crawling peg system of exchange rates', which
allowed for gradual revaluation, was adopted.[25] The debate over
revaluation within Japan was, in the meantime, overtaken by President
Nixon's 'new economic policy' announcement of August 1971, which
suspended the convertibility of the dollar into gold or other reserve
assets and imposed a temporary 10 per cent import surcharge.[26] Soon
after, under the terms of the Smithsonian Agreement of December 1971,
the yen was revalued by nearly 17 per cent. Since other currencies
altered their dollar parity as well, the effective revaluation of the yen
on a trade-weighted basis was 12.5 per cent.[27]

In mid-February 1973 the US dollar was devalued for a second time
and yen-dollar parity was established at around 265 yen to a dollar.
However, Japan agreed to let the yen float and other currencies followed.

As a result, by March 1973 the yen had appreciated by nearly 25 per cent over its pre-May 1971 exchange rate.[28] The revaluation of the yen together with increasing inflationary pressure at home, foreign investment and trade liberalisation measures cut the Japanese trade balance in 1973 substantially. The balance of around $9 billion in 1972 was reduced to £3.7 billion in 1973; the current account surplus of $6.6 billion in 1972 became a deficit in 1973.

One of the major causes of the deterioration in Japan's balance of payments was the oil embargo and subsequent increases in oil prices; by 1974 Japanese oil imports had risen from $4 billion in 1972 to £20 billion.[29] Partly as a result of the unprecedented increase in oil prices the economies of the developed countries suffered a serious recession over nearly six quarters from late 1974 through 1975, with unemployment rates (with the exception of Canada, Italy and Japan) the highest since 1955.[30] In the meantime, inflation continued to run high. Wholesale prices in the developed countries (except West Germany) rose by 20 per cent. The continued world recession resulted in near-stagnation of Japanese exports in 1975 and the balance of payments continued to be in deficit. Business activity in the developed countries recovered substantially in early 1976 led by a recovery in the USA, which resulted in an expansion in imports into USA from her trading partners. As a result, Japanese exports increased by 20.5 per cent in 1976.[31] However, the increase in imports was more modest at 11.4 per cent. This led to a large surplus of $9.9 billion in the merchandise trade balance.[32] On the other hand, Japan's invisible trade balance, which has always been in deficit, recorded a very large deficit of $5.7 billion. In consequence, the current account showed a surplus of only $3.7 billion, in spite of the huge surplus on trade account.

The increased surplus on balance of trade, particularly with the developed countries, revived the old complaints from the USA and the EEC. In October 1976, when a delegation from the Japan Federation of Economic Organisation visited Europe, the EEC 'strongly requested Japan's self-restraint in exports with respect to iron and steel, automobiles, bearings, shipbuilding, etc., claiming that their domestic industries were suffering damage because of import increases or low-price sales of these products'.[33] Similarly, when the US Vice-president, Walter Mondale, visited Japan in January 1977 he voiced his country's grievance with regard to increasing exports of iron and steel products and colour television sets.[34] Subsequently, the US International Trade Commission (ITC) recommended to the President that, in view of the large imports of Japanese television sets and the consequent damage to the domestic industry, the latter be given some relief.

In 1977 Japan's exports showed a further increase of 19.7 per cent over the preceding year while imports went up by only 9.3 per cent. As a result, Japan's trade balance showed a surplus of $17 billion; since the balance on the invisible account continued to be in deficit, the surplus on current account was only $10.9 billion[35] (Table 2.5a, p.42). It must be remembered, however, that the volume of exports both in 1976 and 1977 did not show a very appreciable increase. It was only 2.3 per cent in 1976 and 3.0 per cent in 1977. Therefore the very rapid rate of growth of the value of exports of around 20 per cent in value terms was the outcome of a rise in dollar-based prices resulting from the appreciation of the yen.[36]

While the yen was appreciating during 1977 as a result of the increasing surplus on current account, the US balance of payments registered a substantial deficit. This shook the world's confidence in the US dollar, which lost markedly in relation to other major world currencies between the end of 1977 and the end of 1978.[37] During 1977 alone the value of the yen in terms of dollars increased by 22 per cent. Such an increase had serious implications for Japanese export competitiveness. As is well known, by raising the export price of goods, appreciation of the domestic currency reduces the competitiveness of domestic goods in overseas markets. But by the same token the import of foreign goods becomes cheaper. This has some favourable implications for Japanese industries, including export industries, because they can import raw materials more cheaply. Besides, in a country like Japan, which imports a lot of its food, the appreciation of the domestic currency may also keep domestic retail prices in check and therefore have a considerable price-stabilising effect. Obviously, different sectors of the economy as well as different industries will be affected in various ways by the appreciation of the domestic currency. To assess the situation facing Japanese industries a survey was conducted by MITI in February 1978. It was found that such 'industries as electric appliances, automobiles, general machinery and precision machinery were in the position of meeting favourably even a substantial rise in the exchange value of yen, while those in the textile and chemical industries, for instance, were in for a serious problem in terms of export profitability due to the progress of the higher yen'.[38]

According to MITI estimates, which took into account such factors as the currency composition of export contract prices, the ratio of the burden of exchange risks and the state of raw material imports, industries such as general machinery, electrical machinery, cars and precision machinery would lose substantially from the appreciation of the yen.[39] This is mainly because these industries benefit less from raw material imports, while exports constitute a high proportion of their gross value.

The appreciation of the yen in 1977 and 1978 had a significant impact on the Japanese economy. Even though the dollar value of exports rose by 21.2 per cent in 1978, in terms of the yen exports declined by 5 per cent over the previous year, the first year-to-year decline since 1952.[40] On a commodity basis, iron and steel, boats and ships, television and radio sets, etc., which were traditionally the main items spearheading Japanese exports, showed declining trends. The shrinking of the trade surplus which started in the last quarter of 1978 became even more pronounced in 1979. On the other hand, the invisible trade balance and the transfer balance showed increasing deficits in 1978 and at the beginning of 1979. As a result, the quarterly trend of the current account started showing a downward trend in the last quarter of 1978. It accelerated in the first half of 1979, so much so that in June a Finance Ministry spokesman claimed that 'the government for the present has achieved its goal of reducing Japan's huge payment surplus'.[41]

The current account deficit continued almost unabated until August 1980. The deficits in the first two quarters (April-June, July-September) were substantially higher than in the previous year and some Japanese economists felt that the overall deficit, during the fiscal year ending 30 March 1981, might touch $20 billion.[42] A growing current account deficit led to a fall in the value of the yen to Y260 to a US dollar by early April. In order to defend the yen, the Japanese authorities not only used their foreign currency reserves liberally and raised the discount rate to 9 per cent (a rate traditionally considered too high in Japan) but also actively encouraged capital inflows, particularly the inflow of petrodollars. The total net inflow of foreign capital in 1980 is estimated at roughly $20 billion.[43] As a result of these moves, the yen exchange rate started picking up again. Japanese exports had already benefited in early 1980 because of the weaker yen as well as relative Japanese success in dampening inflation. With the recovery of the yen the dollar value of Japanese exports rose faster from April onwards[44] — leading to a decreasing deficit on current account. According to a Bank of Tokyo estimate the current account deficit in fiscal 1980 may still total anything between $7.5 and $10.0 billion.[45]

In some circles there is a lingering doubt whether this tendency towards deficit on current account is going to be a long-term phenomenon. As the *Japan Times* editorial asked:

> First, questions of a rather practical kind may be raised about whether the shrinking trade surplus is wholly explainable in terms of purely economic relationships. Some artificial steps were taken last year to reduce the trade gap . . ..

It stressed that 'the rapid return to a balance of payments equilibrium in recent months is the combined result of diverse developments here and abroad. Swift changes in the exchange rate, a spurt in domestic demand, artificial efforts to restrain exports and boost imports and the renewed spiral in oil prices — all had a part.'[46]

It is unrealistic to expect that Japan can continue to restrain exports and boost imports by measures such as emergency purchases, etc. In the absence of appropriate structural changes in the domestic economies of the West, even Japan cannot bear the social and economic costs to its own domestic economy indefinitely so as to be a 'net contributor to jobs and income in the rest of the world'.[47]

The long-term future of the Japanese international payments equilibrium depends as much upon Japan as upon the developed countries of the West. Japan has so far shown a considerable willingness as well as ability to make serious efforts in this direction in spite of 'some awkward political repercussions inside Japan'.[48] However, these do not seem to fully satisfy her trading partners who, contrary to international practice and commonsense, concentrate their attention on the bilateral payments situations. It is, as a Japanese economist stressed some time ago, 'an easy assumption that because Japan has, on the face of it, weathered the world recession more easily than most other industrial countries — and because it has also increased the size of its current account surplus — that it has in some way prospered at the expense of the rest of the world'.[49] It is not often realised that Japanese manufacturing industry has had the same difficulties to overcome as its counterparts in other industrial countries from the world recession and the increases in oil prices.[50] If it has fared better than the others it is because of its capacity to maintain better labour relations, to increase productivity and to bring about structural change within the economy more smoothly. Extracting economic concessions from Japan by political 'confrontation' virtually 'boils down simply to wanting to punish the country for happening to be a particularly efficient producer of industrial goods'.[51] Such political pressures have, as a British commentator suggests, 'only a tenuous connection with issues of free competition and unfair trading'.[52] It also shows a callous disregard of the political and social costs that Japan has to face because of the 'beggar thy neighbour' policies of the West. We will now consider some of the economic and social costs suffered by Japan as a result of import liberalisation and export restraints.

Economic and Social Consequences of the Constraints

Since much of the contraction of Japanese industries and the consequent decline in employment is the result of worldwide recession, the increase in oil prices in 1979 and increasing competition from the newly emerging developing countries it is difficult to isolate the influence of trade liberalisation alone on Japan's industrial decline and increasing unemployment. On the other hand, there is no doubt that import liberalisation has been imposed on Japan by the West and at a time when they themselves have been increasing trade barriers in their own countries, particularly against goods originating in Japan and the developing countries. For obvious reasons, this has resulted in industrial decline and increasing unemployment in Japan.

As can be seen from Table 4.1, the overall industrial production index, which was around 112 in 1974 and fell to 100 in 1975, has shown a significant recovery since 1976 and the index stood at 133 in 1979. However, some major industries such as iron and steel, transport equipment and textiles which formed the backbone of Japanese export penetration showed a more sluggish recovery. For instance, the index of production of iron and steel fell from 117 in 1974 to 100 in 1975; even in 1979 it stood at only 123. The Japanese steel industry in early 1979 was working at nearly three-quarters of its capacity; at least 40 million tons out of 145 million tons was lying idle. Against this, most US companies during that period were working at about 90 per cent of their capacity.[53] The industry's earlier production target for 1980 of 150 million tons has been reduced to 110 million tons, which may rise to anything between 120 and 125 million tons by 1985, against an earlier target of 175 million tons.[54] As a result of a rise in the prices of fuel and raw materials, Japanese steel companies had to increase their prices and thereby lost some of their export competitiveness. On top of this came the restrictions in the US and the EEC markets together with the US trigger price mechanism. As a result of the trigger price mechanism, while shipments from Europe

Table 4.1: Industrial Production Index by Sector, 1974-9 (1975 = 100)

Sectors	1974	1975	1976	1977	1978	1979
Total industrial output	112.3	100.0	111.1	115.7	122.9	133.1
Mining	105.8	100.0	100.0	103.1	105.7	101.0
Manufacturing	112.4	100.0	111.2	115.7	123.0	133.3
Iron and steel	116.9	100.0	109.5	108.1	110.1	122.6
Non-ferrous metals	112.6	100.0	119.3	125.0	135.0	142.9
Fabricated metal products	123.0	100.0	116.8	124.9	135.4	137.0
Non-electrical machinery	126.3	100.0	109.9	116.8	126.0	143.3
Electrical machinery	118.0	100.0	128.3	136.5	155.2	177.2
Transport equipment	104.6	100.0	102.2	106.2	106.8	111.1
Precision instruments	108.3	100.0	128.1	165.8	192.0	251.1
Non-metallic mineral products	117.0	100.0	110.4	115.2	121.0	129.0
Chemicals	109.9	100.0	111.5	117.2	131.3	143.7
Petroleum and coal products	104.4	100.0	102.7	104.7	104.0	106.5
Pulp, paper and paper products	113.7	100.0	113.3	115.3	120.8	130.6
Textiles	106.1	100.0	108.4	106.7	107.7	108.5
Lumber and wood products	109.1	100.0	106.8	104.4	107.0	109.0
Foods	97.5	100.0	101.1	104.6	106.2	108.9

Source: MITI, quoted in US-Japan Trade Council, *Yearbook of US-Japan Economic Relations, 1978*, pp.99-100, table 4: and US-Japan Trade Council *Yearbook of US-Japan Economic Relations, 1979*, pp.93-4, table 4.

to the USA increased by 9 per cent in 1978, Japan lost out significantly. Her share in the total steel imports of the USA declined by nearly 13 per cent.[55]

Output in 1980-1 is forecast to fall to 108 million tonnes against 112 million tonnes in the previous year.[56] The export is expected to fall below 30 million tonnes for the first time since 1975.[57] The Japanese mills have been forecasting that their profits during the fiscal year ending in March 1981 will probably be halved because of a decline in domestic demand as well as in exports.[58]

Transport equipment is another sector which has shown sluggish growth. Shipbuilding in Japan had its peak in 1975 when Japanese shipbuilders built 17 million gross tons (GT) and held 50 per cent of the world market.[59] For various reasons (i.e. the cyclical nature of the industry, excess capacity in world tanker capacity, decline in world oil consumption, appreciation of the yen and competition from developing countries such as South Korea, and the centrally planned economies such as Yugoslavia and Poland) there has been a sharp decline in the demand for Japanese ships. In 1978 Japanese shipbuilders built only 7 million GT and their share of the world market was down to 39 per cent.[60] In 1978 only 4.9 million GT were launched. This was the lowest figure since 1965.[61] The impact of the slump has been hardest on the smaller shipbuilders,[62] although large shipbuilders with no other activities have also suffered badly. For instance, Sasebo Heavy Industries, which is the eighth largest shipbuilder in Japan, lost $85 million dollars in 1978, which was equivalent to twice its capital.[63] Large shipbuilders, such as Mitsubishi Heavy Industries, have fared somewhat better since their other operations have served as a cushion. However, during the fiscal year 1979 Japan's six major shipbuilders (Mitsubishi Heavy Industries, Ishikawajima-Harima Heavy Industries, Kawasaki Heavy Industries, Hitachi Shipbuilding, Mitsui Engineering and Shipbuilding, and Sumitomo Heavy Industries) suffered their 'worst ever deterioration' in earnings.[64] If their non-shipbuilding sales are excluded, their sales were half or one-third the level of the previous year.[65]

In view of the serious contraction in shipbuilding demand the Shipping and Shipbuilding Rationalisation Council (SSRC) last year proposed to cut back capacity by 35 per cent. According to this plan, 61 shipbuilding companies capable of building ships larger than 5,000 GT had to reduce their capacities by 35 per cent;[66] smaller shipbuilders were required to cut back by only 18 per cent.[67]

As a result of rapidly rising labour costs since the late 1950s, and the appreciation of the yen, Japan has been fast losing its comparative advantage in labour-intensive industries such as textiles to the developing countries. The export of Japanese textiles was further seriously hampered by the protectionist trends in other developed countries, particularly in the USA and the EEC. More recently Japanese exports have suffered also as a result of the appreciation of the yen, increasing raw material costs and the rise in the self-sufficiency in textiles of Japan's neighbours. As a result the share of textiles in Japanese export earnings fell from nearly 19 per cent to only 4 per cent between 1965 and 1979. Some of the larger companies have shown no profits. For instance, Mitsubishi Rayon Co., a major producer of synthetic fibres, had to sell its main office building; Unitika, another major producer in the field, sold land and bank shares to post a minimal profit.[68]

Small enterprises such as those manufacturing garments, houseware, toys, etc. have suffered even more. Between 1971 and 1977 the number of Japanese textile and apparel-makers dropped drastically from

121,000 to only 10,000.[69] According to the MITI there are over 100 small-scale industries which face a bleak future.[70] For instance, Sabae, a tiny city of 60,000 people which supplied almost 90 per cent of the nation's production of eye-glass frames and sunglasses, is now threatened with serious decline because of increasing imports from developing countries. The appreciation of the yen and the government's efforts to increase imports from the West have further damaged the industry.[71]

The magnitude of the distress is apparent from the fact that in all the industries considered to be depressed (i.e. textiles, aluminium refining, open-hearth and electric furnace steel, shipbuilding, ammonia fertiliser, polyvinyl chloride, machine tools, cardboard, soda, sugar refining and plywood) 'output' levels and operating rates remain below 1973 levels,[72] and the profit/sales ratios of such industries in 1977 were far below their 1973 levels.[73]

The government has recently introduced several measures to help the depressed industries such as the Structurally Depressed Industries Law (May 1978) and the Specially Designated Depressed Areas Medium and Small Firm Countermeasure Law (October 1978). Under the Structurally Depressed Industries Law it was decided to cut electric-furnace and open-hearth steel production capacity by 14.5 per cent; four synthetic fibre industries by 10.5 to 17 per cent; and, as mentioned above, shipbuilding capacity was to undergo a cut by 35 per cent.[74] Other industries such as chemical fertilisers (the ammonia, urea and calcium phosphate industries), cotton spinning, ferro-alloys, corrugated cardboard, plywood, polyvinyl chloride and sugar refining may have to undergo cuts in the very near future. These reductions in production capacities, as a result of planned phasing or otherwise, have led to increasing aggregate unemployment, creating hardship at the national as well as regional levels, together with increasing deprivation of the middle-aged. We will now take a brief look at the unemployment situation in Japan.

Increasing Unemployment

According to estimates of the Statistical Bureau of the Prime Minister's Office, the number of unemployed persons in Japan in March 1979 totalled 1.4 million, giving an unemployment rate of 2.5 per cent.[75] The corresponding rate for the previous year was somewhat higher at 2.7 per cent. The number of jobless passed one million in 1975 and has been increasing ever since. It must be stressed, however, that these numbers do not truly reflect the actual state of employment in Japan. The method adopted by the Statistical Bureau tends to underestimate the number of unemployed. The Bureau estimates this number by a survey covering 33,000 households and the sample districts are changed every two months.[76] To qualify as an unemployed person three conditions have to be met: (1) a person should not have worked for money even for one hour during the last week of the month of the survey; (2) the person must be seeking a job; and (3) a person must attempt to secure the assistance of the employment stabilisation agency and/or job-advertisements in newspapers. These are rather stringent criteria, and would exclude an unemployed person who is earning a very small sum by working only a few hours (it has to be only more than one hour) a week. They would also exclude a housewife who, after losing her job, returns to household chores and fails to register as an unemployed person as well as those who return to their villages to live with their families during the period of unemployment and do odd jobs in those villages. On the other hand, the second criterion (i.e. being a job-seeker) will, in fact, increase the number of unemployed during a period of business upturn since, with the improved expectations of finding a job, the number of job-seekers, particularly housewives looking for part-time jobs, increases.

As reported by *Nihon keizai*, according to the basic surveys on the employment structure in 1977 conducted by the Bureau of Statistics of the Prime Minister's Office, nearly 4.1 million persons were continuing job-seeking activities.[77] This total contained an estimated one million women who lost their jobs and quietly dropped out of the workforce.[78]

In addition to this are the persons who are underemployed. In fact, the number of persons who worked for less than 200 days a year is estimated at 8.4 million.[79] Therefore the official rate of unemployment is probably a gross underestimate. Some experts suggest that if account is taken of unrecorded unemployment and underemployment the rate of jobless could be as high as 9 per cent.[80] Clearly this rate is far in excess of the rates in the USA and the EEC countries with the possible exception of France (Table 4.2).

For obvious reasons, the employment situation deteriorated most in the 'structurally depressed industries' (Table 4.3). It is clear that regular employment has fallen more seriously in industries such as textiles, lumber and wood products, iron and steel, transport equipment and general machinery, leading to distress in the particular regions where

Table 4.2: Number of Unemployed and Rate of Unemployment in the Major Industrial Nations (in millions)

	Japan		USA		West Germany		UK		Italy		France	
	Rate (%)	No.	Rate (%)	No.	Rate (%)	No.	Rate (%)	No.	Rate (%)	No.	Rate (%)	No.
1975	1.9	1.0	8.5	7.8	4.1	1.1	3.9	0.9	3.3	0.7	10.9	0.8
1976	2.0	1.1	7.7	7.3	4.6	1.1	5.3	1.3	3.7	0.7	12.4	0.9
1977	2.0	1.1	7.0	6.9	4.5	1.0	5.8	1.4	7.2	1.6	10.4	1.1
1978	2.1	1.2	6.0	6.1	4.4	1.0	5.8	1.4	7.2	1.6	8.7	1.2
1979 (March)	2.1	1.2	5.7	5.9	4.1	0.9	5.7	1.4	–	–	–	1.3

Source: JETRO, *White Paper on International Trade 1979*, p.10.

Table 4.3: Changes in Regular Employment in Selected Industries (1975 = 100)

	1976	1977	1978	1979
Manufacturing (total)	98.0	97.1	94.9	94.1
Food products and tobacco	104.0	106.3	106.6	108.4
Textiles	97.3	91.6	83.6	80.9
Apparel	103.2	103.2	100.0	102.1
Lumber and wood products	91.8	83.5	79.0	78.9
Pulp and paper products	97.0	95.7	92.9	92.0
Publishing, printing	97.6	95.9	95.1	94.5
Chemical	98.2	95.9	92.1	90.3
Petroleum and coal products	98.0	95.0	93.9	92.5
Non-metallic mineral products	94.1	92.6	93.5	94.5
Iron and steel	93.4	90.0	85.9	82.9
Non-ferrous metals	97.6	96.2	92.7	92.5
Fabricated metal products	96.6	95.0	91.5	92.0
Non-electric machinery	94.7	93.3	90.6	88.4
Electric machinery	101.8	104.1	103.1	105.5
Transport equipment	95.4	93.3	90.4	85.9
Precision instruments	99.5	104.1	106.8	107.6

Source: Japan Ministry of Labour, quoted in US-Japan Trade Council, *Yearbook 1979*, pp.102-3, table 12.

these industries are highly concentrated.

There is further indirect evidence of increasing distress for employees of small industries and the temporary employees of large industries which cannot be reflected in total employment figures. It is well known that in Japan wages and other fringe benefits of employment are customarily higher in larger industries than in small industries. It is also important to note that such fringe benefits are available only to permanent workers. So, by getting rid of permanent workers (through retirement, etc.), industries not only reduce their wage bill (based on seniority-related wage scales) but also the cost of fringe benefits. Wage bills can also be reduced by switching over to female workers, not only because they are not yet getting 'equal wages' for equal work but also because they are more inclined to seek part-time work because of their domestic responsibilities. All these tendencies are now apparent in the employment statistics.

For a time, during the periods of rapid economic growth the differential between wage rates in large and small enterprises was narrowing, but the trend has now been reversed. Recent Labour Force Survey reports suggest that while the large manufacturing enterprises have reduced their workforce substantially[81] there has been some increase in employment by small-sized firms (Table 4.4). There has been a substantial increase in wholesale and retailing as well as in services (Tables 4.4 and 4.5). Part of this trend towards the tertiary sector is the result of higher levels of living but, on the other hand, this increase also reflects a falling back on some forms of employment (as in the case of retailing 'papa-mama' shops) when genuine employment opportunities are lacking.

This point was clearly stressed in the Economic Planning Agency's *Economic Survey of Japan, 1977/78*. It stressed that the 'slow down in employment growth was chiefly concentrated in employed workers. On the other hand there was an increase in the number of self-employed workers. As for employed workers, a decline in the number of regular employees contrasted with some increases in the categories of temporary and day workers. These developments may be interpreted to show increased instability in the employment situation for male workers'.[82] The Economic Planning Agency also confirmed that the 'number of gainfully occupied female workers increased with a remarkably rapidity in fiscal 1977. While some gains were registered in the categories of self-employed and family workers, these were overwhelmed by a major increase in the number of employed workers, especially regular workers. An increase in the number of regularly employed workers was observed even with larger enterprises with a workforce of more

Table 4.4: Changes in Employment by Size of Workforce (1970 index = 100)

	1977 Index
Manufacturing	
over 500 persons	90
100-499 persons	95
30-99 persons	107
1-29 persons	108
Total manufacturing	98
Wholesale and retail	
over 500 persons	133
100-499 persons	133
30-99 persons	132
1-29 persons	124
Total wholesale and retailing	129
Services	
over 500 persons	120
100-499 persons	138
30-99 persons	136
1-29 persons	120
Total services	127

Source: Based on Prime Minister's Office, *Labour Force Survey 1977*: quoted in Economic Planning Agency, *Economic Survey of Japan, 1977/78*, p.183.

than 500.[83] This does not necessarily indicate — although this may be one of the factors — that large companies in Japan have suddenly decided to amend the wrongs inflicted on Japanese women in the past. It is simply that they can still be hired more cheaply than men.

It does not need stressing that the regions closely associated with structurally depressed industries usually suffer higher than average unemployment rates. For instance, Fukui prefecture, which has thrived on textiles since the early Meiji period and on several occasions introduced technological changes by moving into rayon and synthetic fibres to withstand foreign competition, is now fighting for survival. Since 1971, as a result of 'voluntary' restrictions on Japanese exports imposed by the USA and others, Fukui's textile industry has been having a difficult time.[84] Further decline is inevitable if and when

Table 4.5: Changes in Number of Workers Classified by Industry and Employment Form (difference from the previous year: in 1,000 persons)

	1976 April-June	1977 Jan.-March	1978 Jan.-March
Construction			
(1) Self-employed workers and family business employees, self-employed persons	0	0	80
(2) Employees	20	−40	30
Manufacturing			
(1) Self-employed workers and family business employees, self-employed persons	60	80	10
(2) Employees	100	−130	−390
Wholesale, retail, finance, insurance and real estate			
(1) Self-employed workers and family business employees, self-employed persons	−210	110	20
(2) Employees	430	400	50
Transport, communications, power, gas and water			
(1) Self-employed workers and family business employees, self-employed persons	−20	10	40
(2) Employees	100	110	10
Services			
(1) Self-employed workers and family business employees, self-employed persons	−10	−40	200
(2) Employees	290	140	440

Source: Prime Minister's Office, *Labour Force Survey 1977:* quoted in Economic Planning Agency, *Economic Survey*, p.182.

Japan makes further concessions to the developing countries on textiles — such as more favourable Generalised System of Preferences (GSP).

According to a MITI survey, several industries at various locations manufacturing export products were reported in 1978 to be near collapse because of the appreciation of the yen. These included tube matting in Osaka, mosaic tiles in Gifu prefecture, scarf manufacturing in Yokohama, binocular production in Itabashi (Tokyo), ceramicware manufacture in Seto, artificial pearl manufacture in Izu, Osaka, and machine tool manufacture in Sanjo in Niigata prefecture.[85]

Increasing difficulties in obtaining employment in the cities and their suburbs have resulted in the return of workers to the villages at a time when increasing US pressure on Japan to open up its agricultural markets is already threatening employment in agriculture. In a recent conference of the Directors of the Regional Offices of the Ministry of Agriculture, Forestry and Fisheries it was repeatedly reported that the outflow of workers from the agricultural sector has been on the decline. This trend seemed to be conspicuous, especially in the vicinity of large cities.[86] For instance, in the Kinki area, the number of those who left their villages during the first half of 1978 was nearly 37 per cent less than during a similar period in 1977; against this the number of people returning to their villages showed an increase of 60 per cent.[87] This was also true of Chugoku, Shikoku and Kyushu. Many of these people were in the middle and upper age brackets. The Economic Planning Agency recently stressed that 'high unemployment among the middle- and high-aged persons remains the most serious problem on the nation's labour scene'.[88] The proportion of workers between the ages of 45 and 65 currently constitutes nearly one-third of the total labour force, and by the mid-1980s it is likely to increase to around 40 per cent.[89] Because of the lifetime employment system and seniority-related scales older employees cost three to four times as much as new entrants to a job, so large enterprises are increasingly encouraging their older employees to opt for early retirement, at 45 or 50, with a large lump-sum cash compensation.[90] In some cases permanent workers are dismissed on grounds of recession and later employed as temporary workers.[91] Finding alternative employment after retirement is extremely difficult, and those lucky to get employment with medium and small enterprises are paid wages which are even lower than the unemployment insurance benefits.[92] The problem for this group has become so severe that the government has, at least temporarily, introduced a scheme for subsidising the employment of middle-aged and elderly persons. Medium and small enterprises receive a subsidy of 80 per cent and large enterprises 60 per cent of the wage paid to such persons.[93] The period for which this subsidy is paid is likely to be increased from 3 to 12 months for middle-aged persons and from 6 to 18 months for elderly persons. Those elderly workers who manage to hang on to their jobs because of their employers' paternalistic commitments find that life is not all that easy. It is reported that they usually live a life of 'social torment, despised by their worker colleagues, because they are *seki o atatameru dake* (seat-warmers)'.[94] They come to the office daily, sit, chat, drink tea and go home without doing any work because there is none. In view of the contempt shown by their colleagues many are reported to have committed suicide.

The government is also considering the extension of the statutory retirement age from 55 to 60 years. An attempt is also being made to introduce a five-day (instead of six-day) working week. The Japan Federation of Employers' Association (*Nikkeiren*) does not think that reducing working hours will be effective in expanding employment. They argue that since most workers are paid on a monthly or daily basis, a reduction of working hours will ultimately increase costs. This would affect the competitive ability of Japanese exports and consequently future employment prospects. Therefore, the Labour Ministry's proposal to expand employment by shortening the working week or raising the age of retirement is not widely accepted.[95]

It is also predicted that the number of young people, particularly university graduates, among the unemployed will increase.[96] It is likely that to reduce their 'lifetime' commitments, large enterprises will decrease their recruitment of graduates. According to official estimates nearly 1.8 million young people graduate from school every year and at least one million of them want to find work. To create employment for all these people is not going to be easy in coming years. Some circles are already anticipating increased emigration from Japan.[97]

In view of the increasing difficulties of maintaining customary levels of employment in Japan, some trade unions are getting worried about their future roles. They are clearly conscious that 'their solidarity and fighting power have weakened'.[98] It is stressed that:

From the viewpoint of the labour movement, the following points can be pointed out: the inclination to the right, the weakening of struggle power against capital, and the looseness or weakness of the power of solidarity. Some unions openly demand expansion of the defense production industry, and the leaders of many big unions do not try to carry out even strikes against dismissals and for securing wage raises. On the other hand, discriminatory domination by superior employees within workshops and the harsh treatment of activists have now become daily events, so to speak. It has thus become quite impossible for workers to speak out freely.

Under the present economic situation, many temporary and sub-contract workers have been expelled from their workshops, and the annual average number of cases of bankruptcies of medium and small enterprises is over 10,000. However, the actual situation is such that the number of unions resisting these facts violently is extremely small.[99]

To Western liberals the decline in the powers of left-wing labour unions (bearing in mind Western experience) may appear to be a good thing. But it is not readily appreciated that unions such as *Sohyo* basically believe in social democracy and have acted as a bulwark not only against the Communists but also the extreme right-wing conservatives. The decline in their status may easily give rise to a revival of right-wing ultra-nationalism which is being reflected in some recent policy decisions such as the legislation for times of emergency, the expansion of the defence production industry, the recognition of self-defence forces, the legislation of the 'names-of-eras' system and the enshrinement of the wartime Premier Hideki Tojo and thirteen other 'Class A war criminals' in Yasukuni shrine. In fact, Keiichi Takahata, Representative Secretary of the National Consultative Council of Private Workers Union (*Churitsu roren*), openly called for the recognition of the self-defence forces (SDF) and the revision of Article 9 of the Constitution.[100] Business interests want to expand the armaments industry, strengthen Japanese defence capabilities and export armaments.[101] It is probable that with growing unemployment such views will be more generally acceptable.

As Hajime Ohta, a Japanese economist, suggests, the older generation in Japan who lived through the post-war period feel somewhat indebted to the USA for Japan's present well-being and economic success and are therefore often prepared to meet US demands, even though they feel that the USA is forcing its position on Japan.[102] However, the younger generation, who did not experience the war or adversity, do not perceive that they owe anything to any other country and are often convinced that their success is entirely the product of Japanese diligence, ingenuity and racial superiority. Therefore a significant proportion of the younger generation will probably have no qualms about rearmament, particularly if they find their job opportunities shrinking. This would probably be true also of the owners and employees of small businesses as well as farmers and agricultural workers, who usually suffer most during recessions. By temperament they are conservative and they will probably be quite receptive to nationalistic appeals. As a *Far Eastern Economic Review* commentator suggests, even some Japanese liberal scholars are becoming more pessimistic about the 'sturdiness of the democratic political process in Japan'.[103]

It is vital, therefore, for the continuity of democratic values in Japan that its economy continues to grow at a reasonable pace and is not heavily encumbered with unemployment and the other social maladies associated with economic stagnation. Since Japan is so dependent on foreign sources of raw materials and fuel that it has to export for survival, her capacity to export on competitive terms will depend not only on how well and how persistently she can bring about appropriate changes in her own industrial structure, but also on how willing and able the Western developed countries are to bring about such changes in their own industrial structure and to open up their markets to Japan as well as the developing countries, which in their own turn may provide further market access to Japanese manufacturers. If the West's response is inadequate it may not be too long before we find the pace of armament production in Japan beginning to accelerate, with all its possible implications. In so doing Japan will only be taking a page from the West's own history, where armament production and sales have played an important part in the maintenance of exports and employment. It does not need stressing that the Japanese can and do learn fast from the West. These are some of the issues which will concern us in the chapters that follow.

Notes

1. R. Dale, 'Make-or-break Time for a New World Trade Order', *Financial Times*, 16 Jan. 1978.
2. During the negotiations the USA and other countries argued that the Japanese concessions on tariff reduction would not in fact reach 50 per cent. The difference resulted from the fact that the USA and other countries were aiming at a reduction in tariff rates by 50 per cent on the currently applied rates. The Japanese government argued that the unilateral cuts in tariffs in 1978 on 53 items, including 36 mineral and industrial products and 17 agricultural products, were made in anticipation that these reductions would be included as part of Japan's concessions in the Tokyo Round negotiations. The Japanese government, therefore, was conceding a 50 per cent cut in tariffs on GATT-bound rates (the rate which the member countries agreed in previous MTNs not to raise except under extraordinary circumstances) as the base while the other countries were arguing for a 50 per cent cut on the currently applied rates. If the applied rate is used Japan's final offer of tariff reductions on industrial products would average around 28 per cent (US-Japan Trade Council, *Yearbook of US-Japan Economic Relations, 1979*, p.55).
3. Ibid., p.55.
4. *The Japan Times Weekly*, 21 April 1979, p.1.
5. Ibid.
6. Ibid.
7. Ibid.
8. Ibid.

9. M. Subhan, 'Tokyo Round Writes a Progress Report', *Far Eastern Economic Review*, 20 July 1978, p.96.

10. T. Dahlby, 'A Question of Goodwill', *Far Eastern Economic Review*, 27 April 1979, p.104.

11. Ibid.

12. *The Economist*, 10 Feb. 1979, p.87.

13. JETRO, *White Paper on International Trade 1979*, p.48.

14. US-Japan Trade Council, *Yearbook of US-Japan Economic Relations 1978*, p.57.

15. *Task Force Report*, p.35: *On United States-Japan Trade*, 1979, p.35.

16. Ibid., pp.34-5.

17. US-Japan Trade Council, *Yearbook 1978*, p.53. A summary of most of the measures referred to in this book have been taken from this Report.

18. Ibid., p.53.

19. Ibid.

20. Ibid.

21. Ibid., p.54.

22. Ibid.

23. Ibid., p.55.

24. Ibid.

25. For the government's reasons for not revaluing in 1971, see L.B. Krause and S. Sekiguchi, 'Japan and the World Economy' in H. Patrick and H. Rosovsky (eds.), *Asia's New Giant: How the Japanese Economy Works*, p.434.

26. Ibid., p.435.

27. Ibid., p.436.

28. Ibid., p.437.

29. Ibid., p.440.

30. JETRO, *White Paper on International Trade 1976*, p.2.

31. JETRO, *White Paper on International Trade 1977*, p.30.

32. Ibid., p.36.

33. Ibid., p.38.

34. Ibid.

35. JETRO, *White Paper on International Trade 1978*, p.22.

36. Ibid., p.27.

37. Ibid., p.39.

38. Ibid.

39. Ibid.

40. JETRO, *White Paper on International Trade 1979*, p.27.

41. *The Japan Times*, 19 June 1979.

42. C. Smith, 'Fears of a Nightmare Deficit Vanish', *Financial Times*, 3 Dec. 1980.

43. R. Hanson, 'Growing Force in World Markets', *Financial Times*, 3 Dec. 1980.

44. Smith, 'Fears of a Nightmare Deficit Vanish'.

45. Ibid.

46. *The Japan Times*, 19 June 1979.

47. Ibid.

48. *Financial Times*, Editorial, 16 Jan. 1978.

49. T. Nakamae, 'Good Managers or Sharp Traders?' *Guardian*, 4 July 1977.

50. Ibid.

51. Ibid.

52. A. Hamilton, 'Japanese Trade: Time to Rethink', *Business Observer*, 26 Feb. 1978.

53. *Financial Times, World Business Weekly*, 30 April 1979, p.5.

54. Ibid.
55. Ibid., p.6.
56. *The Economist*, 22 March 1980, p 71.
57. *The Economist*, 13 Dec. 1980, p.63.
58. J. Fujii, 'Up-to-date Technologies Help to Counter Falling Sales and Profits', *Financial Times*, 29 Oct. 1979.
59. *Asian Finance*, 15 March 1979, p.40.
60. Ibid.
61. *The Economist*, 30 June 1979, p.77.
62. Ibid.
63. Ibid.
64. *The Japan Times*, 2 June 1979.
65. Ibid.
66. *Asian Finance*, 15 April 1979, p.40.
67. *The Economist*, 30 June 1979, p.77.
68. *Business Week*, 30 Jan. 1978, p.45.
69. Ibid., p.47.
70. S. Awanohara, 'Sabae's Shades May Hide Impending Economic Dam', *Far Eastern Economic Review*, 23 June 1978, p.49.
71. Ibid., p.51.
72. US-Japan Trade Council, *Yearbook 1978*, p.35.
73. Ibid.
74. Ibid., p.36.
75. *US-Japan Trade Council, Yearbook 1979*, p.101.
76. *Asahi*, 15 Feb. 1979.
77. *Nihon Keizai*, 2 June 1978.
78. M. Morita, 'Japan's Despised Seat Warmers', *The New Vanguard*, November 1978.
79. *Nihon Keizai*, 2 June 1978.
80. Y. Hara, 'New For Japan: Rising Joblessness', *Washington Post*, 28 Oct. 1978.
81. Such a trend is the result not only of the recession but also of productivity increases. Declining manufacturing employment is common in many industrial economies.
82. Economic Planning Agency, *Economic Survey of Japan 1977/78*, p.182.
83. Ibid., pp.102-3.
84. Awanohara, 'Sabae's Shades' *Far Eastern Economic Review*, 23 June 1978, p.50.
85. H. Akimoto, 'Era of Heavy Unemployment Coming', *Shukan Yomiuri*, 19 Feb. 1978.
86. *Nihon Keizai*, 22 Jan. 1979.
87. Ibid.
88. Economic Planning Agency, *Economic Survey*, p.181.
89. T. Dahlby, 'Japan's Paternalism is Put to the Test', *Far Eastern Economic Review*, 9 March 1979, p.44.
90. Ibid.
91. Joint Struggle Committee for People's Spring Struggle, *White Paper on The 1980 Spring Struggle*, p.30.
92. Ibid.
93. 'Interview with Labour Minister, Kurihara', *Nihon Keizai*, 19 Feb. 1979.
94. Morita, 'Japan's Despised Seat Warmers', p.13.
95. *Nihon Keizai*, 12 July 1978.
96. Akimoto, 'Era of Heavy Unemployment Coming'.
97. *Financial Times, World Business Weekly*, 22-28 Jan. 1979.
98. A. Iwai, 'Present State of Labour Movement and JSP's Tasks', *Gekkan Shakaito*, Nov. 1978.

99. Ibid.

100. [Japan] *Economist*, 25 April 1978.

101. D. Davies, 'Japan '78; Overview', *Far Eastern Economic Review*, 23 June 1978, p.43.

102. H. Ohta, 'Recent U.S.-Japan Economic Relations: An Overview', *US-Japan Trade Council Report 13*, p.1.

103. Davies, 'Japan '78', p.43.

5   RESTRUCTURING THE JAPANESE ECONOMY

It is doubtful whether the Japanese leadership ever anticipated that the
West would be so critical of their behaviour in international trade but
they were certainly conscious that the unrelenting pursuit of economic
growth would eventually not only create domestic problems (i.e.
environmental pollution, etc.), but also tension with their trading
partners. The *Economic and Social Development Plan* (*1967-71*) had
already emphasised in March 1967 that:

> In Western countries, large-scale investment reflecting the progress
> of technical innovation is being made vigorously, while merger of
> firms to cater for multi-national markets is on the increase. The
> expansion of industries in the developing countries based on low
> wages is threatening some of Japan's industries, together with the
> emergency problem of special tariff reductions for these countries.
> Under these circumstances, Japan is going to face the Kennedy
> Round and the problem of capital liberalization. It is Japan's duty
> to fulfil its responsibility as one of the advanced nations of the
> world and to promote economic cooperation with the developing
> countries . . . Japanese industry's competition in world markets
> must be strengthened through intensified efforts for technical
> development, through improvement of capital structure of firms
> and through reorganization of the domestic economic structure.[1]

The need for restructuring the Japanese economy to face growing
foreign competition was reiterated in the *New Economic and Social
Development Plan* (*1970-75*) published in May, 1970. It was stated that:

> Following the rise of Japan's economy and creation of a world
> economy without national borders, it is believed that the
> internationalization of the economy and society will progress
> swiftly in future. It is our intention to tackle this situation
> positively and by concentrating our efforts on renovation of our
> country's economic structure, as well as by active cooperation with
> the rest of the world, to establish a foundation for the future
> development of the Japanese economy.[2]

However, the most significant step towards a rethinking of Japanese economic, particularly industrial, priorities came in May 1971 when the Industrial Structure Council, an Advisory Committee of the MITI, submitted an interim report on 'International Trade and Industrial Policy for the 1970s'. It stressed that the short- and medium-run objective of the Japanese economy, to 'catch up with the advanced European and American countries', had already been attained. But this had a 'price of its own' and had 'extracted its price by aggravating environmental problems, accelerating over-congestion and delaying the development of social capital'.[3] Besides, it was felt that with genuine affluence the Japanese people would demand qualitative improvements in their standard of living so that the industrial structure would have to be appropriately remodelled to meet these changing demands. Naturally, such a restructuring towards a higher quality of life had to keep in view the resource-poor character of Japan, with its implications for exports, foreign competitiveness, etc. Therefore, the Council recommended that 'only those industries that satisfy four standards — the standard for the income elasticity of demand, the standard for the growth rate of productivity, the standard for congestion and environment and the standard for work content — are desirable in the 1970's'.[4] The first and third were aimed to ensure a higher quality of life, the second was a higher productivity criterion for rapid growth as well as for maintaining export competitiveness abroad. The last, relating to work satisfaction, may be treated both as a component of the quality of life as well as a means to increase labour productivity. On these criteria it was felt that the research and development-intensive industries, highly sophisticated assembly industries, fashion industries and knowledge industries were the most appropriate and needed priority. Thus the Council's interim report heralded a shift away from heavy and chemical industries.

The Japanese experience in the early 1970s, with the problems created by the currency realignment of 1971, the emergence of the OPEC as a major force pushing up oil prices since 1973, the food shortage in 1973-4 with rocketing grain prices and the unilateral embargo by the US government on even commercial exports of grain and soybean, the increasing militancy of the Third World and the potential risk of confrontation between the rich and poor countries, with its implications for an uninterrupted flow of raw materials into Japan, made her increasingly aware of her dependence on the world outside. In addition, the impact of increasing oil prices and the resulting chains of recessions made the capitalist nations of the West even more alarmed at the increasing Japanese 'threat'. As a result they started forcing Japan to open up her markets, while at the same time imposing increasing restrictions on Japanese exports entering their markets. With a view to diverting Japanese productive resources into the non-productive blind-alley of defence and rearmament, some US politicians started blaming Japan for having a 'free-ride' in defence and security matters on the back of the USA. The US government also started putting direct or indirect pressures on Japan to share the increasing burdens of the security of the Far East and South-east Asia, regions vital for the political and economic security of Japan.

Together with the economic shocks, came the political ones when President Nixon sent Kissinger to the PRC in 1971 without informing the Japanese, sowing seeds of suspicion in Japanese minds whether the Japan-US alliance was really meaningful. All these events in the early 1970s added urgency to the need for Japanese rethinking about their future economic and political priorities. The debate still goes on. So far, four major directions can be discerned: the technocratic view still pins its hopes on restructuring industry towards 'technology-intensive industries which can maintain their dynamic comparative advantage' to form a basis for a stable development of the economy.[5]

Another variant of the same approach (i.e. the restructuring of industries) is presented by the economic-technocracy, which believes in the conventional Keynesian wisdom of public works policy, stressing the role of the tertiary and 'service' sectors in creating additional employment opportunities and in a stable economic environment. Prime Minister Ohira's visions of a 'garden city' came into this category.

These policies may create job opportunities (or keep unemployment within manageable proportions) and increase or stabilise incomes, but they will not eliminate the need for imports of raw materials and energy. Therefore continued access to raw material sources is imperative. This need can be met by increasing foreign investment in sources of raw materials. Since a large proportion of raw materials and energy originate in developing countries there is increasing pressure in Japan to invest in these countries while at the same time developing friendly relationships with developing countries through 'aid' and trade. Foreign investments also provide a back-door entry into the protected markets of the West. Besides, foreign investment initially represents an outflow of capital from Japan to the West and thereby reduces Japan's bilateral or multilateral balance of payments surplus with her trading partners. In view of these advantages, foreign investment and 'aid' are also being emphasised under the broad category of 'international-ization of the Japanese economy'.[6]

Similarly, increased welfare expenditure on improving the quality of life and the environment will certainly create more employment, but this may have some adverse implications for the economy as well. For instance, increasing the expectations of the people may increase wage costs and thereby reduce export competitiveness both at home and abroad. Besides, such activities do not necessarily use up the products (such as sophisticated electronics, ships, cars) which have been the basis for the prosperity of large companies in Japan. Some of their losses can be compensated by foreign investment and, at least for the present, there may be ample scope for doing so despite the local opposition of the host-country's industrialists and trade unions. Therefore, large companies cannot regard foreign investment (except for securing sources of raw materials) as a long-term solution of their problems. It is in this context that a new dimension is added to the current debate. Growth in defence expenditure and increases in armament production and export, particularly in the high technology area which becomes obsolete every few years, can create an almost insatiable demand for steel, electronics, ships, etc. As mentioned earlier, the large Japanese companies have already begun suggesting this alternative. It has also been mentioned that some trade unions have spoken in favour of increasing defence expenditure. Since foreign investment is often tantamount to exporting employment, with increasing unemployment in Japan trade unions may oppose massive investment in foreign manufacturing industries. The trade unions, particularly of the loft, who currently oppose rearmament may, in future, support this when the trend in unemployment shows significant increases. The potential threat from the rapidly increasing Soviet naval presence in the Pacific and a growing Japanese suspicion that the US government lacks both the ability and willingness to defend Japan against such a threat has added credibility to such proposals.

In fact, all these four major directions are not mutually exclusive. It is likely that the Japanese leadership will opt for a mix of all four — restructuring the Japanese industries towards more technology-oriented industries as well as towards service industries; increasing foreign investment in developed and developing countries and increasing defence expenditure and expanding armament production. Each of these directions has problems and implications, some of which we shall attempt to analyse in the remaining sections of this chapter.

Restructuring Industries

It has already been mentioned that the basic course of Japan's new trade and industry policies was set by the Industrial Structure's Council's interim report of May 1971. However, in view of the rapidly changing circumstances in the wake of currency readjustments in the post-Smithsonian world, the third world's growing demand for the New International Economic Order (NIEO) and the increasing risks of interruption in the supplies of raw materials and energy, the MITI asked the Industrial Structural Council in July 1974 to look into the matter again. After careful study of various options, the Council came out with 'The Direction of Japan's Industrial Structure', which was subsequently published under the title *Japan's Industrial Structure: A Long Range Vision*. The Council stressed that their report represented the Council's value-judgements on national needs and therefore not only ought to be critically examined by the people, but also that the 'Vision' ought to be continuously revised in view of the changing circumstances within and outside the country and the changing needs of the economy. Therefore the 'Vision' came to be seen as a 'rolling plan' to be reviewed annually.[7]

In view of the recent economic and political changes at home and abroad, the subsequent reviews have added new dimensions to the original plan prepared in 1974. These include 'the effects of slower economic growth, relationships between changing world economic trends and the nation's industrial structure, regional economic development including distribution of the tertiary industry and distribution of goods, and an updated outlook on energy, industrial location, and supply and demand for labor for the next twenty years'.[8]

The original 1974 plan and its subsequent modifications included a large number of numerical estimates about the health of the economy (e.g. changing consumer demand) and on that basis attempts were made to highlight the necessary directions of change. In the original plan it was anticipated that gross domestic product (GDP) would increase 'from Y162 trillion in fiscal 1970 to Y418 trillion in fiscal 1985 – a 2.6 fold increase and an average annual growth of 6.6%'.[9] It was indicated that the annual growth rate of the primary industries would slow down to around 1.9 per cent during this period, while secondary industries would grow by nearly 6.8 per cent. Tertiary industries were expected to grow by 6.6 per cent. Among the individual industries it was anticipated that electrical machinery would experience an annual growth rate of 9.2 per cent, fabricated metal products by 8.3 per cent, machinery 7.9 per cent, construction 7.1 per cent and services 6.9 per cent.[10] Low growth of anything between 2 and 3 per cent per annum was anticipated in agricultural-forestry-fisheries and textiles, while intermediate growth rates of around 5 or 6 per cent were anticipated for iron and steel, transport equipment, etc.[11] In subsequent reviews these rates were modified slightly. But the changes in the production structure continued to 'suggest a shift towards greater technology-intensiveness and higher value added, reflecting diversifying needs and growing preference for quality'.[12]

The plan emphasised that the future industrial structure should contribute to the growth of national welfare and the quest for qualitative improvements in the people's life.[13] With a view to promoting the attainment of the 'true needs of national life' it advocated the development of technology in the three following areas: (1) areas directly connected to the needs of human life;[14] (2) fundamental areas capable of responding to the needs of society as a whole; and (3) fundamental areas oriented towards responding to future needs.[15] It was acknowledged that although the technological level in the private sector manufacturing enterprises was well advanced, in the public sector, particularly in relation to urban development, housing, traffic and transportation, it was fairly backward. It was also conceded that the level of research in health and medical care had not reached the desired level of sophistication.[16]

Therefore, the plan suggested for each of these areas the type of technologies to be developed in future. Similarly, a long list of technological developments for environmental protection was also drawn up. It was also emphasised that even in the private sector the 'entrepreneurs supplying goods and services, not just technicians and researchers, should review the relationship of man and nature to industrial technology, abandon the dependence on Europe and America, and actively endeavour to develop technology for the progress of the Japanese economy and society'.[17] It was this aspect of technological development, i.e. abandoning the dependence on Europe and the USA, that led to a conflict between the Japanese and the US government with regard to the NTT affair. As has been suggested before, in this area the Japanese had a technological lead over the West and they did not wish to share their secrets with their trading partners.

It was hoped that with the change in industrial structure, the composition of exports would be transformed. For instance, it was anticipated that while the shares of iron and steel products and textiles in total exports would fall considerably, the share of mechanical equipment and chemical products would rise, particularly of 'high quality sophisticated goods backed by new technology — for example, electronic computers, industrial mechanical equipment which is integrated with electronic devices and systems products among machinery goods'.[18] The plan also indicated that the export of industrial plant would grow as a result of increasing Japanese overseas investments.[19] Among chemical products, the export of new chemical compounds was expected to increase while that of petrochemicals and plastics was thought likely to decline.[20] It was thus hoped that the commodity composition of Japanese exports would move away from energy-intensive products like steel and petrochemicals to less energy-intensive industries such as fine chemicals, sophisticated textile goods, etc. It was stressed that 'the Japanese exports structure will promote horizontal trade among developed countries centering on quality goods which emphasize non-price competitive factors with a high value-added productivity, or on new machinery developed to meet the needs to construct a welfare society in Japan while simultaneously contributing to the harmonious development of a new international community and promoting trade relations with developing countries'.[21]

In terms of imports the aim of the plan was also to reduce the share of raw materials and fuels mainly by locating basic industries such as iron and steel and petrochemicals overseas.[22] It was anticipated that because of the increasing horizontal trade between Japan and the West the impact of high-quality sophisticated machinery would increase. It was also expected that the import of semi-finished products, low-grade textiles and low-grade machinery from newly industrialising developing countries would increase.

According to the plan, the changing structure of industries would be reflected in a changing structure of employment. It was felt that the 'share of the agriculture-forestry-fisheries industries as a percentage of the total employed population will drop substantially from 17.4% to 9.1% while the share of fabricated metal products and machinery will increase somewhat. The share of construction and services will also expand from 7.7% to 9.9% and from 18.4% to 23.5% respectively'.[23] However, productivity in the manufacturing sector was expected to experience a slowdown largely as a result of a decline in the utilisation rate of equipment and of the introduction of shorter working hours and more holidays.[24] On the other hand, an increase in labour productivity was anticipated in the tertiary sector because of the development of new technologies and labour-saving equipment.[25]

It seems that the underlying strategy incorporated in the 'Vision' has already started bearing fruit, in spite of the continuing world recession and increasing trade restrictions by the West and increasing competition at home and abroad. The three major sectors which are spearheading the new industrial policy of Japan are large computers and computer systems, aerospace and nuclear power.[26] So far, the indigenous Japanese computer industry controls only about 57 per cent of the domestic market, with a major slice of around 29 per cent controlled by a wholly-owned subsidiary of IBM.[27] Exports, though increasing steadily, account for less than 2 per cent of the total value of production.[28] Japanese producers have so far been fairly successful in narrowing the technological gap between themselves and IBM. They have been subsidised by the government to develop their own software. However, the export of Japanese hardware has been limited to those units which are compatible with IBM software.[29] If Japanese firms succeed in developing their own software, which seems imminent, they may make significant inroads into IBM supremacy in the world computer market.

The Japanese aerospace industry is still in its infancy and is geared mostly to military demand. However, the industry already produces various jet aircraft, including fighters, and helicopters under licence. It has also independently developed an intermediate jet trainer.[30] In design Japan's aerospace industry is catching up with European and US industries. It has successfully bid for subcontracts from some leading aircraft manufacturers such as Boeing against leading international firms and it is now being approached by various foreign aerospace industries for joint ventures.[31]

Nuclear power is another growth sector to which Japan is now fully committed. The aim is not only to ensure a regular source of domestic fuel but also to develop a growth industry with export potential. The government is not in favour of continued dependence on foreign technology and is subsidising efforts to develop indigenous heavy-water reactors as well as fast-breeder reactors. Japan is already exporting, though in small quantities, nuclear power equipment such as turbine generators and power-plant core-pressure vessels.[32] It is hoped that Japan will be able to put on the market a commercially viable fast-breeder ractor by the end of this century which will place the industry on a firm footing. Because of the interrelationships between the development of nuclear energy and the defence build-up, this subject will be dealt with in greater detail later.

One of the other fast-developing sectors is electronic medical diagnostic equipment, which includes conventional X-ray, computer tomography ('brain-scanning'), ultrasound equipment and nuclear medicine.[33] Japan has made rapid strides in drug technology and is transforming itself into a major exporter of vitamins, antibiotics and amino acids.[34] She has also made spectacular progress in the technology of producing artificial blood.[35] The Japanese pharmaceutical industry is making a considerable research effort to develop new drugs, and it is reported that, in 1978, of the 104 drug agents from 23 world leaders in drug manufacture pending clinical evaluations, 56 were developed entirely by the Japanese.[36] Other growth sectors are numerical control machines, office machines, communications equipment, small computers, industrial robots and small, possibly automated, tractors.

While major efforts are being directed towards developing new growth sectors, the traditional sectors are not necessarily being neglected. For instance, the car industry is developing increasingly sophisticated electronic equipment for the car of the future. The new Cedric/Gloria series recently exhibited by Nissan Motor is reported to have 21 separate functions controlled by the electronic system and is considered to be the most electronic-intensive car in the world.[37] Television manufacturers are also developing 'no-defect' colour television sets.

Thus Japanese industry, with the leadership and assistance of the government, will certainly aim at restructuring the industrial base towards more sophisticated technology-intensive industries. By so doing it may retain a 'dynamic comparative advantage' over its trading partners. Such an industrial transformation requires the Schumpeterian 'process of creative destruction', i.e. the phasing out of declining industries. This they are already doing or planning to do by exporting raw material and energy-intensive industries such as iron and steel, cement, etc. to the developing countries. This process of creative destruction has both positive and negative aspects. The positive aspect relates to the income- and employment-generating capacity of such industries in the developing countries. Foreign investment may provide a basis for processing the raw material domestically for export and may replace the export of raw material. Such a substitution has an employment-creating affect in raw-material-producing countries. Such an increase in employment and income may not only reduce poverty in those countries but will also create a demand for Japanese technology, engineering goods and other sophisticated products which the developing countries cannot produce themselves. Against some of these positive advantages of foreign investment one has to take account of various malpractices such as bribery and corruption, political interference and evasion of taxation through manipulation of 'transfer pricing', which are well discussed in the literature.[38] Even developed countries have found it difficult to control and regulate the activities of multinational enterprises. Thus developing countries (or any country for that matter) do not want excessive foreign control of their basic minerals and key industries. The ultimate weapon of nationalisation often does not work because the major powers do not hesitate to interfere covertly or overtly to destabilise the government of a developing country if there is a nationalisation threat to their multinationals.

Besides, Japanese investment itself will create more favourable conditions for these countries to catch up with Japan in less sophisticated products, and Japan will have to continue with an accelerated pace of 'creative destruction' and scientific and technological inventions and innovation to maintain her position. So long as Japan can maintain her technological lead this strategy will succeed, but this will require running faster and faster. With a rapidly ageing population there is a risk that Japan may lose her dynamism. Besides, such 'creative destruction' will bring about structural unemployment and regional decline in its wake, the social distress of which can be minimised mainly by constant retraining for new jobs and possibly by moving populations from one region to another. Even if the government and entrepreneurs are able to plan and implement such retraining and transfers, people may not be psychologically prepared to cope with such changes. There is always a limit to people's tolerance in these matters; excessive strains may create social and psychological tensions which are not conducive to physical and mental wellbeing. In the long run, therefore, there may be a conflict between industrial restructuring and meeting the human and social needs which the 'Vision' has postulated.

Restructuring towards the Service Sector

Some analysts — both official and unofficial — look to the expansion of the tertiary sector as the best means of absorbing the suplus labour displaced by the manufacturing sector. A report on 'Problems of the Shift to the Service Economy', prepared in April 1978 by the Price Task Force of the Economic Planning Agency, suggested that the tertiary sector will absorb increasing numbers of people mainly because of the slower growth of the economy and the changing composition of demand towards 'miscellaneous' items such as entertainment and recreation, medical and sanitary services and social and cultural expenditures.[39] The demand for recreation and leisure-related industries will also increase because of shorter working hours. Attempts to introduce regulations for the control of pollution and for environmental conservation will further increase employment in the tertiary sector. According to Nukazawa, some other societal factors will strengthen these trends.[40] For example, state provision of welfare and medical care will require people to run such services. With increased longevity of the Japanese people demands for leisure activities will rise significantly and so will the need for care of the aged. With the improvement of women's social status and the increase in their employment opportunities much of the services now provided by housewives (cooking, nursing, cleaning) may have to be provided by commercial sources. The expansion of tourism will encourage the use of credit cards and other similar financing facilities requiring additional personnel. In order to reduce the dependence on imported technology, expenditure on indigenous research and development is bound to increase. This in itself will increase employment in the tertiary sector. It can also be argued that with increasing domestic and foreign competition, an increasing proportion of manufacturing industry's value-added is devoted to buying the products of the tertiary sector, e.g. advertising, transportation, insurance and executives' expense accounts.[41]

Some of this is certainly true. But Japan's tertiary sector is already large by international standards.[42] In 1976 it accounted for 58.9 per cent of GNP against 64.4 for the USA, 49.2 for West Germany and 54.8 for France.[43] In 1976 it accounted for 52.6 per cent of the labour force against 69.6 per cent for the USA, 47.8 for West Germany, and 51.9 for France.[44]

In view of such a high share of the tertiary sector both in the GNP as well as in the labour force a major expansion of this sector is unlikely. Isao Nishimura, the Director of the First Research Department of the Sumitomo Bank, feels that the absorptive capacity of the tertiary sector is rather limited.[45] On the basis of a comparative study of the employment situation in this sector in Japan and in the USA, he argues that some service trades are already heavily manned. There are others who think that the streamlining of the distributive trade (under the pressure of increasing costs as well as the political pressures exerted by the West) may, in fact, reduce employment in this sector.

It is possible, however, that such increased productivity will reduce trading margins, will lower retail prices and consequently will increase the real income of consumers.[46] On the other hand, if such a stream-lining results in increasing foreign penetration of the Japanese domestic market, the employment effect would be transferred to other countries. Even the MITI's long Range Vision (1978 edition) expects that by 1985 the tertiary industries would absorb only 55.6 per cent of the workforce,[47] a mere 3 per cent increase over 1976.

Admittedly, there is some scope for the expansion of the service sector within the domestic economy in welfare or leisure activities; there will also be some scope for expansion in the service sector in terms of business advertising. On the other hand, many of these activities increase the 'unproductive' burden on the economy and therefore indirectly increase labour costs. This may adversely affect the domestic and international competitiveness of Japanese manufacturers. The technology-intensive restructuring of industries is likely to put considerable emphasis on industrial robots and other means of automation both in the manufacturing industries and in the distributive trades. In the sphere of international services relating to merchandising, banking, finance and transport (which are the broad headings of invisible earnings) Japan has a deficit with the West. An effort can be made to increase relative self-sufficiency in this field. Attempts can be made also to provide consulting services for the construction of roads, bridges, railways, etc. in developing countries. But all this will mean that Japan will have to allow foreigners to operate in her domestic markets for both goods and services. Under these circumstances, it is difficult to say whether the overall gain in employment will necessarily be substantial.

Japanese Foreign Investment

As a result of her defeat in World War II Japan forfeited all her foreign investment in 1945. A new start was made in 1951 but up to 1960 the total volume of Japanese investment abroad was only $209 million. However, the net outflow gathered momentum in the late 1960s and by 1973 it had reached nearly $2 billion, a figure comparable to that of West Germany, though still considerably less than that of the USA.[48] The cumulative total rose from $3.6 billion in 1970 to $6.8 billion by March 1973. At the end of the fiscal year 1978 this had increased to $26 billion.[49]

The geographic distribution of Japanese foreign investment is shown in Table 5.1. In the 1960s and early 1970s, the US share was the highest, closely followed by Asia. Gradually, the relative importance of Asia has outstripped that of North America, accounting for nearly 28.5 per cent of total Japanese foreign investment in 1977. Both as a supplier of raw materials and as a market the role of North America, particularly the USA, has been extremely important. The USA alone accounted for nearly 21.5 per cent of total Japanese investment in 1977. Latin America has also been quite important, with nearly 17 per cent of the total Japanese foreign investment. Europe received only 11.3 per cent of foreign investment in 1969. However, with the hardening of the US attitude towards imports from Japan in the early 1970s Japanese manufacturers started paying much greater attention to Western Europe. Joint ventures with Europeans, which provided a means of back-door entry into the highly protected markets of the EEC, became quite attractive to Japanese manufacturers. There was a significant upsurge in Japanese investment in Europe during the first half of the 1970s, and in 1973 the European share stood at around 24.5 per cent. However, except for the UK, Japanese foreign investments

Table 5.1: Geographical Distribution of Japanese Foreign Investment in 1969, 1973 and 1977 (in million US $)

Regions	1969 Value	1969 Percentage	1973 Value	1973 Percentage	1977 Value	1977 Percentage
Asia[a]	604	22.5	1,350	20.5	6,328	28.5
North America	720	26.8	1,549	22.9	5,401	24.3
Latin America	513	19.2	989	13.3	3,752	16.9
Europe	303	11.3	1,659	24.5	3,075	13.8
Oceania	158	5.9	432	6.4	1,257	5.7
Africa	79	2.9	148	2.2	913	4.1
Middle East	306	11.4	606	8.9	1,479	6.7
Total	2,683		6,773		22,211	

a. Includes only South and East Asia.
Sources: UN Economic Commission for Asia and Far East, 1970: The Far Eastern Economic Review, 18 March 1974: and *Look Japan*, Aug. 1978. See also R.P. Sinha, 'Japanese Foreign Investment', *The World Today*, April 1975.

in Europe did not make much headway, and the European share
declined gradually to 14 per cent in 1977, half of which was in the UK
alone. This trend has continued. The share of the Middle East has
progressively declined from 11.4 per cent in 1969 to 6.7 per cent in
1977. However, the recent annual flow of Japanese foreign investment
suggests that investment in the Middle East is picking up once again
(Table 5.2).

*Table 5.2: Share in the Annual Flow of Direct Overseas Investment
by Regions, 1976, 1977, 1978 (fiscal years) (%)*

Regions	1976	1977	1978
Asia	36.0	30.8	29.9
North America	21.6	26.2	30.8
Latin America	12.1	16.3	13.0
Europe	9.7	7.8	5.9
Oceania	4.7	5.9	3.1
Africa	7.9	5.0	5.0
Middle East	8.0	8.0	12.4

Source: JETRO, *White Paper on International Trade 1979*, p.53.

There has been a substantial increase in the proportion of Japanese
investment going to North America in recent years. In the fiscal year
1978, total investments in the USA increased by $1.3 billion against
$688 million in 1977. The increase in Canada amounted to $34 million.
Japanese investors are attracted to the USA and Canada because they
are not only important sources of raw materials and substantially large
markets but also because land is cheaper and labour costs are
comparable. Besides, with the increasing criticism of Japan's growing
trade deficits, the export of capital can perform a useful role in
bringing about a balance of payments equilibrium. There was a significant
increase in the flow of investment to Asia as well. In the 1978 financial
year, Japanese investments in Asia totalled $1.3 billion against only
$865 million in the previous year.[50]
     In terms of the relative importance of individual countries, the USA
continues to be much the most important country both in terms of
the cumulative total of investment as well as the annual flow (Table
5.3). Indonesia is next in importance, followed by Brazil. Among the
developed countries the UK has nearly 7.6 per cent of the cumulative
total but the annual inflow in recent years has been rather small.

Table 5.3: Relative Importance of Countries for Japanese Foreign Investment (in million US $)

| | Inflow 1976 (FY) | | Inflow 1977 (FY) | | Cumulative 1951-77 | |
	Total	Percentage	Total	Percentage	Total	Percentage
USA	663	19.2	686	24.4	4,767	21.5
Indonesia	929	26.8	425	15.1	3,128	14.1
Brazil	270	7.8	267	9.5	2,071	9.3
UK	88	2.5	50	1.8	1,690	7.6
Australia	137	4.0	146	5.2	964	4.3
Saudi Arabia, Kuwait	67	1.9	49	1.7	879	4.0
South Korea	102	2.9	95	3.4	785	3.5

Source: *Look Japan*, August 1978.

The attraction of particular countries to Japan is self-evident. Market considerations, particularly entering protected markets, play an important part in directing foreign investment to North America and Western Europe. In the case of developing countries such as Indonesia, Brazil and Saudi Arabia a secure supply of raw materials and fuel are the main considerations. On the other hand, developing countries may also represent a cheap source of labour. This was the main reason for Japanese interest in Taiwan, South Korea and Indonesia.

Table 5.4: Composition of Japanese Foreign Investment (%)

Sectors	1973 FY	1976 FY	1977 FY	1978 FY
Manufacturing	42.9	29.6	38.3	45.3
Mining and agriculture, fisheries and forestry	16.6	30.6	21.5	9.2
Commerce	12.6	11.7	12.3	18.5
Finance and insurance		6.3	6.3	4.0
Others	27.9	21.8	21.8	23.0

Source: For 1973 see H. Ishihara, 'Japan Inc. Goes Overseas' *Euromoney*, March 1978: for other years see JETRO, *White Paper on International Trade, 1979*, p.53.

Manufacturing is the major sector attracting Japanese foreign investment (Table 5.4). Because of the world recession in 1973-5 there was a significant decline in manufacturing investment, but this has now picked up and by 1978 its share exceeded that of 1973. The period 1973-5 was also one of considerable militancy on the part of the developing countries, many of whom are the major sources of supply of raw materials and fuel. For a resource-poor country like Japan the trend towards increasing investment in sources of raw materials was not surprising. Since 1976 this trend has, in fact, been slowing down. Commerce accounted for nearly 12 per cent of investment, jumping to 18.5 per cent in 1978. It is too early to say whether this trend is going to continue or not. On the other hand, the trend for commerce in the USA, the biggest recipient of Japanese investment, is one of significant decline. Between 1951 and 1972 commerce accounted for as much as 43 per cent of Japanese investment in the USA. The relative share of manufacturing was only 13.8 per cent.[51] Clearly, Japanese manufacturers were initially interested in the import potential of the US market and in securing a firm foothold there, so they concentrated their efforts on creating a distribution network (commerce, finance and services). Now, with increasing protectionist trends in the USA, they find it essential to actually produce in the USA in order to maintain and/or increase their market share. As mentioned above, this trend has been facilitated because of the relative cost of land and labour in North America. These two factors of production, particularly land for building sites, have become much more expensive in Japan in recent years.

Future Prospects for Foreign Investment

On present trends, Japanese investment abroad will increase rapidly, both in the developed as well as in developing countries. With growing shortages of land and increasing pressures from the environmental lobby, Japanese industries will continue to look for foreign bases with cheaper sources of labour. Besides, there will be a growing need for ensuring a continued supply of raw materials and fuel. Another reason for increasing Japanese foreign investment in developing countries, especially in Asia, is that the last few years have made it increasingly obvious that Japanese export prospects in the markets of the richer countries in North America and Europe will continue to be severely restricted. Moreover, the pressure on Japan to reduce her bilateral trade balance with the West will also continue.

Thus at least four distinct motives are discernible in Japan's foreign investment drive. One of the main motives is the procurement of raw materials and fuel from diverse sources such as Brazil, Indonesia, the Middle East and Australia. The second, aiming at export promotion, leads to concentration on commercial enterprises, distribution networks, finance and other services, such activities being extended worldwide. The third motive for securing markets has resulted in large Japanese companies starting actual production or assembly in the highly protected markets of the USA and Western Europe. This process is likely to be further strengthened by the demands of the West to reduce bilateral balance of payment surpluses. Finally the aim to reduce labour costs has taken them mainly to developing countries such as South Korea, Malaysia and Taiwan.

As a result of all these factors Japanese enterprises are likely to continue expanding their overseas activities. However, their success in this endeavour will depend on the readiness of other countries to accept Japanese investment. From the Japanese point of view, two areas, North America and Asia (particularly South-east Asia), will be the most crucial, although in order to diversify their sources of raw materials and markets the Japanese will not ignore Australia, Latin America or Africa. But these regions will continue to be less significant than Asia. The Japanese leadership has at least tacitly seen Asia as their zone of influence, while Africa is considered to be the zone of influence of Europe and Latin America of the USA. It might be useful to see how North America and Asia have reacted so far to Japanese investment.

Direct Japanese investment in the USA was relatively insignificant until about 1970, but equity investment has increased rapidly since then (Table 5.4). However, even at the end of 1978, direct Japanese investment in the USA was around $2.7 billion out of a total of $49.8 billion. This represented only 6.6 per cent of the total foreign investment in the USA against 23.9 per cent for the Netherlands, 18.1 per cent for the UK and 15.1 per cent for Canada. Thus the overall share of Japan in total direct foreign investment in the USA is rather small (Table 5.5), and there are no immediate reasons for resentment against a further inflow. Both the federal and state governments are at present keen to invite Japanese capital into the USA. 'Invest-in-USA' missions are being sent to Japan under federal as well as under state government leadership.[52] Several state governors visited Japan to approach Japanese enterprises. The state of California is undertaking a reform of local tax laws in order to attract more Japanese industries.[53] At present the US government is willing to accept any industry. On the other hand, there is a general awareness that concentration in a few sectors may bring unfavourable reactions. The *Task Force Report*

Table 5.5: *Foreign Direct Investments in the USA, 1973-8 (in million US $)*

	1973		1974		1975		1976		1977		1978	
	Amount	Percentage	Amount	Percentage	Amount	Percentage	Amount	Percentage	Amount	Percentage	Amount	Percentage
Japan	152	0.7	345	1.4	591	2.1	1,178	3.8	1,755	5.1	2,688	6.6
Canada	4,203	20.4	5,136	20.4	5,352	19.3	5,907	19.2	5,650	16.3	6,166	15.1
Europe	13,937	67.8	16,756	66.6	18,584	67.2	20,162	65.5	23,754	68.7	27,895	68.3
UK	5,403	26.3	5,744	22.8	6,331	22.9	5,802	18.9	6,397	18.5	7,370	18.1
Europe (excl. UK)	8,535	41.5	11,013	43.8	12,253	44.3	14,360	46.7	17,356	50.2	20,525	50.3
Others	2,264	11.0	2,907	11.6	3,135	11.3	3,523	11.4	3,436	9.9	4,081	1.0
Total	20,556	100.0	25,144	100.0	27,662	100.0	30,770	100.0	34,595	100.0	40,831	100.0

Source: G. G. Fouch, 'Foreign Direct Investment in the United States in 1978', *Survey of Current Business*, August 1979.

stressed this point in the course of their discussions with the Japanese parliamentarians:

> It is important for foreign investors in the U.S. to provide some balance between joint ventures which simply exploit our natural resources (and through mining and smelting operations use our energy and destroy our environment) versus those that provide high technology manufacturing (not just assembly) jobs. To treat America only as a place to extract resources will soon create resentments.[54]

The *Task Force Report* also stressed that people in the USA are sensitive to foreign investments in farmland. The Japanese firms investing in the USA might have to face some trade union opposition as well. The UAW, which has been persuading Japanese car-manufacturers to build plants in the USA, has already started complaining that Japanese companies 'are trying so hard to block unionization that they're violating U.S. labor laws'.[55] They have also filed unfair-practices complaints with the National Labour Relations Board against three employers.[56]

Nevertheless, it can be concluded that, for the time being, the USA will be prepared to accept a substantial inflow of Japanese foreign capital if concentration in specific industries is avoided. In the long run, if the Japanese presence is too obvious this may give rise to resentment. On present trends, Western Europe will not become a significant importer of Japanese capital. Outside the UK, Japanese investment in manufacturing in Europe on a rather limited scale is mainly in Italy, Ireland, Spain and West Germany. As mentioned earlier, the European market is not as important to·Japan as the USA. For political and security reasons as well Japan does not like to displease her largest trading partner. An additional reason for Japanese reluctance to come to Europe, particularly to the UK, emanates from their apprehensions about difficult labour relations, even though Japanese companies in Britain have a fairly successful industrial relations record.[57] In addition is the opposition of local industries and sometimes the trade unions to Japanese investment. This became very clear to the Japanese in 1977 when Hitachi, in the face of opposition by the British television manufacturers and the trade unions, had to withdraw its proposals for a television set factory in north-east England.[58]

A more recent proposal by Nissan to set up a car-manufacturing plant in Britain to produce 200,000 cars a year has been welcomed by the Conservative government, but in some political circles as well as among trade unions 'there was apprehension about possible repercussions for U.K. motor manufactuers'.[59] Grenville Hawley, the secretary of the Transport and General Workers Union, is reported to have said that 'there was no space in the U.K. market for anyone to increase the number of vehicles for sale in the U.K.'[60] EEC car-manufacturers (Fiat, Renault, Peugeot, Volkswagen and British Leyland) have already started lobbying for a change in the EEC rules on 'source of origin'.[61] According to their proposals, a car should be designated as originating in the EEC only if 80 per cent of the car is manufactured in member-countries. Nissan had indicated that initially (i.e. 1984, when production starts) the local content will be around 60 per cent. This would be raised to 80 per cent 'as soon as practicable after full production is reached'.[62] EEC car manufacturers are demanding a rigorous enforcement and monitoring of the 80 per cent local content. The EEC Commission and some of the member states have already described the proposal as a 'Trojan horse'. It is not yet clear whether Nissan now will be more welcome than Hitachi in 1977. After all, even in the case of Hitachi, the UK government had initially made favourable noises. It is well known that Japanese manufacturers intending to invest abroad do not like adverse publicity, so Nissan might decide against investing in Britain if there is too much opposition.

The USSR has shown some willingness to accept Japanese technology and know-how for the development of Siberia's natural resources. With Japan's political and ideological commitment to the USA it is difficult to visualise substantial economic cooperation between the USSR and Japan.

The People's Republic of China (PRC), of course, is a different matter. She fits very well, at least at present, into the grand Western design for the encirclement of the USSR. The PRC may provide a large market for Japanese technology and skills, but the initial optimism generated by the 'opening up' of the country by the successors to the 'gang of four' is already on the wane. Foreign technology imports are being cut back; chemicals and metallurgical industries, particularly iron and steel, are likely to be worst hit.[63] Japan has been blamed by the Chinese authorities for inappropriate site-selection for the Baoshan steel plant near Shanghai. However, it is hoped that the PRC would continue to import light industrial and textile machinery, as well as port-handling, oil-drilling and coal-mining equipment.[64] A significant part of such machinery imports may come from Japan. Besides, Japan will continue to see the PRC as a significant source of supply of raw materials and fuel and will, therefore, continue to woo her.

As to the South-east Asian countries it is undeniable that the availability of technical and managerial skills will facilitate their economic development, but the 'image of the ugly Japanese businessman is very real in many South East Asian minds'.[65]

The attitudes, pronouncements and behaviour of Japanese businessmen and administrators do not always help. As mentioned earlier, culturally the Japanese people always think of countries (as people) in hierarchical order. As a result, they cannot negotiate on equal terms. Their 'big brotherly' behaviour often offends countries which have only recently won their freedom from their colonial masters and are very sensitive to any suggestions of encroachment on their sovereignty. Japanese leadership, in recent years, has identified more with the richer countries of North America and Europe, many of which have dubious colonial records. As a result, the 'Asianness' of Japan has come to be seriously questioned. This was articulated a few years ago by Lee Kuan Yew, the Prime Minister of Singapore, who stressed that 'Japan will have to ask itself whether it is part of Asia or not'.[66] In Asian eyes, the Emperor's journey to Europe in 1971 and the repeated Japanese claim to a permanent seat on the UN Security Council reflect this Japanese feeling of superiority over other Asians, which comes out clearly in public opinion surveys. For instance, in a survey conducted recently on cultural friction between Japan and South Korea, 58.8 per cent of the respondents indicated that they felt superior to South Koreans. The ghost of the 'East Asian Co-Prosperity Sphere' haunts any efforts towards economic co-operation between Japan and South-east Asia. The threat of economic expansion weighs heavily on the minds of South-east Asian leaders, in spite of repeated assurances by Japanese leaders that Japan had no intention of re-emerging as a military power and is merely interested in what Prime Minister Fukuda termed a 'heart-to-heart' relationship.[67] How genuine these overtures are it is difficult to say. But governments, academics and industrialists do stress the need for active co-operation between Japan and the South-east Asian countries. For example, the chief executive of one of the major companies is reported to have said:

These [Taiwan, Korea] are countries we can co-operate with economically. Europe has its EEC. America is sufficient within itself. We coloured peoples who have become the world's problem people must even now unite our strength. I believe the old East

Asian Co-prosperity Sphere was essentially right. The only trouble
is that Japan looked only to its own advantage and resentment of
this persists still. From now on we must meet a new age by
changing our thinking both about giving aid and about being aided.[68]

Such statements revive Asian fears of Japanese 'neo-colonialism'. After
all, not many Asians will take seriously the suggestion that the Japanese
consider themselves as 'coloureds' and therefore closer to the developing
countries. Most developing countries in the region (with the sole
exception of the PRC) have ample reason to suspect that the Japanese
leadership has not given up 'superpower' ambitions and that any
scheme of mutual co-operation between Japan and themselves cannot
be evolved on the basis of equality and mutual self-respect. This is
clearly reflected in the promotion of the idea of the 'Pacific Era' by
Jiro Tokuyama, the Managing Director of Nomura Research Institute.[69]
The point that 'the flow of history is going to leave Europe behind
and shift to the Pacific region' has been made by others before, but
the relish with which Nomura Institute is advocating it is a clear
reflection of Japanese superpower ambitions and the role the
Japanese expect of other countries in the region. Let us examine some
of Tokuyama's statements: 'The Pacific economic basin has the edge
over the Atlantic economic basin in growth potential. Moreover,
this dynamism is sustained by the existence of ample food and energy
resources and the increasingly close relations between the United
States and Japan.'[70] He has his eyes not only on the food surplus of
North America and Australia but also on the Mekong Delta; the
petroleum reserves in the continental shelves from the East China
Sea to the coast of Vietnam; Australian uranium, Indonesian
petroleum and the abundant coal deposits of the Pacific area. Given
the hinterland rich in raw materials and fuel that Japan lacks so
badly, Tokuyama conceives a group of nations 'Japan, the United States,
Australia, New Zealand and Canada as the nuclei for solving the
problems' in much the same way as the EEC is the nucleus for the
Atlantic basin.[71] The interesting thing about this statement is the
placing of Japan before the USA on this list, which is not alpha-
betically arranged. This slip is intentional; probably many Japanese
do sincerely believe in this 'destiny' of Japan to lead the world. Of
course, as a second thought, he does concede that there is a risk of
being misunderstood.

Especially since Japan will have to take the initiative, there is a

possibility that the true intention of restoring global order will
be misunderstood and that formation of a Pacific basin will be
criticized as a Japanese attempt at hegemony or even a
reincarnation of the Greater East Asia Co-Prosperity Sphere.
It is thus imperative that Japan's intentions be fully understood
by the United States and Western Europe, both of which have
closely interdependent relations with Japan, and that there be
full communication of views with Australia, New Zealand,
Canada and ASEAN, all of which are economically very much
intertwined with Japan. Japan should actively undertake the role
of honest broker and must be prepared to ungrudgingly bear the
costs incurred in the basin's formation.[72]

The idea of an organisation for the Pacific countries is certainly not a
new one. As early as 1966 Kiyoshi Kojima and Hiroshi Kuromoto
proposed the idea of a Pacific Free Trade Area in their article 'A
Pacific Economic Community and Asian Developing Countries'.[73]
The idea was subsequently put forward in a slightly modified form in
Kojima's book *Japan and a Pacific Free Trade Area*, published in
1971. In the meantime bankers, industrialists and businessmen from
the so-called 'Pacific Five' (USA, Japan, Australia, New Zealand and
Canada) formed a Pacific Basin Economic Council 'to promote the
study and discussion of issues raised in regional trade and investment
and greater cooperation between public and private interest'.[74] The
Council now has a membership of about 400 major companies largely
from the 'Pacific Five' nations.[75] One of the outcomes of the
deliberations of Council has been the establishment of the Private
Investment Cooperation for Asia. Several conferences, mainly with the
Japanese Foreign Ministry support, have been held to discuss the
Pacific Free Trade Area concept. Out of such discussions has emerged
a new concept of the 'Organisation For Pacific Trade, Aid and
Development' (OPTAD), sponsored jointly by Kojima and Drysdale.
According to Drysdale, the OPTAD proposal has four broad aims:

(1) 'To provide a more effective safety valve . . . for the discussion of
trade and economic grievances among Pacific countries in a rational
and cooperative atmosphere . . .'
(2) 'To provide a stimulus to aid and investment flows for the
developing countries of Asia and a framework for a radical improvement
in the quality and structure of their aid, investment and trade relations
with developed countries in the Pacific';

(3) 'To provide a forum for consultation and discussion about the longer term development in and economic transformation of the region';
(4) to provide 'a more secure framework of economic alliance among the countries of Asia and the Pacific, an alliance within which participant's could feel free to develop closer economic integration in smaller grouping . . .'[76]

The OPTAD is conceived to 'develop along the lines of the OECD in Europe'[77] but at the same time incorporating the objectives of GATT and UNCTAD. The authors of the idea make no secret of the fact that OPTAD is conceived as a counterbalance to the growing economic power and trade protectionism of the EEC. They stress that:

> global institutions and mechanism no longer provide an adequate framework for dealing with the Pacific economy for reasons both of commercial diplomacy and of political strategy. The weight and structure of established Atlantic and European interests in international economic diplomacy are heavily directed towards trade share stabilisation and reactive protection of the present international order, and against constructive adjustment to dynamic economic growth such as that taking place in Asia and the Pacific. The preoccupations of the major European industrial economies in their individual and collective approaches to external adjustment during the 1970's have led them further away from automatic support for a free and open international trading environment.[78]

One can sympathise with the feelings of the promoters of the ideas of OPTAD that the existing power structure of the global organisations (including the UN agencies) gives much more weight to the US and European countries at the neglect of Japan, Australia and the Third World countries, and therefore does not adequately represent present-day reality. Nor can one deny that in order to revitalise such organisations there is a need for drastically altering their power structure. This is essentially what the Third World has been asking for under its (often misunderstood) slogan of the New International Economic Order (NIEO). Strangely enough, both Japan and Australia have consistently made a common cause with the USA and the EEC and thwarted the Third World's effort to bring about such a restructuring. There is hardly any reason to suggest that the behaviour of Japan or Australia would suddenly change towards the developing countries once a new organisation such as OPTAD is created. If these two countries are looking for a 'role' they are reasonably well represented in the regional as well as in global organisations. They can, if they wish, play a significant role in co-operation with the Third World and the Scandinavian countries. After all, the Scandinavian countries have played a reasonably active role in the UN system without having much political power.

By and large, it is almost certain that South-east Asian countries will continue to accept Japanese foreign investment, but the suspicions will continue. It is for this reason that the ASEAN is now developing more links with the EEC. It is also possible that with growing experience, ASEAN and other developing countries will impose stricter conditions in future and demand reciprocity in trade, particularly in the import of labour-intensive goods such as textiles. It must be remembered that Japan, under the Generalised System of Preferences (GSP), provides duty-free treatment on imports of most manufactured and semi-manufactured products from a large number of developing countries.[79] Japan's list of beneficiaries is broader than those of the USA and the EEC, but it excludes many products originating in Hong Kong and, among manufactured products, agricultural and fisheries items and textiles. As in the case of the USA and the EEC, Japan places a ceiling on the value of imports receiving GSP treatment.[80] It has been estimated that trade benefits of GSP in the absence of any MFN reductions to developing countries from imports to Japan did not exceed $25 million in 1971.[81] The corresponding figure for the USA and the EEC respectively were $236 million and $217 million. Naturally, many developing countries — particularly the East and South-east Asian countries — expect better access to the Japanese market. For instance, in a recent choice of foreign companies to be allowed to manufacture diesel engines in the Philippines, the Japanese firm was ruled out on the grounds that Japanese firms have an excessive share of the manufacturing of transport equipment.[82] Four other major Japanese companies are under sharp criticism for allegedly attempting to corner a power project in the Central Philippines.[83]

On the whole, in the foreseeable future the prospects for Japanese foreign investment both in the USA and South-east Asia are not bad. However, a substantial outflow of capital overseas from Japan may have serious consequences for the domestic economy. Foreign-based Japanese industry will attempt to export products to Japan and will compete with domestic producers at a time when the export market may already have shrunk because of increasing supplies from foreign subsidiaries. This, together with the fact that foreign investment often amounts to 'exporting employment', will have serious consequences for domestic employment. Therefore the pace of foreign investment will not only depend on the tolerance of foreigners to receiving foreign investment but also on the sensitivity of the domestic population to increasing unemployment, and its social and political implications.

Overseas Aid

Another subject which has attracted considerable attention in the current controversy between Japan and the West is the question of aid to developing countries. This featured prominently both in the Ushiba-Strauss joint statement as well as in the Joint Communiqué between President Carter and Prime Minister Ohira. In the Ushiba-Strauss joint statement it was reaffirmed that the government of Japan intended to double its aid within five years and that the quality of the official development assistance would also be improved through an increase in the grant element in the aid package, as well as an untying of such financial assistance. The Joint Communiqué between President Carter and Prime Minister Ohira reiterated that the

> United States and Japan should improve their official development assistance to developing countries. It is particularly important for them to strengthen aid in the field of human resources development and to strengthen support of research and development in such areas as health, food and energy. The two countries will explore, through bilateral discussions and consultation with developing countries, how to promote cooperation in technical assistance and in research and development in these areas.[84]

Although Japan has emerged in recent years as a major aid donor, on various criteria her performance has been rather poor compared to that of the other developed countries. Between 1970 and 1979 Japan's financial assistance (total new flow of resources) increased nearly four times (Table 5.6). In 1979 it was the fourth largest donor after the USA, the UK and France, and was closely followed by West Germany. The total net flow of resources from Japan to developing countries in 1979 fell from $10.7 billion to only $7.6 billion.

Table 5.6: Net Flow of Resources by Selected Development Assistance Countries (DAC), 1979 (in million US $)

| | Total | | Official development assistance | |
	1969-71 Average	1979	1969-71	1979
Japan	1,742	7,555	468	2,637
Belgium	294	2,290	127	631
Canada	625	2,542	314	1,026
France	1,723	8,685	1,001	3,370
West Germany	1,810	7,289	638	3,350
Italy	800	4,055	153	273
The Netherlands	417	1,948	185	1,404
Switzerland	167	5,534	29	207
UK	1,293	11,219	528	2,067
USA	5,905	18,674	3,214	4,684
Total[a]	15,743	73,943	7,131	22,375

a. Includes other OECD countries not included here.
Source: OECD, *Development Cooperation Review, 1980*, pp.178-9, tables A2 and A3.

The Japanese share in the total assistance provided by the DAC countries jumped from 3.4 per cent in 1962 to 10.2 per cent in 1979. However, much of the total flow of resources is directed towards export promotion and securing sources of raw materials and should not qualify as 'aid', which refers mainly to assistance on concessional terms.[85] Net official development assistance (ODA) in 1979 constituted only 34.9 per cent of the total net outflow of resources (Table 5.7). Against this, ODA constitutes nearly 25.1 per cent of resource flows in the case of the USA, 38.8 per cent for France, 46 per cent for West Germany and 18.4 per cent for the UK. Although there has been a substantial increase in the volume of ODA, from $1,424 million in 1977 to $2,637 million in 1979, Japanese aid performance continues to remain unsatisfactory in terms of the International Development Strategy for the Second United Nations Development Decade, which stipulated that the richer countries would progressively increase their ODA to the developing countries to reach a minimum net amount of 0.7 per cent of their gross national product at market prices by the end of the decade.[86] It also recommended a 1 per cent target for total flows. In the case of Japan, the target for total flows was met in 1978 but in 1979 it fell to only 0.8 per cent of the GNP. Net ODA as a proportion

Table 5.7: The Flow of Japanese Financial Resources to LDCs, 1979
(in million US $, share in percentages)

		Total	Share
I	Official development assistance (A + B)	2,637.5	34.9
	A. Bilateral official development assistance (1 + 2)	1,921.2	25.4
	1. Grant and grant-like contribution	560.2	7.4
	Technical assistance	241.9	3.2
	Food-aid	21.4	0.3
	Other grants	296.9	3.9
	2. Development lending and capital	1,361.0	18.0
	New development lending	1,243.4	16.4
	B. Contribution to multilateral institutions (1 + 2 + 3)	716.3	9.4
	1. Grants	112.7	1.5
	2. Capital subscription payments	610.7	8.1
	3. Concessional lending	−7.1	
II	Other official flows (A+B)	210.1	2.8
	A. Bilateral other official flows (1 + 2)	440.4	5.8
	1. Official export credit	−235.1	
	2. Equities and other bilateral assets	675.4	8.9
	B. Multilateral Institutions	−230.2	
III	Grants by private voluntary agencies	19.0	0.3
IV	Private flows at market terms	4,689.0	62.1
	1. Direct investment	690.6	9.1
	2. Bilateral portfolio investment	2,715.2	35.9
	3. Multilateral portfolio investment	640.7	8.5
	4. Private export credit	642.5	8.5
Total resource flows (balance of payment basis)		7,555.6	

Source: OECD, *Development Cooperation Review, 1980*, pp.186-7, table A.9.

of GNP increased from 0.2 per cent in 1978 to 0.3 per cent in 1979.
This figure was substantially lower than the average of the DAC
countries at 0.4 per cent. As seen in Table 5.7, the net flow of private
capital from Japan in 1979 was nearly twice as high as ODA.

The geographical distribution of Japanese assistance clearly
underlines the Japanese concern for securing stable sources of energy

and other raw materials. Bilateral ODA, which accounted for 73 per cent of the total disbursement in 1979, continues to be directed to the developing Asian countries, with Indonesia as the leading recipient.[87]

The breakdown of bilateral official development assistance, for obvious reasons, also reveals a bias in favour of Japanese export promotion or of securing supplies of raw materials and components for Japanese industries (Table 5.8). This is reflected clearly in the major share of ODA being directed towards public utilities, industry and mining. Official sources clearly indicate that 'economic cooperation should help Japan secure the steady supply of resources and energy which are necessary to keep its economy moving . . .'[88] So far, technical co-operation, agriculture and social infrastructure have received low priority in Japanese ODA. The share of technical co-operation in bilateral developments aid is much higher in the cases of other major donor countries. The overall figure of the DAC countries in 1979 was 40 per cent. For France it was as high as 59 per cent, for West Germany 37 per cent, the UK 26.6 per cent and the USA 60.9 per cent.

Table 5.8: Purpose Breakdown of Bilateral Official Development Assistance, 1979 (in million US $)

		(%)
Bilateral ODA allocable by sectors	2,143.2	
Agriculture	419.5	19.6
Public utilities, industry, mining and construction	1,340.7	62.6
Trade, banking, tourism, etc.	35.7	1.7
Education, health, social infrastructure	168.9	7.9
Technical assistance	285.9	13.3
Financing current imports	345.1	16.1
(of which, food-aid)	171.6	8.0
Debt reorganisation	4.9	0.2

Source: OECD, *Development Cooperation Review, 1980*, pp.204-7, tables B.4 and B.5.

With respect to the terms on which economic assistance has been provided the Japanese record is poor compared to the other major donors. For example, the grant element in total ODA commitment at only 77.7 per cent was by far the lowest of all the DAC countries. (The average for the DAC countries was 92.8 per cent.) For France, the USA and the UK it was between 92 and 93 per cent.

The loan interest terms offered by Japan are somewhat better than those of France but significantly higher than those of West Germany, the UK and the USA (Table 5.9). With respect to maturity Japanese terms are better than those of France and the UK but much inferior to those of West Germany and the USA. Grace periods allowed by Japan are substantially longer than those of the UK, France and West Germany but a little less than those of the USA.

Table 5.9: ODA Loan Terms of Repayments and other Related Payments, 1979 (%)

Countries	Interest rates	Maturity (years)	Grace period (years)	Grant element of total ODA commitments
Japan	3.1	27.7	9.1	77.7
France	3.9	19.8	7.0	93.5
Germany	2.2	34.6	7.7	85.1
UK	2.7	13.5	2.6	96.6
USA	2.8	37.0	10.0	91.6
Total DAC countries	2.6	31.2	8.5	92.8

Source: OECD, *Development Cooperation Review, 1980*, p.201, table B.1.

A major part of Japanese ODA continues to be tied. In 1979 only 45.7 per cent of ODA was untied. Nearly 32.4 per cent of ODA was tied and about 22 per cent partially tied. Against this, nearly 80 per cent of West German ODA was untied; in the case of France the figure was 39.1 per cent, with 47.5 per cent for the UK and 37.1 per cent for the USA. The figure for the DAC as a whole was 53.8 per cent.

The Japanese government concedes that 'the Official Development Assistance extended by Japan is not necessarily satisfactory, in terms of either quantiy or quality'.[89] It also accepts that 'it is necessary that Japan devote further effort to the quantitative and qualitative improvement of its Official Development Assistance in order to assume full international responsibility appropriate to its power in world economy'.[90]

There is no doubt that the total amount of Japan's net financial flows to developing countries will continue to increase; it is also possible that Prime Minister Fukuda's commitment at the Bonn summit in July 1978 to double Japan's ODA by 1980 will also be met. It is doubtful whether the target of 0.7 per cent of gross GNP set by the

International Development Strategy will be met in the foreseeable
future. The prospects become still bleaker if the present trend of a
deficit on the balance of payments continues.

On the other hand, the developing countries, particularly in Asia,
may not be so keen to welcome Japanese ODA in future for fear of
increasing political interference by Japan. After all, Japanese ODA has
been largely directed towards facilitating Japanese access to sources of
raw materials and energy.

No country desires a considerable penetration of its basic resources
by a foreign power with a colonial history. There may also be another
reason for conflict between Japan and her aid-recipients. It is almost
inevitable that with increasing industrial capabilities the developing
countries will want to obtain increasing access to the Japanese market
for their products. In this respect the Japanese official stance, at least in
theory, is more positive than that of the West. It is clearly acknowledged
that 'the growing competition from these countries is a natural
consequence of the development of the world economy — a path
which cannot be bypassed. Seen in this light, a case can be made that in
the long-run it will be in the best interest of Japan to accept the
competition as inevitable and tackle the problem with a forward-
looking stance. Such competition can best be accommodated through
positive steps for industrial adjustment.'[91] However, restrictive policies
have not been ruled out. It is stressed that 'if and when competition
from the developing countries intensifies so rapidly as to allow Japan
little time to adjust, Japan may be compelled to take some sort of
emergency measures in the area of trade. But such measures, if
implemented at all, should be of the shortest duration necessary for
making the necessary adjustments.'[92] If such restrictive policies are
introduced by Japan it is possible that the tension between Japan
on the one hand and developing countries on the other may increase,
with adverse consequences for economic and technical co-operation
between them.

On the whole, one can expect a continued increase in the net flow
of Japanese financial resources to developing countries but it will not
be large enough to have a significant impact on the Japanese balance
of payments with the rest of the world. In any case, increased ODA by
Japan will not, in any way, affect the bilateral trade balance between
Japan and the USA or the EEC, which has rather erroneously become
the focus of the trade controversy.

Notes

1. Economic Planning Agency, *Economic and Social Development Plan, 1967-1971*, 1967, p.5.
2. Economic Planning Agency, *New Economic and Social Development Plan, 1970-1975*, 1970, p.1.
3. JETRO, *Japan's Industrial Structure: A Long Range Vision*, p.5.
4. Ibid.
5. Ibid.
6. This also includes the opening up of Japanese markets for foreign goods and investments.
7. JETRO, *Japan's Industrial Structure*, p.7.
8. MITI, *Japan's Industrial Structure — A Long Range Vision, 1976 Edition*, p.1.
9. JETRO, *Japan's Industrial Structure*, p.20.
10. Ibid.
11. Ibid.
12. MITI, *Japan's Industrial Structure*, p.9. see also MITI, *Japan's Industrial Structure — A Long Range Vision, 1978 Edition*.
13. JETRO, *Japan's Industrial Structure*, p.6.
14. Human needs were classified into five groups: dietary life, clothing life, dwelling life, health care, and culture and recreation. The list of appropriate commodities for respective groups were: dietary — chemical fertilisers, agricultural machinery, cultured seafood resources, health food, foods utilising micro-organisms, artificially photosynthesised foods; clothing — clothes, wearing apparel and ornamental accessories, fashion clothes and related products, footwear, precious metals, raw materials for clothing; dwellings — home decorations, furniture and fixtures, carpets and *tatami*, ornaments, air-conditioners and heaters, products for construction, electrical goods, interior fixtures, plywood and assembly materials, plastic products, cement, prefabricated housing units, prefabricated high-rise flats, etc.; health care — sports equipment, pharmaceuticals and medicines, medical machinery, opticals, fire prevention and fire fighting equipment, crime prevention equipment, anti-pollution machinery, etc.; culture and recreation — fishing equipment, seaside recreation, camping articles, telecommunication machinery and apparatus, bicycles, opticals, musical instruments, toys and athletic equipment, pens, pencils and painting materials, sports guns, horticultural equipment (JETRO, ibid., p.33).
15. Ibid., p.136.
16. Ibid.
17. Ibid., p.150.
18. Ibid., p.36.
19. Ibid.
20. Ibid.
21. Ibid., p.37.
22. Ibid.
23. Ibid., p.22.
24. Ibid.
25. Ibid.
26. R. Hanson, 'Japan's New Industries', *Financial Times*, 6 Nov. 1979.
27. R. Hanson, 'High Hopes for the Future', *Financial Times*, 6 Nov. 1979.
28. Ibid.
29. Ibid.
30. P.J. Rubin, 'Flair for Design Work', *Financial Times*, 6 Nov. 1979.
31. Ibid.
32. R. Hanson, 'A Major Force Emerges', *Financial Times*, 6 Nov. 1979.

33. C. Smith, 'Large Market is Growing Rapidly', *Financial Times*, 6 Nov. 1979.
34. C. Dale, 'Great Strides in Drug Technology', *Financial Times*, 6 Nov. 1979.
35. Ibid.
36. Ibid.
37. R. Hanson, 'In-Car Electronics', *Financial Times*, 6 Nov. 1979.
38. Some of which are R. Barnet and R.E. Muller, *Global Reach: The Power of the Multinational Corporation:* G. Ball, *Diplomacy For a Crowded World*, particularly pp. 291-8: L. Turner, *Multinational Companies and the Third World*: S. Lall, 'Transfer Pricing by Multinational Manufacturing Firms', *Oxford Bulletin of Economics and Statistics*, pp.173-95: S. Lall, 'Transfer Pricing and Developing Countries: Some Problems of Investigation', *World Development*, vol.7, no. 1: S. Lall, 'Financial and Profit Performance of MNC's in Developing Countries: Some Evidence from an Indian and Columbian Sample', *World Development* vol.4, no.9: P.P. Streeten and S. Lall, *Main Finding of a Study of Private Foreign Investment in Selected Developing Countries* (UNCTAD, TD/B/C 3/111): UN Department of Economic and Social Affairs, *Panel on Foreign Investment in Developing Countries*, E.69, II D.12.
39. Quoted in K. Nukazawa, 'Japan's Emerging Service Economy and The International Economic Implications', unpublished, p.16.
40. Ibid., p.17.
41. M. Shinohara, '*Sangyo Kozo Ron*', *Chikuma-Shobo*, (1976), p.58, quoted in Nukazawa, 'Japan's Emerging Service Economy', p.23.
42. C. Smith, 'Sector's Growth Rate Outstrips that of Manufacturing Industry', *Financial Times*, 29 Oct. 1980.
43. Ibid.
44. Government of Japan, *Economic White Paper, 1978*, pp.214-15, quoted in Nukazawa, 'Japan's Emerging Service Economy, p.5.
45. Quoted in Nukazawa, ibid., p.10.
46. Ibid., p.12.
47. MITI, *Japan's Industrial Structure, 1978 Edition*, p.16.
48. GAO, *United States-Japan Trade: Issues and Problems*, p.163, Table 4.
49. JETRO, *White Paper on International Trade, 1979*, p.51.
50. *Asian Wall Street Journal*, 7 July 1979.
51. *Japan Report*, 1 Feb. 1979.
52. *Nihon kogyo*, 4 Oct. 1978.
53. *Nihon kogyo*, 27 June 1978.
54. US Congress, *Task Force Report on United States-Japan Trade*, 1979, p.48.
55. R.L. Simison, 'After Coaxing Japanese Car Makers to U.S., UAW Finds They Resist Union Organizing', *The Wall Street Journal*, 26 Aug. 1980.
56. Ibid.
57. D.R. [D. Ramsey], 'Cautious Approach to Setting up Abroad', *Financial Times*, 26 July 1977.
58. *Financial Times* (editorial), 8 Dec. 1977.
59. *Financial Times*, 30 Jan. 1981.
60. Ibid.
61. S. Alexander, 'Europe Unites to put Skids under Nissan', *Sunday Times Business News*, 8 Feb. 1981.
62. Ibid.
63. D. Bonavia, 'Another Turnabout in China', *Far Eastern Economic Review*, 12 Dec. 1980, p.60.
64. Ibid.
65. R. Tasker, 'The Ugly Japanese Image is Still Very Alive, *Far Eastern Economic Review*, 23 March, 1979, p.44.

66. Ibid., p.45.

67. Ibid., p.44.

68. Quoted in J. Halliday and G. McCormack, *Japanese Imperialism Today: Co-prosperity in Greater East Asia*, pp.117-18.

69. J. Tokuyama, 'Japan's Role in the Pacific Era', *Japan Echo*, vol. VI, no.1 (1978).

70. Ibid., p.43. 'Pacific basin' refers to all the countries encircling the Pacific Ocean.

71. Ibid., p.45.

72. Ibid., p.47.

73. K. Kojima, 'An Organisation For Pacific Trade, Aid and Development: A Proposal', Australia-Japan Economic Relations Research Project, Australian National University (mimeo), p.1n.

74. C. Williams, 'The Pacific Community: A Modest Proposal', Australia-Japan Economic Relations Research Project, Australian National University (mimeo), p.7.

75. P. Drysdale, 'An Organisation For Pacific Trade, Aid and Development: Regional Arrangements and the Resource Trade', Australia-Japan Economic Relations Research Project, Australian National University (mimeo), p.10.

76. Ibid., p.14.

77. Ibid.

78. P. Drysdale and H. Patrick, 'Evaluation of a Proposed Asian-Pacific Regional Economic Organisation', Australia-Japan Economic Relations Research Project (mimeo), p.19.

79. R.E. Baldwin and T. Murray, 'MFN Tariff Reductions and LDC Benefits under the GSP', *The Economic Journal*, vol. 87, no.345, (March 1977), p.34.

80. Ibid.

81. Ibid., p.37, table 1. See also R.E. Baldwin, 'Measuring Trade and Employment Effects of Various Trade Policies' in R.E. Baldwin *et al.* (eds.), *Evaluating the Effects of Trade Liberalization*, pp.20-1.

82. L. Gonzaga, 'The Headaches caused by Over-visibility', *Far Eastern Economic Review*, 23 March 1979, p.64.

83. Ibid., p.65.

84. Joint Communiqué between President Jimmy Carter and Prime Minister Masayoshi Ohira: 'Productive Partnership for 1980's', 2 May 1979, reproduced in GAO, *United States-Japan Trade*, p.202.

85. R. Sinha, 'Japan's Aid to Developing Countries', *World Development*, vol.2, no.8 (1974), p.15.

86. OECD, *Development Cooperation Review 1973*, p.40.

87. OECD, *Development Cooperation Review, 1980*, p.116.

88. MITI, *Economic Cooperation of Japan, 1978*, p.29.

89. JETRO, *White Paper on International Trade, 1979*, p.54.

90. Ibid.

91. MITI, *Economic Cooperation of Japan, 1978*, p.48.

92. Ibid., p.43.

6 THE MILITARY SITUATION IN THE FAR EAST AND THE THREAT TO JAPAN

It has been mentioned earlier that the increasing pressures from the West on Japan to restrict her exports and to liberalise her import policy together with the continued world recession have led to a significant contraction of capacity in various sectors of the economy and a consequent rise in unemployment, particularly of middle-aged people. As a result both industry and some trade unions are already looking to the defence industries to create a favourable climate for industrial investment and additional employment opportunities. According to Kiyoshi Tamaki, the director of the Central Procurement Office of the Japan Defense Agency (JDA), 'more enterprises are coming to show understanding for defense production, which can secure an average profit rate of 5 to 7 per cent, and they are coming to attach expectation on it'.[1]

The shipbuilding industry (which has been forced to cut its capacity[2]) is placing its 'hopes on the concrete materialization of the JDA's naval vessel consolidation and expansion plan, and are seeking the way to overcome the depression in the planned building of MSDF [Marine Self Defence Force] ships, including the early replacement of superannuated ships'.[3] *Tokyo Shimbun* reported in August 1978 that the Shipbuilders Association of Japan made representations to the JDA Director-General to promote the building and replacement of MSDF ships at a more rapid pace.[4] The JDA ordered nine ships in the budget for the 1978 fiscal year. It is reported that some businesses have come to believe that 'if public-works projects will not be as helpful for the buoying up of businesses as in the past, then the quickest way will be to construct naval vessels'.[5] Some major enterprises such as Tokyo Shibaura Electric and Fujitsu have already indicated their intention to strengthen the defence production sector.[6] Japanese industries are also trying to pressurise the government into relaxing the restrictions on the export of armaments.[7] Japan currently adheres to the 'Three Principles Concerning Weapons Exports', which forbid exports (1) to the Communist bloc, (2) to areas to which such exports are banned by the UN and (3) to nations which are party to conflicts or where there is a potential risk of their being so involved.[8] As early as 1975 the Japanese Aeronautics and Space Industry Association requested the government to allow them to export multipurpose US-1 seaplanes, medium-size C-1 jet transport planes and helicopters.[9] It is reported that Bunichiro Tabe, the President of Mitsubishi Shoji, made a public statement that 'Anything that can be exported should be exported, even if they are goods which are close to being weapons.'[10] Recently a government report suggested that Japan should develop its nuclear industry as an export industry.[11] In fact, the MITI has already decided to actively promote the development of small reactors for export.[12] Japanese industries are also aiming at raising the ratio of domestic production of licensed items such as the F-15 fighter planes and the P3C anti-submarine patrol planes.[13] The emphasis is shifting towards developing their own weapons system. More recently, Yoshihiro Inayama, who is informally designated as the next Chairman of *Keidanren* (Federation of Economic Organisation), argued that 'The peace of the world is being maintained by the nuclear balance between the US and the Soviet Union. However, disputes arise constantly. Japan is under the US nuclear umbrella, but it cannot depend upon the US as to all disputes. National defense to prevent them is necessary.'[14] Similarly, Takeshi Sakurada, the Chairman of *Nikkeiren* (Japan Federation of Employers' Associations), advocates that 'Article 9 of the Constitution should be revised and matters concerning defense power should be clearly written in it. Also, it is necessary to make it possible to declare a state of emergency, and to increase the stockpile of munitions . . .'[15] The Chairman of Mitsui Shipbuilding, Isamu Yamashita, recommends possessing 'at least medium-range missiles for defense at the first stage though not intercontinental ballistic missiles'.[16] However, the boldest among them is Hosai Hyuga, the Chairman of *Kankeiren* (Kansai Federation of Economic Organisation), who made the controversial suggestion that Japan should look into 'a draft system for an emergency'.[17] He feels that the 'Afganistan problem is the best chance to enhance [the people's] awareness of national defense' and argues that:

> The core of over-all security is defense power. The defense expenses in advanced nations in Europe and America are on the level of 3-6 per cent of the GNP. Even in Switzerland, where the defense expenses are the smallest among advanced nations, the rate is 1.9 per cent. Japan . . . should increase the amount at least to the level of Switzerland.[18]

Leading Japanese businessmen, as in the West, have always clamoured for increased military expenditure. As Halliday and McCormack point out, as early as 1953 Japanese businessmen began 'to draw up plans for the rearmament of Japan, in 1954 to press for research into guided missiles; in 1955 it succeeded in getting orders for a start on the production of jet fighters'.[19] Leading members of large Japanese firms have never made a secret of their intentions. As early as 1952 a Defence Production Committee was set up within the *Keidanren* for lobbying and marketing of arms and ammunitions.[20] Office-bearers of the *Keidanren* have openly advocated expansion of defence capability and possession of nuclear arms.[21] In May 1969, at the 30th General Conference of the *Keidanren*, the then President remarked that Japan had 'a duty to contribute to the preservation of peace in the Far East and to gradually increase self-defense capacity, as well as to hold strongly to Security Treaty System'.[22] Several other examples of similar views by leading Japanese businessmen have been listed by Halliday and McCormack. In the current atmosphere of recession and high unemployment together with the increasing opposition by the West to Japanese exports, it is no surprise that leaders of firms in Japan have become much more vocal on defence issues.

Under the pressure of increasing unemployment, some trade unions have also come to support increased defence production. For instance, as early as 1975 the All-Japan Shipbuilding and Machine Industry Workers Union proposed the domestic manufacture of weapons. Similarly in autumn 1977 the Consultative Council of Aircraft Industry Labour Unions urged the government to encourage the indigenous development of the mainstay fighters.[23] We have already mentioned the views of Keiichi Takahata, the Representative Secretary of the National Consultative Council of Private Workers Union, who has called for the recognition of the SDF and the revision of Article 9 of the Constitution.

Nevertheless, the trend towards increasing defence expenditure and the strengthening of Japanese defence forces cannot be explained purely in terms either of deepening world recession and slowdown in Japan's economic activity and high unemployment or of a conspiracy of the large companies. There are several other forces at work. US pressure on Japan (and other allies) to increase military expenditure and to make greater efforts towards defence of her sea-lanes is certainly one of the major factors accounting for a renewed debate on Japan's defence capabilities. There is also a genuine concern about increasing Soviet military presence in the Pacific and a growing worry that the USA may not possess either the ability or the willingness to defend Japan in the event of a Soviet invasion. As *Nihon*

Keizai put it:

> As for the recent military balance between the East and the West, the West's predominance is becoming unstable, due to the stumbling of the strengthening of US military power partly because of the effects of the consistent strengthening of Soviet military power and of the Vietnam War. The actual situation is such that as can be seen in the Soviet invasion of Afganistan and the US Embassy hostage incident in Iran, the US cannot necessarily cope properly with the complicated military situation.
>
> In the Far East, during the past one or two years, the Soviet Union's high-handed actions have become conspicuous, such as the deployment of the aircraft carrier *Minsk*, the Backfire supersonic bomber, and the SS-20 intermediate-range missile and the construction of full-scale bases on three of the four islands in the northern territory. Therefore, the focal point of the present situation would be whether the US-Japan Security Treaty Structure with US military power and the SDF as the two pillars, will function effectively if a dispute in Europe or in the Middle East is extended to the Far East after a part of US Forces in the Western Pacific are dispatched to that disputed area under the United States' Swing Strategy.[24]

Above all, there is a growing feeling of self-confidence and assertiveness among the Japanese elite. It is argued that 'In terms of economic activities, Japan has grown to be a world power. However, the U.S. military power on which Japan has depended for the safety of it sea routes has come to a relative decline. Unless Japan tries to secure the safety of these sea routes on its own . . . Japan will perish.'[25] To such people military power is not only a means of self-defence but it provides Japan with more room for manoeuvre and influence and ultimately the status of a world power. In the words of Ikutaro Shimizu

> When Japan shatters its post-war taboos and banishes its illusions and comes to possess military power commensurate with its economic capacity, *a political power of no small magnitude* will be born. In its relations with the U.S., the Soviet Union and other countries, Japan will gain more room for manoeuvring and influence. Either because of inertia or self-debasement, Japan has so far behaved like a handicapped person on the world stage when, in fact,

it has the qualities to become a world power.[26] (italics mine)

Such a 'hawkish' statement by Shimizu would come as a surprise to those familiar with his active involvement in the anti-Japan-US Security Treaty Campaign of 1960 and the anti-government peace movement. In recent years he has not only supported increased military expenditure but also possession of nuclear arms by Japan. As we shall see later, he is not alone in this; there are others — within the government, in large companies and among the intellectuals — who believe in the 'great power' destiny of Japan and who pose a 'threat' to Japan's pacifism. Ultimately, it is this ambition of the Japanese elite to be a major power which may tilt the balance towards the militarisation of Japan. However, the current defence debate is being conducted mainly around two factors — the increasing Soviet military presence in the Far East and a growing Japanese doubt about the US willingness and/or ability to come to Japan's rescue in the event of a Russian attack. The growing concern about the Soviet threat was highlighted in the Defense White Paper approved by the Japanese cabinet on July 1979. It stressed that 'over the past 10 years . . . the Soviet Union has continued to strengthen its military power at a far greater pace than Western Countries and the United States seems to have failed to retain an advantage over the Soviet Union in strategic and theatre [area] nuclear weapons, naval and airpower. Above all, not only has the quantity of Soviet strategic nuclear weapons increased but a remarkable improvement in accuracy has been achieved.'[27] It also stressed that the 'Reinforcement of the Soviet Far Eastern military forces has started to have an influence over the military balance between the United States and the Soviet Union in the Western Pacific. It must be said that the Soviet Union has built up a military capability which must be watched carefully by Japan.'[28]

While it is true that defence and rearmament is becoming more respectable in Japan for economic as well as political reasons, the magnitude of the Japanese defence build-up, at least in the foreseeable future, will largely depend on the perceived Soviet threat. Therefore to understand the nature of the current defence debate in Japan it is important to understand the nature of the Soviet threat. Our intention is to present a bird's-eye view of the military situation in the Far East so that a reader can assess the 'growing Soviet threat' and Japanese military potential.

The Soviet Military Build-up

All the evidence indicates that 'North East Asia ranks second only to
Central Europe as the most heavily armed region of the globe.'[29] Apart
from the military strength of the USSR and the USA there is the
PRC, with the second largest armed force of 4.5 million[30] (about twice
the number of US armed forces) and the third largest annual defence
budget of nearly $57 billion.[31] Then come the two Koreas, with their
armed forces of a little over half a million each with annual military
budgets of around $1.3 billion for the North and $3.5 billion for the
South.[32] Taiwan comes next with an army of nearly half a million
and a $1.8 billion annual defence budget.[33] Compared to these,
Japan's military budget around $10-11 billion exceeds the combined
total of the two Koreas and Taiwan, while it has an army of just under
a quarter of a million men.[34]

According to the International Institute for Strategic Studies (IISS)
out of a total of 1.8 million in 173 divisions in the Soviet Army, nearly
500,000 men in 46 divisions are positioned along the Sino-Soviet border
and at least 31 divisions are in Transbaykal and the Far Eastern military
districts.[35] They are more lightly equipped than the Soviet divisions
in Eastern Europe and are in a relatively low state of readiness.[36] The
army bordering on the PRC has 40 motorised rifle and six armoured
tank divisions supported by a single airborne division of nearly 7,000
men and possesses limited offensive capabilities.[37] Some Soviet
groundforces are also deployed in the Sakhalin islands, the Kamchatka
Peninsula and the Kurile islands. Since 1970 the Soviet troops in this
region have received new weapons such as the T-62 tank (with its
115-mm gun), the BMP-76 armoured personnel carrier (with a 76-mm
gun and anti-tank missile), the BM-21 multiple rocket launcher (with a
122-mm gun, 40 barrels), the FROG-7 tactical nuclear rocket, etc.[38]

The Soviet naval strength in the region consists of 755 ships with a
total tonnage of 1.3 million. The fleet, based in Vladivostok, has 10
cruisers, 80 destroyers and 125 submarines of which 50 are nuclear
powered.[39] Two naval infantry regiments (which correspond to the US
Marine Corps) for amphibious missions are also deployed in the region
but, because of their small size and poor amphibious lift-capability,
their offensive capability is limited to 'lifting a task force of modest
size to a nearby objective'.[40] The Pacific Fleet is also augmented by
30 naval combat aircraft.[41]

However, the quality of the naval forces deployed in this region has
improved significantly as a result of the deployment of anti-ship

missiles capable of being launched from submarines or surface warships.[42] The recent modernisation of the Soviet surface fleet by the introduction of Kresta-class cruisers and Kotlin-SAM class and Krivak-class destroyers has improved considerably the ocean-going capability of the Soviet navy.[43] Similarly, the introduction of nuclear-powered submarines with anti-ship cruise missiles, some of which can launch missiles while remaining submerged, has added considerably to Soviet anti-submarine warfare (ASW) capabilities.[44] Recently there has been an addition to the Soviet Pacific Fleet based at Vladivostok of Minsk-class 40,000-ton aircraft carriers with vertical take-off and landing (VTOL) planes, a guided-missile cruiser and an amphibious-assault transport dock.[45]

The Soviet air power in the Far East consists of nearly 2,000 aircraft, including 500 bombers, 1,400 fighters and 140 patrol planes.[46] This air strength is being upgraded by retiring old models (such as the TU-16 medium bomber and the MIG-17, MIG-19 and MIG-21 fighters) and substituting them with SU-19, MIG-23 and MIG-25 fighters and the TU-26 Backfire. These modern aircraft have a longer range than those being replaced and can carry a much bigger payload of ammunition. In recent years out of the five wings of the Soviet Air Force (air defence command, naval aviation, long-range aviation, frontal aviation and military transport aviation) the air defence command has lost ground relative to frontal aviation.[47] The latter is the tactical arm which is responsible for supporting groundforces by advance attack on enemy positions and strategic sites, including airports. It is estimated that the frontal aviation's fixed-wing assets have increased by nearly a third while its load-carrying capacity has been doubled.[48]

The Soviet Union has accorded a high priority to its strategic nuclear capability which increased, both in tonnes of targetable warheads and equivalent megatonnage, nearly five-fold between 1964 and 1976.[49] It is estimated that the Soviet Union has 1,398 intercontinental ballistic missiles (ICBMs) and 1,003 submarine-ballistic missiles (SLBMs).[50] Several of these can be equipped with multiple independently targetable re-entry vehicles (MIRVs).[51] The new generation of missiles in the Soviet arsenal can carry tremendous destructive potential,[52] can hit their targets with a great deal of accuracy and have a range of up to 12,000 km for the ICBM and nearly 7,700 km for the SLBMs.[53] The number of these strategic weapons located in the Far East is not known, but analysts suggest that it may be only a small proportion of the Soviet strategic nuclear capability,[54] most of which is certainly directed at US and Western European targets.

The US Military Presence in the Far East

The total strength of the US army in Asia is around 57,000, out of
which nearly 38,000 are deployed in South Korea while another
19,000 are stationed in Hawaii. In addition to these there are about
2,700 liaison and support personnel in Japan and 500 elsewhere
in the Western Pacific.[55]

The Pacific Air Force (PACAF), consisting of the US 5th and
13th Air Force, has nine fighter squadrons, six with F-4 and three
with F-15 fighters.[56] The force is supported by one tactical reconnaissance
squadron with RF-4 fighters and one special operations squadron. For
tactical airlift they have 32 C-130 transport planes and 12 smaller
aircraft in addition to nearly 100 logistic support helicopters.[57] Two
Airborne Warning and Control Aircraft, E-3A (AWACS), have been
deployed with the US Air Force detachment in Okinawa. By 1983
the number of AWACs will be increased to four.[58] Apart from the
PACAF currently deployed in the Pacific, at least 15 fighter/attack
wings from the continental US are potentially available for reinforcements
in Asia.[59]

But the major strength of the US armed forces lies in the US
Seventh Fleet based in Hawaii. It has two aircraft carriers, 26 surface
combat ships, seven attack submarines, some mobile logistic support
ships and an amphibious lift capability.[60] One of the aircraft carriers,
together with eight combat ships and two support ships are based at
Yokosuka in Japan.[61] The two aircraft carriers of the Seventh Fleet
between them carry a total of 160 fighter, attack, reconnaissance,
electronic counter-measure (ECM) and Anti-Submarine Warfare (ASW)
aircraft.[62] According to the assessment of the US Arms Control and
Disarmament Agency 'In several respects, the 7th Fleet presently
surpasses the capabilities of other navies in East Asia. Its ASW
capabilities are unrivaled. It is the only navy deployed in the region
with extensive sea-based fleet air defense capability — a vital asset
in any extended conflict in open ocean theatres.'[63]

On the other hand, according to the Japan Defense Agency, while
'the Seventh Fleet has substantial anti-submarine capability for its
own defense, it does not have sufficient capability to protect merchant
shipping; and therefore will have difficulty in completely fulfilling
its assigned mission of maintaining sea lanes in the face of Soviet
attempts to sever such lanes'.[64]

Some tactical nuclear weapons are also deployed by the US forces
in South Korea and the number of warheads is estimated at around

650.[65] They have a short range of up to 50 km and carry a small pay-load.[66]

The PRC's Military Strength

Although there is no immediate threat of military confrontation between the PRC and Japan, in any military equation in the Far East the PRC's military strength cannot be ignored. In the present atmosphere of continuing distrust between the USSR and the PRC, Japan has to tread rather carefully but, on the other hand, the continuing 'confrontation' between the two Communist giants works to the advantage of Japan in at least two ways. First, it ties up considerable military resources of both the USSR and the PRC, and second, in an effort to modernise its armed forces the PRC has to import Western technology to create and develop her strategic industries. Japan is one of the main beneficiaries of such efforts. On the other hand, Japan cannot be oblivious to the increasing military capability of the PRC because it may eventually have adverse consequences for the South-east Asian region and, as a result, on Japanese sea-lanes and foreign investment.

At present, nearly 75 of the PRC's total of 140 divisions, consisting mostly of infantry divisions, are deployed in the north-east, northern and western regions near the common border with the USSR.[67] These troops are supported by millions of highly trained armed militia who can be mobilised at short notice.

The Chinese airforce possesses nearly 5,200 combat aircraft and about 800 naval combat aircraft.[68] The majority of them consist of the old-generation Soviet-designed MIG-17, MIG-19 and F-9 fighters, and a Chinese version of the MIG-19.[69] She also has some TU-16 medium and IL-28 light bombers. Both in terms of pay-load and their range of operation and speed, these virtually outdated planes are no match for the new generation of Soviet aircraft.

The PRC navy consists of 38 major combat ships and 97 submarines, including a nuclear-powered one.[70] She also has an assortment of around 1,500 fast-attack and patrol craft mainly suited for coastal patrol. The submarines are slow, noisy and can be easily detected by modern ships with ASW equipment.[71]

Among her tactical weapons, the PRC has deployed 50-70 intermediate-range ballistic missiles (IRBMs) and 40-50 medium-range ballistic missiles (MRBMs); the latter can reach up to 2,800 km and can carry a 1- to

3-megatonnes warhead.[72] She has also one or two 'limited-range' intercontinental ballistic missiles with a range of 6,437 km.[73] These can reach the heartland of the USSR, but, given the PRC's economic and technological capabilities, a full-scale deployment of such strategic weapons will take some time.

Japan considers the maintenance of peace on the Korean Peninsula to be essential for peace and security in the whole of East Asia, including Japan. On the other hand, Japan does not want — at least at present — to become militarily involved in Korea.[74] By and large, she prefers to see a military balance maintained in the Peninsula. Currently, North Korea has a groundforce of nearly 600,000 troops, including two tank divisions, two independent tank regiments and three motorised infantry divisions.[75] It also has 100 battalions of powerful artillery and 82 rocket battalions together with surface-to-surface missiles[76] within striking range of Seoul, the capital of South Korea. North Korea has around 2,650 tanks.[77] But many of these tanks are old and have limited fire power and poor armour-plate protection.[78] The North Korean airforce has about 615 combat aircraft, consisting largely of MIG-19 and MIG-21 fighters. Most aircraft, except for the supersonic SU-7, are old and have limited capability. However, the airforce is supported by nearly 250 surface-to-air missiles (SAMs) of limited effectiveness.[79] The North Korean navy consists of four frigates, 16 submarines and about 317 fast attack craft, some with missiles and torpedoes, others with guns.[80] Many of these are old but they can be particularly effective against South Korean merchant shipping.

South Korean groundforces, at around 520,000 regular troops,[81] are somewhat smaller than those of North Korea. They also have about a million reservists who can be mobilised easily, against North Korean reserves of 260,000.[82] The South Korean airforce, with only 362 combat planes, is considerably smaller than the North Korean one. But South Korean combat planes include more sophisticated US fighters such as the F-4D/E Phantom and the F-5A/E Tiger.[83] The South Koreans also possess 80 Hawk and 45 Nike-Hercules SAM launchers.[84] The South Korean navy has 10 destroyers, seven frigates and six corvettes in addition to some fast attack and patrol craft. Four out of seven destroyers are fitted with ASW detection equipment but South Korea does not have submarines.[85]

The Taiwanese army of nearly 310,000 troops is supported by a tank force of 200 medium and 625 light tanks.[86] The airforce has around 388 combat aircraft of varying capability. Many of these are old and have limited usefulness as interceptors or bombers. The army also possesses 80 launchers of Nike-Hercules and Hawk missiles and 20 Chaparral and surface-to-air missiles.[87] The main core of Taiwan's navy consists of 22 destroyers, nine frigates and two submarines.[88] Most of these ships are more than 30 years old but they have been modernised. They are supported by a few ASW patrol craft and gunboats and nine Tracker ASW aircraft.[89] However, the total defence capability of the Taiwanese navy is rather small.

Japan's Military Capability

While the constitutional nature of the Japanese Self-Defense Forces (SDF) is still being questioned by some political parties in Japan, the SDF has emerged from its modest beginnings as a Police Reserve Force in 1950 to become one of the most sophisticated armed forces in the world. Even though as a percentage of GNP military expenditure continues to be around 1 per cent,[90] the total amount of such expenditure has increased from a little less than $2 billion in 1965 to nearly $11.8 billion in the draft defence budget of 1980 presented in December 1980.[91] Japan's military expenditure is considerably less than that of West Germany, France and the UK but it is much more than any other Western European country. In terms of numbers of armed personnel Japan is not far behind the UK. The sophistication of a military machine can be broadly gauged by the military expenditure per head of armed personnel, and it can be seen from Table 6.1 that Japan is very much in the European league. Her expenditure per head of armed personnel is much higher than that of Italy, compares favourably with that of France, is almost three times as high as that of the PRC and almost nine times that of India. It is seven times higher than South Korea and sixteen and nineteen times higher than that of North Korea and Taiwan respectively. It is well known that only about a quarter of the resources of the USSR are in the Far East and these forces are not as well armed there as in Europe. Therefore it is probable that in term of sophistication the Japanese armed forces, in spite of their 'peace' Constitution, are the best equipped in the region. Other countries in the region certainly have an overwhelming superiority in numbers of armed personnel but in modern warfare numbers are less important than military hardware, the technical ability to man sophisticated equipment and the industrial capability to sustain the supply of hardware and spare

Table 6.1: Military Expenditure in Selected Countries

	Military expenditure (million US $) (1980)	Military expenditure as % of GNP (1979)	Total armed personnel (millions) (1980)	Military expenditure per head of armed personnel (US $)
Developed countries				
Japan	8,960	0.9	0.24	37,178
Denmark	1,404	2.0	0.04	40,114
France	20,220	3.9	0.50	40,848
West Germany	25,120	3.3	0.50	50,747
Italy	6,580	2.4	0.37	17,978
The Netherlands	5,239	3.4	0.12	45,556
Norway	1,570	3.1	0.04	42,432
Sweden	3,588	3.3	0.07	54,364
Switzerland	1,832	2.1	0.02	101,778
UK	24,448	4.9	0.33	74,310
USA	142,700	5.2	2.05	69,610
USSR[a]	165,000	11.0-13.0	3.57	46,218
Developing countries				
The PRC	56,941	9.0	4.45	12,796
India	4,406	3.9	1.10	4,005
Indonesia	2,070	3.4	0.24	8,554
Korea (North)	1,300	11.2	0.68	1,917
Korea (South)	3,400	5.5	0.60	5,757
Malaysia	1,465	n.a.	0.07	22,196
Pakistan[b]	1,050	n.a.	0.44	2,392
Philippines	962	n.a.	0.11	8,513
Singapore	574	n.a.	0.04	13,667
Taiwan[c]	1,007	n.a.	0.44	2,299

a. For 1979. Estimates range from $124 billion to $165 billion (IISS, *The Military Balance: 1980-81*, p.137.
b. 1979.
c. 1975.
Source: Ibid., pp.96-7, table 4.

parts to keep the military machine running. In all these respects Japan
is far superior to her Asian neighbours.

Currently the Japanese Defence Forces are divided into three
components, the ground (GSDF), the maritime (MSDF) and the air
(ASDF) forces.

The Ground Self-Defence Force (GSDF)

The GSDF is responsible for dealing with land-bound invasions,[92] and has
a total authorised strength of 180,000 personnel. Currently nearly 86
per cent of this quota is being maintained. The GSDF also maintains a
force of 39,000 reserve personnel for rear-support duties during
emergencies.[93] Its total strength is divided into 12 divisions and a
composite brigade.[94] The entire country is divided into 14 districts:
Hokkaido has three districts, Tohoku two and Kyushu two. Kanto,
Koshin-etsu, Tokai-Hokuriku, Kinki, Chugoku, Shikoku and Okinawa
have one each. Each district has one division of the GSDF except
for Okinawa, which has a composite brigade, and Shikoku, which
currently has none.[95] Because of its proximity to the Soviet bases in
the Sakhalin and Kurile Islands, Hokkaido is considered to be 'the
first line of Japan's defence', and has also been given the 7th Division,
which is the only mechanised division of the GSDF. It is estimated
that nearly 50,000 troops are deployed in Hokkaido, together with
the 1st Tank Corps and almost half the guns of the GSDF.[96] For
mobility, the GSDF possesses about 830 tanks and 560 armoured
personnel carriers.[97] This amounts to roughly one armoured vehicle
per 128 troops, which is a much lower ratio than in the other developed
countries. For instance, the USSR has one armoured vehicle per
twenty troops and West Germany has one per thirty.[98] Since Japan
does not have a land frontier with other nations the need for armoured
vehicles is somewhat less than that for the other countries, although
even the UK possesses one armoured vehicle per 26 troops. However,
it is estimated that nearly 5 per cent of tanks are outdated M-41 models
given to Japan by the USA. The other model, the Type 61, comprising
75 per cent of Japan's tank inventory, was developed fifteen years ago
and since then has been the mainstay of the GSDF armoured force,[99]
though it is now somewhat outdated. Twenty per cent of the tanks
are Type 74, which has been developed in Japan. This tank is considered
to be well suited to the Japanese terrain and compares favourably with
the modern tanks possessed by other major powers. It carries a

105-mm turret gun which can fire accurately even while traversing rugged terrain because of its 'altitude control system' which correlates tank altitude with changes in terrain. It is claimed to be the only make of tank to possess such a device.[100]

The GSDF artillery possesses a total of 830 field guns.[101] At least half of these are World War II types and are already obsolete.[102] To help the increasing mobility of the artillery the carriage-drawn 155-mm howitzers are being replaced by self-propelled Type 75 155-mm howitzers, which have considerably greater firepower and mobility. The GSDF is also deploying the Type-75 130-mm self-propelled multiple rocket launchers, which can fire up to 30 rockets almost simultaneously. It is expected that, because of its mobility and firepower together with its armour protection for the crew, it will provide close support to the infantry and tank units.[103]

The GSDF has only a limited anti-tank capability but this is being ameliorated by the acquisition of anti-tank helicopters (AH-IS) which are equipped with anti-tank guided missiles with a range twice that of anti-tank guns. An attempt is also being made to develop ground-to-ground short-range guided missiles with a view to enhancing long-range anti-tank attack capability.[104]

For defence against aircraft coming at low and medium altitudes the GSDF maintains 8.5 anti-aircraft artillery groups equipped with Hawk missiles.[105] These have been operational in Japan since 1964. It is felt that the existing Hawks cannot cope with recent improvements in aircraft performance, so an attempt is being made to replace these by improved ones. Deployment of a short-range surface-to-air missile (SAM) is also being contemplated.[106] Nevertheless according to the US Arms Control and Disarmament Agency, the GSDF lacks adequate transport equipment for moving large numbers of troops and much of the artillery. Anti-tank and air-defence capabilities and groundforces are not impressive by modern standards.[107]

The Maritime Self-Defense Force (MSDF)

According to the JDA the 'primary missions of the Maritime Self-Defense Force (MSDF) are to defend Japan from seaborne invasion forces and to secure the safety of maritime transportation in the peripheral waters around Japan'.[108] The MSDF has a total strength of nearly 40,500 personnel. In 1978 the MSDF had 32 destroyers, 15 frigates, 16 submarines, 42 mine-warfare ships, 29 patrol ships and six amphibious landing ships.[109] It had nearly 294 aircraft.[110]

Japanese destroyers and destroyer escorts have ASW (anti-submarine warfare) capabilities similar to those of the navies of the other major powers.[111] Five of the MSDF submarines are most suited to coastal defences while the remaining ten have long-range mission capability.[112] For defence capability the MSDF has commissioned anti-aircraft missile destroyers and helicopter destroyers. As for submarines, a new generation with a 'teardrop-type' hull for greater underwater manoeuvrability has been commissioned.[113] These submarines possess computerised high-speed data processing: with the improvement in submarine capability, particularly after the development of nuclear-powered submarines, ASW requires more sophisticated detection and data capabilities. The land-based anti-submarine capability of the MSDF consists mainly of 120 fixed-wing patrol aircraft of three types: the S2F-1, the P2V-7 and the P12J.[114] The first two were supplied by the USA in the mid-1950s and are now obsolete. The P-2J, an improved version of the P2V-7, is now produced in Japan but it cannot accommodate the sophisticated equipment necessary for detection and data processing. Therefore the National Defence Council decided on 28 December 1977 to acquire 45 Lockheed P-3C aircraft, mainly through domestic production under license.[115] The P-3C is considered a versatile aircraft which can be used both for patrol and ASW operations and can be easily 'armed with homing torpedoes, anti-submarine depth charges, anti-submarine rockets and other weaponry'.[116] The USA is investigating the possibility of arming the P-3C with nuclear depth charges. Under the three 'nuclear policies', Japan is currently not interested in such possibilities.

The US Arms Control and Disarmament Agency suggests that 'the MSDF is a relatively modern force capable of conducting effective ASW and minesweeping operations near Japan's coastal waters'.[117] According to the Agency, with respect to ASW operations 'the Japanese destroyers are comparable to their U.S. counterparts' and 'the Japanese minesweeper force is one of the world's most modern.'[118] However, for lack of seagoing replenishment and air-defence capability Japanese naval operations have to be restricted to coastal waters, even though Japanese destroyers possess the range to operate in large areas of ocean.[119]

The Air Self-Defense Force (ASDF)

The ASDF is responsible for dealing 'speedily and appropriately with not only isolated cases of casual airspace violations during peace time but also airborne invasion'.[120] In order to perform its functions satisfactorily the ASDF maintains an air defence system based on fighter interceptors and ground-to-air guided missiles.[121] The Japanese airforce consists of 44,000 men, 356 combat aircraft, 395 trainer planes and 40 transporters.[122] Out of 10 fighter squadrons five are based on F-4EJs and five on F-104Js.[123] The F-104J is a supersonic fighter which was commissioned in the mid-1960s. However, in terms of low-altitude interception or aerial combat capability it is no match for modern fighters. Nor can it compare favourably in its electronic warfare capability such as electronic jamming, etc.[124] and it is already being phased out. The F-4EJ, a Japanese version of the US Phantom, is considered to be comparable with current foreign fighters.[125] However, it is felt that it may not continue to be effective against those supersonic bombers which can maintain high speeds even at low altitudes.[126] In view of this, the ASDF aims at acquiring 100 F-15s as the mainstay fighter-interceptor, through domestic production as well as through imports.[127] This aircraft is considered to be 'capable of effectively dealing with the aircraft of the late 1980's'.[128] The programme of airforce modernisation also includes the development of the F-1 support fighter. Six air-defence missile groups are armed with Nike J missile units.[129] To increase the efficiency of the transport units the ASDF has been developing C-1 medium transport aircraft. Domestic development began in 1966 and the first flight was made in 1970 with the delivery of the first aircraft in 1973.[130] A domestically built supersonic trainer aircraft came into service in 1976.

The ASDF is also responsible for the Base Air Defense Ground Environment (BADGE), which maintains surveillance of Japanese air and sea space. The BADGE consists of 28 land-based radar sites located throughout the country.[131] However, this land-based radar often fails to detect modern higher performance aircraft operating at low altitudes. This weakness came to light when a Soviet MIG-25 landed undetected in Japan in September 1976. To remedy this, arrangements are being made to establish an aircraft unit equipped with surveillance radar units. Equipment modernisation also includes the installation of interchangeable, mobile three-dimensional radar units.[132] This radar unit has been domestically produced and is capable of computerised estimation of the co-ordinates, speed and altitude of incoming aircraft. The air-defence capabilities are being enhanced by the procurement of a number of E-2C early warning aircraft. It is estimated that up to eight E-2Cs may be operational with the ASDF by the mid-1980s.[133]

Nuclear Weapons

Japan believes in the three non-nuclear principles of 'not possessing, manufacturing, or allowing the introduction of nuclear weapons'.[134] But she has not forgone the right to develop nuclear energy for peaceful purposes. By now Japan has developed a huge nuclear power generation programme. According to the annual White Paper on Atomic Energy Development published in December 1979, Japan had a total of 21 nuclear reactors with a total output capability of nearly 15 million KW, which is roughly equivalent to 12 per cent of the country's total power generation capacity.[135] The White Paper indicated that the Japanese nuclear power generation capacity would be expanded to 30 million KW by 1985 and 78 million KW by 1995.[136] At present Japan is totally dependent on imports for enriched uranium. She has already designed and produced an advanced thermal convertor reactor (ATR) named 'Fugen', which was commissioned in March 1977.[137] A spent-fuel reprocessing plant located at Tokai Mura, about 85 miles from Tokyo, is operating on an experimental basis. Japan has already produced a small experimental breeder reactor, 'Joyo', which went critical on 24 April 1977. It is also planned to build a prototype fast breeder reactor, 'Monju', which is aiming at criticality in 1984.[138] The first domestically developed Japanese uranium-enrichment pilot plant went into operation in September 1979. It is estimated that this plant will produce enough enriched uranium to supply a nuclear power plant with an output capacity of 500,000 KW.[139] This fuel will be used by the reactor 'Fugen'. The Atomic Energy Commission of Japan plans to have a commercial uranium-enrichment plant by the second half of the 1980s. With a view to meeting this target the Japan Science and Technology Agency is planning to build a bigger prototype uranium-enrichment plant with five times the processing capacity of the one recently commissioned.[140] So far, the only disaster has been the attempted nuclear-power ship *Mutsu*, which developed a radioactive leak and had to be abandoned because of mounting public criticism. Observers believe that Japan probably has the 'capability to manufacture nuclear weapons and systems for their delivery within a few years following a national decision to do so'.[141] This statement was made by the former head of the US Atomic Energy Commission, Glann Seaborg, in 1971. Since then Japan has progressed significantly.

Japan certainly has the industrial technology and capacity to produce most of her warships, some of her aircraft, tanks, missiles and almost all her ammunition and artillery.[142] A number of warships, aircraft, tanks and missiles are indigenously designed and produced. Most of the others are produced under license. Important items in this category are the Swiss-designed L-90 anti-aircraft machine-guns, the US-designed ground-to-air guided missiles (Nike and Hawk), fighter-interceptors (F-86F, F-104J, F-4EJ), anti-submarine patrol aircraft (P2V-7), various types of helicopters and the BADGE 'air defence system'. It also has its space satellite programme which, at present, is based on US rocket technology.[143] However, a domestically designed and built multi-stage N-2 rocket was being completed in Spring 1981.[144]

The importance of research and development for the domestic production of defence equipment has repeatedly been emphasised in Defence White Papers. It has been noted that Japan has successfully developed and produced indigenously tanks (Type-61, Type-74), armoured personnel carriers (Type 60, Type 73), anti-tank missiles (Type-64 guided missiles and launchers), anti-submarine flying boats (PS-1), support fighter aircraft (FS-T2 MOD), trainers (T-1, T-2) and transport aircraft (C-1).[145] For the present the research and development funding available is less than 2 per cent of the defence budget as against 10 to 12 per cent in the US and UK defence budgets and 5 to 8 per cent in the French and West German budgets. In future, with increasing pressure for relative self-sufficiency in defence needs, it is probable that this expenditure will increase.

On the whole, the Japanese defence capability is already formidable. One analyst in the Japan Defense Agency has suggested that by the early 1970s Japan had 'the most well-balanced force in Asia' and the 'seventh in the world in terms of total strength'.[146] This may not necessarily be an exaggeration.

The Nature of the Military Threat to Japan

However, military strength and defence capability cannot be judged in isolation. It has to be seen in the perspective of a potential threat or a perceived threat. In the foreseeable future Japan's security can be threatened primarily in two ways: (a) political and/or military instability in the region and (b) direct Soviet military action against the Japanese mainland or the sea-routes which are so vital for the health of the Japanese economy. The second worries the Japanese leadership much more than the first.

Instability in East Asia

The emergence of the PRC as a major military power with some nuclear capability has altered the configuration of power in the region from a bipolar to a multipolar one, consisting of the USA, the USSR, the PRC and Japan.[147] The stability of the region is maintained by an extremely complex set of interactions between these four powers and their interactions with the smaller powers in the region. For instance, while the PRC and the USSR are 'locked in hostile confrontation' and 'the possibility of a large-scale war cannot be totally excluded',[148] both countries are individually committed to the survival of North Korea. Similarly, while Japan continues to be committed to her close military alliance with the USA she has, in terms of trade and investment in the region, become a major economic rival of the USA.

Continued stability in the region depends on the maintenance of the four-power equilibrium. Anything that upsets this equilibrium is likely to bring about increased instability and conflict. Among the main developments which may bring about a change in the military balance in the region, the most important are the following: (1) a rapproachment between the two Communist giants; (2) military imbalance on the Korean Peninsula; (3) political instability and a possible increase in the influence of Communist powers in South-east Asia; and (4) an imbalance between the military presence of the USA and the USSR. Any of these four developments may directly or indirectly have adverse consequences for Japanese security and may lead to a Japanese decision to expand her military capability. A heavily 'armed' Japan will certainly be suspect in the eyes of one or both of the Communist giants, although at present the PRC leaders are encouraging Japan to enhance her military capability. It is debatable whether the USA herself wants Japan to rearm heavily. The US Arms Control and Disarmament Agency has argued that any departure from gradual growth would not only 'engender sharp and vociferous domestic political opposition' but also 'could be seen as implying a threat to the U.S.S.R. and even to China over the longer-term, and could therefore prompt very different Chinese or Soviet attitudes towards Japan. One could speculate, in fact, that a rapid and significant military build-up could even contribute to Sino-Soviet rapprochement.'[149] She might be conceived as posing a serious threat to smaller nations, not so much in terms of direct invasion but of political and military intervention such as supplying military hardware or blockading sea ports in support of convenient regimes. For the present, however, in fear of the growing military strength of Vietnam and her involvement with the USSR some of the smaller South-east Asian nations such as Singapore are urging Japan to strengthen her defence capability.[150] It is difficult to speculate whether this attitude will continue if Japan begins to assert her weight as a military power. It can therefore be argued that a major thrust towards projecting Japan as a major military power may itself become a major disequilibrating factor.

Sino-Soviet Relations

The possibility of open military conflict between the two Communist giants cannot be discounted. Apart from their ideological disputes 'both Chinese and Russians are acutely aware of their profound cultural differences and have a deep sense of distrust based on revised historical memories'.[151] Differences have also arisen in the past because of conflicting perceptions of national interests. The serious divergence of views came to the fore in relation to the Taiwan Straits crisis of 1958, nuclear co-operation and the Sino-Indian dispute.[152] The hostility was also intensified as a result of numerous border incidents which occurred in the early 1960s. Tension is reported to have reached a peak at the time of the 1969 clashes, when war looked a distinct possibility.[153] So long as the dispute continues and military concentration on either side persists, the risk of serious clashes and an escalation into war cannot be ruled out.[154]

However, Barnett feels that, in spite of the definite military superiority of the USSR over the PRC in both conventional as well as in nuclear weapons, at least for the foreseeable future, war between the two 'can be viewed as an improbability'.[155] It is argued that the acquisition of nuclear weapons by the PRC and the improved Chinese dialogue with the West, particularly the USA, together with the growing status of the PRC in the Third World will act as a restraint on the USSR. But at the same time the prospects for any far-reaching *rapprochement* in the foreseeable future seems also limited.[156] It is possible that in coming years the new leadership in the PRC, once they are fully entrenched in power, will take a more conciliatory approach towards the USSR with a view to reaching a possible detente, but it is highly unlikely that an effective alliance between the two countries will be restored.[157] The Japanese leadership seems to believe that no major change is likely to take place in the Sino-Soviet relationship in the foreseeable future. This is reflected in the following statements of the

Defense Agency of Japan:

> The Sino-Soviet confrontation has led to the deployment of the
> enormous military strengths of these two rival powers along their
> border areas. As a result, threat is directed toward the inland
> districts of the Asian continent, rather than towards the peripheral
> areas. This is an unignorable factor contributing to the military
> stability of the peripheral areas.
>   While no major changes are expected in the current international
> environment, the expanding military potential of the Soviet Union
> and the withdrawal of American ground forces from the Republic
> of Korea demand close attention.[158]

The Korean Peninsula

The Korean Peninsula is certainly a potential zone of conflict. However,
observers tend to agree that 'large scale war is unlikely in Korea in the
near future'.[159] It must be recognised that the power balance in Korea
is not necessarily determined by the power balance between the two
Koreas. In fact, the North probably, in military terms, has a slight edge
over the South. Seoul, but for the presence of the US army and its
tactical nuclear weapons, is certainly vulnerable to a quick thrust by
the North. However, as stated earlier, the power balance is maintained
because of the multipolar balance between the four major powers,
and none of these powers is particularly keen to alter the *status quo*.
The US government continues to be committed to defending South
Korea. In fact, in March 1979 the Carter administration decided to keep
in abeyance the decision to withdraw combat troops and nuclear
weapons from South Korea. In the shadow of the Afghan crisis and
particularly in view of the 'hawkish' stance of the Reagan administration,
it is difficult to visualise an early withdrawal of US forces from Korea,
especially when South Korea is, at least for a time, passing through a
period of uncertainty resulting from the assassination of President
Chung-Hee Park in October 1979. The PRC leadership is not keen to
encourage any adventurist policies by the North Korean leadership
because they are interested in the US presence in the region as a
counterweight to the Russians. Under pressure from the North
Korean leadership, the officially stated policy of the PRC is that she
regards the North Korean regime as the 'sole legal sovereign state of
the Korean nation'.[160] On the other hand, the leadership stresses that
the unification of Korea ought to be attained by *peaceful* means.[161]
Observers feel that the USSR, like the PRC, does not want to change the

status quo on the Korean Peninsula.[162] In fact, there have been
occasions when the Soviet leadership has shown some indication of
favouring a two-Koreas solution.

The Japanese themselves seem to prefer a two-Koreas solution even
though they pay lip-service to the goal of Korean unification.[163] Under
the circumstances, there is a general consensus that the risk of
immediate armed conflict on the Korean Peninsula is limited. The
Japanese Defense Agency corroborates this:

> It seems obvious that the United States, China and the Soviet Union
> have no desire to see any major change in the present Korean
> situation through armed conflict, and it is therefore highly probable
> that the present situation will remain unchanged, though the severe
> North-South confrontation will continue unabated. Although the
> possibility for small-scale conflict cannot be denied, it is hardly
> conceivable that any large-scale conflict will break out on the Korean
> Peninsula.[164]

The stability of peace in South-east Asia is also important for Japan
not only because of her considerable foreign investments but also
because of the sea-lanes passing through South-east Asian waters which
are so vital for Japanese trade, particularly for the import of oil from
the Middle East. The disengagement of the US forces in Vietnam from
1968, the final collapse of the non-Communist regimes in both
Kampuchea and Vietnam in 1975 and the subsequent takeover of
Laos by Communist forces has led to the emergence of Vietnam as
the dominant military power in the region. This has inherent risks
for Thailand and other South-east Asian countries. In this context
South-east Asia is rapidly becoming a potential zone of conflict.

The invasion of Kampuchea in December 1978 by the Vietnamese
Army and the subsequent installation of a new government in that
country has aggravated such risks. The PRC had continuously supported
the previous regime in Kampuchea and mounted a punitive military
intervention in Northern Vietnam in February 1979.[165] This has driven
'Vietnam deeper into the political embrace of the Soviet Union'.[166]
The ASEAN states together with the PRC, Japan and the USA continue
to recognise the ousted Pol Pot regime. In protest against the Vietnamese
invasion of Kampuchea, Japan not only voted in the United Nations for
a withdrawal of the Vietnamese forces from Kampuchea but has also
suspended all economic aid to Vietnam.[167] Japan prefers a political
rather than a military solution to the problem of Kampuchea. In her

view military pressure on Vietnam will push her more and more into the Soviet camp and she may have 'to make naval base facilities available to the Soviet Union on full operational terms and then such an enhancement of Soviet naval power and reach will not necessarily be matched or countered by the United States'.[168]

The stalemate in Kampuchea continues. It is almost certain that for a time Vietnam is likely to be involved in the consolidation of its gains in Indochina. But once its aim of establishing at least a loose Indochina Federation of Vietnam, Kampuchea and Laos is achieved there may be the risk that she will become increasingly involved in subversive activities in the other countries of the region – but so can the PRC. The Southeast Asian countries are apprehensive about the future intentions of all three Communist countries, the PRC, Vietnam and the USSR. This is clearly reflected in a statement by Singapore's Prime Minister, Lee Kuan Yew:

> Our dilemma is acute. If there had been no 'Chinese' intervention, we would face Vietnamese supremacy which in this case means Soviet supremacy. If the intervention is over-successful, it means that in ten, fifteen years there will be an assertion of influence, perhaps not amounting to hegemony, by a Communist power that has influence over all guerilla movements in the countries of Thailand, Malaysia, Singapore and Indonesia.[169]

Because of the continued military presence – though on a limited scale – of the USA and the growing economic involvement of Japan, together with the rivalry of the two Communist giants, a major military conflict in South-east Asia seems unlikely in the foreseeable future. While the risk of internal subversion continues, the internal Communist movements are not very strong. Besides, the rapid economic development of the ASEAN in recent years has reduced this risk. Therefore, as Barnett suggests, 'even though the prospects for genuine stability within most South-east Asian nations, or in their regional relationships, are clouded, there is no imminent danger that these countries will rapidly succumb, in domino fashion, to internal Communist takeovers'.[170]

In view of the growing understanding between the USA and the PRC during the Nixon and Carter administrations the Taiwan issue seemed to have been defused. The USA seemed, effectively, to have accepted the sovereignty of the PRC over Taiwan. The new administration under President Reagan has been making sympathetic noises towards Taiwan and the PRC suspects that the US Administration may be veering

towards a 'two-Chinas' solution.[171] This would certainly be
unacceptable to the PRC. However, the PRC cannot afford a military
action on Taiwan because she not only needs Western (particularly US)
technology and capital for her 'four modernisations' but also Western
support against a potential Soviet threat. On the other hand, the PRC
fits well into the US strategy of the encirclement of the USSR.
Therefore it is highly unlikely that either the PRC or the USA will
precipitate the Taiwan issue.

Thus, barring any sudden catastrophic changes in the international
environment, the Japanese do not anticipate any major military
conflict in the region. Their main worry for some time has been the
growing Soviet military presence in East Asia and the nagging doubt
that the USA may not respect its obligations under the existing
US-Japan security arrangements.

Japanese Perception of the Military Threat

As to the nature and the extent of the Soviet threat to Japan, expert
opinion in Japan is divided. The 'hawkish' view is voiced by people
like Hiroomi Kurishu, a former chairman of the Joint Staff Council of
the SDF, who was asked by the government to resign in 1978 for his
outspoken criticisms of the existing laws constraining the SDF
operations in an emergency situation. In the February (1981) issue of
Gendai, Kurishu argued that the Soviet Union has 'a concrete
capability' to attack not only Hokkaido but also the Japanese mainland,
because of the introduction of the Backfire, the strategic bomber,
the *Minsk*, the aircraft carrier, and the medium-range missiles.[172]
Other experts feel that the landing of Soviet troops on Hokkaido is
somewhat unrealistic because the USSR lacks adequate amphibious lift
capability. This view was reflected in a fourteen-instalment series entitled
Soren Wa Kyoi Ka (Is the Soviet Union a Threat?') carried by *Asahi
Shimbun* between 28 November and 13 December 1980.[173] *Asahi
Shimbun's* editorial committee and its defence commentators have
consistently held a balanced view that

in almost all cases, Soviet military power in the Far East is directed
at China. As for another problem, it is certain that importance is
being attached to competitive relations with the US. In other words,
it cannot be said that this means the strengthening of military power,
with Japan as a direct object. However, when it comes to the

problem of whether it will have no effects on Japan, that is not
necessarily so. If Soviet power increases relatively, it will have effects
on the security of Japan . . . To be sure, visible reinforcement is
being carried out in the field of military capability. It will provide
a potential threat. So far, however, there is nothing which shows
that the Soviet Union considers that it must militarily confront
Japan.[174]

Similar views have been echoed by some leading US sources. For
instance, the US Ambassador to Japan, Mike Mansfield, in an interview
for *Sankei* is reported to have clearly stated that he did not think that
'the Soviet forces' were 'marking Japan as their primary target. However,
the military strength of a potential enemy is a potential threat, and
there must be preparedness to cope with it.'[175] Similarly in an interview
for *Sankei*, a former CIA Director, William Colby, in his capacity as a
consultant on Japan-US problems, stated that he is 'of the opinion that
while the Soviet Union certainly holds powerful military power, its
nature is rather "defensive"'.[176]

The 'defensive' nature of the Soviet military build-up is stressed by
some Japanese experts on the USSR. For instance, Hiroshi Kimura
suggests that it is the 'Russian inferiority complex, feeling of
vulnerability, persecution complex and encirclement complex born
of . . . geographical and historical conditions have formed an attitude
towards security peculiar to the Russians. One important element of
this is an attitude of seeking excessive defense power.'[177] According to
this view 'unless certain circumstances prevail in Japan, a Russian
invasion' of Japan 'is unlikely'.[178] These circumstances include the
setting up of a Communist government in Japan, the abandonment of
the Japan-US security arrangements, the conclusion of a Japan-Soviet
treaty of friendship, amity and co-operation with a clause on
'co-operation in times of emergency' and political chaos in Japan.[179]
Kimura feels that 'Unless all these conditions exist, no Russian invasion
is likely. To say that Hokkaido will be the next Russian target after
Afganistan, as some have implied, is nonsense.'[180]

However, the dominant view in Japan regards 'Russia as a threat
because of its traditional expansionism as well as the sense of mission
to spread Marxism-Leninism to where it has not yet been accepted and
to protect a regime espousing this ideology when its existence is
threatened'.[181] By and large, public opinion in Japan is not very
friendly to the USSR. In a nationwide public opinion survey carried
out by *Yomiuri* in February 1980, in an answer to the question 'with

which nation do you think Japan should be especially friendly, in the future?' only 12.9 per cent respondents mentioned the USSR, against 65.4 per cent for the USA and 61.8 for the PRC. For the Middle East nations the proportion was 31.8 per cent, while for Asian nations, other than the PRC, and Western European nations it was only 17 and 16 per cent respectively.[182] Public displeasure against the USSR was recently expressed vehemently when all the six opposition parties including the Japan Communist Party (JCP) endorsed the Japanese Government's week-long campaign for the return of the four northern islands (Etorofu, Kunashiri, Habomai and Shikotan).[183] The dispute over these islands has continued for thirty-five years and stands in the way of a peace and friendship treaty between Japan and the USSR.[184] The Soviet position, as outlined by Nikita Khrushchev in a letter to Prime Minister Ikeda in August 1961, still remains unaltered. Khruschev had indicated that the 'Soviet Union' desired 'to completely normalize relations with Japan resolving through discussions all outstanding issues'.[185] The main barrier to the normalisation was 'Japan's military alliance with the United States of America and continued maintenance of foreign military bases on Japanese soil'.[186] The Soviet position has probably hardened after the conclusion of the Japan-China Treaty of Peace and Amity signed between the two countries in August 1978.[187] Swearingen feels that 'the Northern Territories issue is not likely to be resolved to Japan's satisfaction in our life time'.[188]

The other outstanding dispute between Japan and the USSR is the fisheries issue.[189] After the Japanese surrender in 1945 SCAP had delineated a limited area for Japanese fishing operations. The Northern Pacific, Kurile, and Soviet and Chinese coastal waters were excluded.[190] Until the signing of the 1975 Fisheries Accord, as the *Japan Times* wrote 'the yearly talks have always marked a period of great anxiety, for they have seldom proceeded smoothly. Hard bargaining, to be sure, is a part of any negotiation. But the results of Japanese-Soviet fisheries talks have invariably presented disappointments to the Japanese side.'[191] The Fisheries Accord of 1975, a three-year renewable agreement, called for a 'closer fishing cooperation between the two nations'.[192] It provided for restriction on the volume of fish to be caught by both sides. The USSR agreed to 'take into consideration' Japan's rules for fishing control. It was also decided that the two countries would co-operate in programmes for salmon breeding in the Sakhalin area.[193] The overall reaction to this agreement within Japan was negative. As the *Mainichi* wrote, the agreement was disadvantageous to Japan because in principle it included all of the Soviet demands while the Japanese fishing industry was forced to make 'a big withdrawal'.[194]

None of these disputes are likely to be settled in the foreseeable future, particularly when open criticism of the USSR is gathering momentum in Japan. Besides the Soviet leadership has increasingly come to believe that Japan, at least tacitly, has agreed to join an anti-Soviet axis with the USA and the PRC.

As mentioned earlier, in addition to the increasing Soviet military threat, there is a growing worry in Japan that the USA may not possess either the willingness or ability to defend Japan in the event of a Soviet attack. As we have already seen, the military balance between the two superpowers is reached by maintaining a large deployment of both conventional and strategic nuclear capability. Both superpowers possess a 'deterrent' strategic nuclear capability consisting of ICBMs, SLBMs and strategic bombers. Both believe in maintaining a 'second strike capability', which can be broadly defined as 'strategic forces of such size and character that they can survive a well-planned, large-scale surprise attack with sufficient strength remaining to penetrate the attacker's defenses and still destroy him'.[195] This does not preclude hitting civilian targets. The superpowers also provide a 'nuclear umbrella' to their non-nuclear allies.

With the growth of Soviet nuclear power doubts have been raised about the value of the US commitments as a deterrent to both nuclear and conventional aggression against Japan.[196] Similar doubts have been expressed in Western Europe as well; some of the arguments which can be put forward against a nuclear war to save Western Europe from Soviet domination can be equally applied to Japan. As a French military strategist suggested:

> If resort to force no longer merely implies the loss of an expeditionary army but hazards the very substance of national life, it is clear that such a risk can be taken for oneself and not for others including even close allies.[197]

This point was made as early as 1959 by Kissinger, who had stated that the 'defense of Europe cannot be conducted solely from North America, because . . . however firm allied unity may be, a nation cannot be counted on to commit suicide in defense of a foreign territory'.[198]

Some US defence analysts argue that the 'loss of Europe could have serious psychological and geopolitical ramifications, but it would not necessarily pose a serious military threat to the United States'.[199] The loss of Western Europe's industrial capacity, it is argued, will not add significantly to the nuclear capabilities of the USSR. On the other hand, a nuclear attack on the USSR could not prevent the Warsaw Pact conventional forces from capturing Western Europe anyway, so that, 'little would be accomplished other than the destruction of over 100 million Americans and perhaps between 5 and 100 million Soviet citizens'.[200] Under the circumstances, the US leadership does not seem keen to use the nuclear deterrent except in the event of direct attack on the USA itself. This was clearly underlined by Schlesinger, the Secretary of Defence, in his annual report to Congress:

> Today such a massive retaliation against cities, in response to anything less than an all-out attack on the U.S. and its cities appears less and less credible.[201]

European allies have also been worried for some time that the superpowers may decide to fight a 'limited war' over Europe 'possibly using tactical nuclear weapons as a countermeasure against a conventional attack, but not allowing that war to escalate to intercontinental warfare involving the territories of the superpowers themselves'.[202] European leadership has always considered such a prospect as catastrophic for Europe. As early as 1971 Helmut Schmidt had categorically stated that 'A war which, though regarded as a "limited war" by the superpowers would be no less than a war of annihilation for the countries of the battlefield.'[203] With the announcement of President Carter's Directive 59, which accepts 'limited war' as a part of the US nuclear strategy, such fears have become more real. Some doubts have arisen also in relation to the use of US conventional forces. The debate is built around the US capability as well as a willingness to come to the rescue of the allies. Such doubts have been raised in the USA itself particularly in the wake of the Soviet intervention in Afganistan and the failure of the US efforts to rescue the American hostages held in Iran. After investigating the US military establishment the *New York Times* published a series of seven articles in September 1980 highlighting some major US military shortcomings. It reported that 'pilots, skilled technicians and weapons specialists are in short supply in virtually all the services. Planes are grounded for lack of maintenance and shortages of spare parts. Ships, ranging from destroyers and frigates to aircraft carriers, are often deemed unprepared for a crisis because of lack of skilled technicians'.[204] It further added: 'Key parts of the American strategic arsenal are wearing out. The B-52, for example, the mainstay of the Air Force's nuclear bomber forces, is about 20 years old and afflicted with aging equipment such as frequently faulty bombing and navigation computers.'[205] The US armed forces are reported to be facing 'problems of too few men, too little equipment and too many skilled people dropping out, especially in the Navy and Air Force, leaving serious gaps in critical jobs'.[206]

The Japanese leadership is particularly worried about the reduction in strength of the US Seventh Fleet. They point out that the number of personnel assigned to the Seventh Fleet has continued to decline since 1969, i.e. the peak of the Vietnam war, when the Seventh Fleet had 225 ships and the number of personnel was around 87,000. (This did not include the marines on combat duty in Vietnam.) The number of ships declined to 145 in 1970, and by December 1979 the number had come down to only 50 ships with a total personnel of 28,000.[207] On the basis of an analysis by the US Naval Institute, 'an authoritative auxiliary organ of the US Navy' there is growing apprehension that in the event of large-scale war between the USA and the USSR the already depleted strength of the Seventh Fleet will 'not be reinforced by the 3rd Fleet assigned to the sea areas east of Hawaii . . . the 3rd Fleet will be used to reinforce the Atlantic Fleet . . . the 7th Fleet will probably engage mainly in operations for the maintenance of the present situation, in various ways, such as the defence of Japan's shipping lanes'.[208]

This suspicion that Western Europe has priority over the Far East in the US calculation has been further confirmed by the leakage of a strategic plan that the US government and the NATO allies approved in the early 1950s. This strategy for fighting a global war (known as the 'swing strategy') called for the USA to shift their forces from Asia and the Pacific to Western Europe in the event of a Soviet attack there.[209] Such a 'swing' would include the transfer of aircraft carriers, amphibious ships, Army and Marine divisions and B-52 bombers. This strategy has been reaffirmed by various US administrations. President Carter's Secretary of Defense, Harold Brown, and other senior officials have stressed that NATO takes precedence in US strategic planning.[210] With regard to conventional forces, the US government believes in what is known as a 'one and a half strategy'.[211] This implies that US conventional forces would remain in preparation to fight one large and one small war simultaneously. If the US strategy assigns greater priority to its Western European allies and to the Middle East because of its vital oil supplies then this casts doubt on the US capacity to counter a Soviet attack on its Asian allies.

Another factor which has been worrying the Asian allies relates to the growing 'isolationist' tendencies in the USA. For instance, polls conducted by the Harris Organisation between 1968 and 1974 found that the proportion of 'internationalists' had declined from 60 to 41 per cent of the US population.[212] By mid-1969 the Organisation found that a substantial number of Americans did not support the idea of defending the allies by the use of force. In fact in 1974 less than half were prepared to use American troops in defence of Japan or Western Europe,[213] although a more recent poll taken by the Kettering Foundation in early 1978 indicated that around 54 per cent of Americans supported keeping US troops in Japan. Against this the proportion supporting the stationing of troops in Western Europe was 62 per cent.[214]

The Japanese Defense Agency has come to believe that 'because of the continuing fluidity of the Middle East situation, the U.S. will have no choice but to keep its naval fleet, centering on aircraft carriers, in the Indian Ocean and the Middle East sea areas, for some time to come'.[215] As a result the JDA is extremely 'worried that U.S. naval strength in the Western Pacific cannot but be weakened correspondingly'.[216] This worry has, in fact, been reflected in the White Paper on Defense (1979) which stresses the need for strengthening Japanese defence forces. Such worries have been further aggravated by the Afghan crisis. In this context, a statement by Saburo Okita, the then Foreign Minister of Japan, though in line with the Defense White Paper (1979), represents something of a departure from earlier Japanese thinking. He states:

> Japan's foreign policy had served its national interests well in two-and-a-half decades since the Second World War.
>
> In the 1980's, however, conditions would be different. Japan could no longer take for granted the existence of an international climate guaranteeing its prosperity. It must therefore start trying to make a positive contribution to global stability.[217]

He stressed, however, 'that he was not suggesting any radical changes in Japan's relationship with individual countries. The U.S. alliance would remain the corner-stone of foreign policy but could no longer be taken for granted as in the past.'[218] In a later speech he clearly indicated that he was thinking in terms of 'Japan's increasing of its defense power' which 'will also come to lead to Japan's deterrent power against a Soviet invasion'.[219] He further stated 'that it will be impossible to cope with overwhelming military power, and calling for unarmed neutrality will come to lead to some sort of defeatism'.[220] He stressed that Japan had the economic capability in terms of the GNP matching those of the USSR and also has highly advanced technology. Under the circumstances, if 'Japan increases its self-defense power, and if the Soviet Union should come to invade Japan, it will cost too much (due to the Japanese side's resistance). Therefore, the Soviet Union cannot but abandon its attempt to invade Japan.'[221] If Okita's views reflect the growing consensus among the members of the LDP and Japanese business leaders on the future of Japan's defence commitment, it is probable that the SDF will be strengthened considerably in the foreseeable future. Whether the people of Japan will accept such a change continues to remain a debatable issue. An attempt will be made in the next chapter to examine the Japanese people's attitude towards the strengthening of the SDF.

Notes

1. Quoted in a report by Y. Funabashi, 'Slowly Turning to the Right' (part 8), *Asahi*, 20 March 1978.
2. See pp.113-14.
3. *Tokyo Shimbun*, 6 Aug. 1978.
4. Ibid.
5. Funabashi, 'Slowly Turning to the Right'.
6. Ibid.
7. H. Scott-Stokes, 'It's All Right to Talk Defense in Japan', *The New York Times Magazine*, 11 Feb. 1979, p.20.
8. Funabashi, 'Slowly Turning to the Right' (part 9), *Asahi*, 21 March 1978.
9. Ibid.
10. Ibid.
11. *The Japan Times Weekly*, 5 Jan. 1980, p.5.
12. C. Smith, 'Tokyo Backs Reactor Sales Plan', *Financial Times*, 15 Jan. 1981.
13. Funabashi, 'Slowly Turning to the Right' (part 8).
14. *Nihon Keizai*, 20 Feb. 1980.
15. Ibid.
16. Ibid.
17. Ibid.
18. Ibid.
19. J. Halliday and G. McCormack, *Japanese Imperialism Today: Co-Prosperity in Greater East Asia*, p.108.
20. Ibid., p.115.
21. Ibid., p.117.
22. Quoted in Halliday and McCormack, *Japanese Imperialism Today*, p.117.
23. Funabashi, 'Slowly Turning to the Right' (part 8).
24. *Nihon Keizai*, 16 May 1980.
25. I. Shimizu, 'Nuclear Weapons For Japan – Why Not?', *The Japan Times Weekly*, 16 Aug. 1980, p.4.
26. Ibid.
27. Quoted in *Los Angeles Times*, 25 July 1979.

28. Ibid.
29. S.E. Johnson and J.A. Yager, *The Military Equation in North East Asia*, p.1.
30. International Institute For Strategic Studies (IISS), *The Military Balance: 1980-81*, (1980), p.62.
31. Ibid., p.64. According to the Chinese official figures it is only $12.9 billion but this figure is not comparable to Western defence estimates since it excludes items such as pay and allowances for the troops. If the Chinese estimates were made consistent with the Western estimates the total would come to around $50 billion, possibly $56.9 billion for 1980.
32. Ibid., pp.70-1.
33. Ibid., p.67.
34. Ibid., p.69.
35. Ibid., pp.10-11.
36. Ibid., p.11.
37. Johnson and Yager, *The Military Equation*, pp.11-12.
38. Japan Defense Agency, *Defense of Japan, 1977*, pp.33-4.
39. ———, *Defense of Japan, 1978*, pp.31-2.
40. Johnson and Yager, *The Military Equation*, pp.12-13.
41. US Arms Control and Disarmament Agency, *Japan's Contribution To Military Stability in Northeast Asia* (1980), prepared for the subcommittee on East Asian and Pacific Affairs of the US Senate Committee on Foreign Relations, p.70.
42. Japan Defense Agency, *Defense of Japan*, 1978, p.32.
43. Johnson and Yager, *The Military Equation*, pp.13-14.
44. Ibid., p.14.
45. *Los Angeles Times*, 25 July 1979.
46. Japan Defense Agency, *Defense of Japan*, 1978, p.31.
47. B.M. Blechman *et al.*, *The Soviet Military Build-up and U.S. Defense Spending*, p.12.
48. Ibid., p.12
49. Ibid. (Equivalent megatonnage 'is a measure of the area destruction capability of a nuclear arsenal' (p.8, note to table 4).).
50. IISS, *The Military Balance*, p.9.
51. Ibid.
52. For instance, the largest ICBM, the SS-18, can deliver one warhead with a yield of up to 50 megatons (over 3,000 times the capacity of the bomb dropped on Hiroshima) or eight independent warheads. (See D. Richardson, 'World Missile Directory', *Flight International*, vol. II (1977), pp.1350-1. It is reported that on new and larger ICBMs the Soviets can deploy up to ten large-yield warheads (see R.D. Speed, *Strategic Deterrence in the 1980s*, p.32).
53. Johnson and Yager, *The Military Equation*, p.20.
54. Ibid.
55. US Arms Control and Disarmament Agency, *Japan's Contribution*, p.67.
56. IISS, *The Military Balance*, p.9.
57. US Arms Control and Disarmament Agency, *Japan's Contribution*, p.66.
58. Ibid.
59. Ibid.
60. IISS, *The Military Balance*, p.7.
61. US Arms Control and Disarmament Agency, *Japan's Contribution*, p.63.
62. Ibid.
63. Ibid.
64. Japan Defense Agency, *Defense of Japan, 1978*, pp.37-9.
65. Johnson and Yager, *The Military Equation*, p.47.
66. Ibid.

67. Japan Defense Agency, *Defense of Japan, 1978*, p.40.
68. IISS, *The Military Balance*, p.63.
69. Japan Defense Agency, *Defense of Japan, 1978*, pp.41-2.
70. IISS, *The Military Balance*, p.68.
71. Johnson and Yager, *The Military Equation*, p.25.
72. G. Treverton, 'China's Nuclear Forces and the Stability of Soviet American Deterrence' in IISS, *The Future of Strategic Deterrence*, Part I, pp.38-9.
73. Ibid.
74. S.S. Harrison, 'The United States, Japan and the Future of Korea' in F.B. Weinstein (ed.), *U.S.-Japan Relations and the Security of East Asia*, pp.205-7.
75. IISS, *The Military Balance*, p.70.
76. Ibid.
77. Ibid.
78. Johnson and Yager, *The Military Equation*, p.39.
79. Ibid., p.40.
80. IISS, *The Military Balance*, pp.70-1.
81. Ibid., p.71.
82. Ibid., p.70.
83. Ibid., p.71.
84. Ibid.
85. Johnson and Yager, *The Military Equation*, p.42.
86. IISS, *The Military Balance*, p.67.
87. Ibid.
88. Ibid.
89. Johnson and Yager, *The Military Equation*, p.37.
90. If Japan's defence expenditure is calculated by the NATO formula, which includes pensions and annuities for military personnel, the ratio to the GNP reached 1.5 per cent (see *Tokyo Shimbun*, 5 March 1980).
91. J. Lewis, 'The SDF's New, Sharp Teeth', *Far Eastern Economic Review*, 16 Jan. p.25.
92. Japan Defense Agency, *Defense of Japan, 1978*, p.88.
93. Ibid., p.89.
94. A composite brigade is smaller in scale than a division but posseses similar ground combat capabilities (see Japan Defense Agency, *Defense of Japan, 1977*, p.61).
95. Ibid., pp.60-1.
96. H. Kase, 'Defense Lifeline of Japanese Archipelago' in *Jiyu*, Jan. 1979.
97. US Arms Control and Disarmament Agency, *Japan's Contribution*, p.38.
98. Johnson and Yager, *The Military Equation*, p.30: see also IISS, *The Military Balance 1977-78*, pp.5, 8-9, 19, 53, 54.
99. Japan Defense Agency, *Defense of Japan, 1978*, p.91.
100. ——, *Defense of Japan, 1976*, pp.96-7.
101. US Arms Control and Disarmament Agency, *Japan's Contribution*, p.38.
102. Japan Defense Agency, *Defense of Japan, 1978*, p.91.
103. ——, *Defense of Japan, 1976*, p.98.
104. ——, *Defense of Japan, 1978*, p.92.
105. US Arms Control and Disarmament Agency, *Japan's Contribution*, p.38.
106. Japan Defense Agency, *Defense of Japan, 1978*, p.93.
107. US Arms Control and Disarmament Agency, *Japan's Contribution*, p.39.
108. Japan Defense Agency, *Defense of Japan, 1978*, p.95.
109. US Arms Control and Disarmament Agency, *Japan's Contribution*, p.33.
110. Ibid.
111. Johnson and Yager, *The Military Equation*, pp.33-4.
112. Ibid., p.34.

113. Japan Defense Agency, *Defense of Japan, 1976*, pp.99-100.
114. ——, *Defense of Japan, 1978*, p.113.
115. Ibid., p.112.
116. Ibid., p.118.
117. US Arms Control and Disarmament Agency, *Japan's Contribution*, p.34.
118. Ibid.
119. Ibid.
120. Japan Defense Agency, *Defense of Japan, 1978*, p.99.
121. Ibid.
122. IISS, *The Military Balance*, p.70.
123. Ibid.
124. Japan Defense Agency, *Defense of Japan, 1976*, p.107.
125. Ibid.
126. Ibid., p.108.
127. Japan Defense Agency, *Defense of Japan, 1978*, p.123.
128. Ibid., p.125.
129. IISS, *The Military Balance*, p.70.
130. Japan Defense Agency, *Defense of Japan, 1976*, pp.106-7.
131. ——, *Defense of Japan, 1978*, p.86.
132. Ibid.
133. US Arms Control and Disarmament Agency, *Japan's Contribution*, p.38.
134. T. Kubo, 'The Meaning of the U.S. Nuclear Umbrella for Japan' in Weinstein (ed.), *US-Japan Relations*, p.109.
135. *The Japan Times Weekly*, 5 Jan. 1980, p.5: see also M. Dickson, 'Regenerating the Nuclear Option', *Financial Times*, 4 Feb. 1981.
136. *The Japan Times Weekly*, 5 Jan. 1980, p.5.
137. L. Richardson, 'Nuclear Power in Japan – The New Age Turns Sour', unpublished, (1978), p.9: also *The Japan Times Weekly*, 14 Jan. 1978.
138. Richardson, ibid., p.19.
139. *The Japan Times Weekly*, 15 Sept. 1979.
140. Ibid.
141. G. Seaborg, *Man and Atom*, p.319.
142. R. Whymant, 'Officially Japan doesn't have an Army but this is what it has for Self-defence', *Sunday Times*, 5 Feb. 1978.
143. Ibid.
144. *The Japan Times Weekly*, 12 Jan. 1980, p.10.
145. Japan Defense Agency, *Defense of Japan, 1976*, pp.125-6.
146. Hisao Iwashima, 'Trends in Peace Research and Military Studies in Japan' (1972), quoted in A. D. Barnett, *China and the Major Powers in East Asia*, p.150.
147. Barnett, ibid., p.288.
148. Ibid., pp.291-3.
149. US Arms Control and Disarmament Agency, *Japan's Contribution*, p.61.
150. *The Japan Times Weekly*, 17 Jan. 1981, p.1.
151. Barnett, *China and the Major Powers*, p.60.
152. Ibid., p.72.
153. Ibid.
154. Ibid., p.80.
155. Ibid., p.81.
156. Ibid., p.82.
157. Ibid., p.83.
158. Japan Defense Agency, *Defense of Japan, 1978*, p.50.
159. R. N. Clough and T. Yano, 'Commentary: Two Views on Peace and Dialogue in Korea' in Weinstein (ed.), *US-Japan Relations*, p.230: see also F. Kamiya, 'The Prospects for Peace in Korea', ibid., p.168: Barnett, *China and the Major Powers*, pp.311-12.

160. *Peking Review*, 2 May 1975, p.9.
161. Barnett, *China and the Major Powers*, p.311.
162. Kamiya, 'The Prospects for Peace in Korea', p.182.
163. Clough and Yano, 'Commentary', p.235: see also Barnett, *China and the Major Powers*, p.310.
164. Japan Defense Agency, *Defense of Japan, 1978*, p.51.
165. M. Leifer, *Conflict and Regional Order in South-east Asia*, Adelphi Papers, no. 162, p.3.
166. Ibid., p.15.
167. Ibid., p.19.
168. Ibid., p.20.
169. L. Kuan Yew, *Singapore Bulletin* (Aug. 1979), quoted in Leifer, *Conflict and Regional Order*, p.16.
170. Barnett, *China and the Major Powers*, p.323.
171. T. Walker, 'Peking Fears Shift of Policy under Reagan', *Financial Times*, 2 Dec. 1980.
172. K. Murata, 'The Soviet Threat: It is a Subject of Many Discussions in Mass Media', *The Japan Times Weekly*, 24 Jan. 1981, p.3.
173. Another series entitled 'Soren wa Kowai Kuni Ka?' ('Is the Soviet Union a Fearsome Country?') was carried by *Tokyo Shimbun*, in Jan. 1981.
174. T. Sakanaka, the editor of *Asahi Shimbun*, in a dialogue with Shinohara, a member of the *Asahi Shimbun* editorial committee, reported in *Asahi*, 7 Feb. 1980. Both are responsible for defence affairs.
175. M. Mansfield, in an interview with T. Miyamoto and J. Kusano, *Sankei*, 7 Jan. 1980.
176. W. Colby, in an interview with O. Yoshida, *Sankei*, 6 April 1980.
177. H. Kimura, 'Relax – The Russians Are Not Coming', *The Japan Times Weekly*, 22 Nov. 1980, p.4.
178. Ibid.
179. Ibid.
180. Ibid.
181. Murata, 'The Soviet Threat', p.3.
182. *Yomiuri*, 15 March 1980.
183. P. Hazelhurst, 'Soviet Anger over Japan Campaign', *The Times*, 9 Feb. 1981.
184. For details of the conflict see R. Swearingen, *The Soviet Union and Postwar Japan*, Ch.13.
185. Quoted in Swearingen, ibid., p.194.
186. Ibid.
187. Ibid., p.196.
188. Ibid., p.89.
189. For details see ibid., Ch.12.
190. Ibid., p.173.
191. *The Japan Times*, 9 March 1974.
192. Swearingen, *The Soviet Union and Postwar Japan*, p.177.
193. Ibid.
194. *Mainichi Shimbun*, 16 May 1975, quoted in Swearingen, *The Soviet Union and Postwar Japan*, p.178.
195. A.C. Enthoven and K.W. Smith, *How Much Is Enough? Shaping the Defense Programme, 1961-69*, p.175.
196. M. Momoi, 'Are There Any Alternative Strategies for the Defense of Japan?' in Weinstein (ed.), *US-Japan Relations*, pp.73-4.
197. P. Gallios, 'United States Strategy and the Defense of Europe' in H.A. Kissinger (ed.), *Problems of National Strategy* (1965), p.295.
198. H.A. Kissinger, 'The Search for Stability', *Foreign Affairs* (July 1959), p.548.

199. R.D. Speed, *Strategic Deterrence in the 1980's*, p.110.
200. Ibid.
201. Quoted in Speed, ibid., p.110.
202. A. Myrdal, *The Game of Disarmament*, p.39.
203. H. Schmidt, *The Balance of Power: Germany's Peace Policy and the Superpowers* (translated by Edward Thomas), p.76.
204. B. Weinraub, 'Nation's Military Anxiety Grows as Russians Gain', *The New York Times*, 21 Sept. 1980.
205. Ibid.
206. Ibid.
207. T. Takubo, 'U.S. Studies on "Emergency in the Far East — Analysis of U.S. Naval Institute Report"', *Bungei Shunju* (December 1978). This estimate was based on the report *Guide to Far Eastern Navies*, prepared by the US Naval Institute, Annapolis, Virginia.
208. Takubo, ibid.
209. *The New York Times*, 9 Oct. 1979.
210. Ibid.
211. *Nihon Keizai*, 27 April 1979.
212. J.A. Nathan and J.K. Oliver, *The Future of United States Naval Power*, p.172.
213. Ibid.
214. Ibid.
215. *Tokyo Shimbun*, 22 April 1979.
216. Ibid.
217. *Financial Times*, 24 Jan. 1980.
218. Ibid.
219. *Tokyo Shimbun*, 16 July 1980.
220. Ibid.
221. Ibid.

7 THE STRAINS ON JAPANESE PACIFISM

A revival of 'militarism' in Japan is not going to be easy. Apart from the international implications of such a revival, there are domestic obstacles. The so-called 'Peace Constitution' is still popular among the people; the opposition parties continue to question the wisdom of a substantial increase in defence expenditure; and the majority of people are content with the present size of the SDF. However, the country's mood is changing because of the changes in the international economic and political environment together with the structural changes in Japanese society itself which is undermining the militancy of the *Kakushin* parties. This has encouraged the 'hawks' to advocate increased military expenditure in order ultimately to create an independent deterrent. Increasing Soviet military presence in the Far East has added credibility to these arguments. The Japanese leadership, in search of an international role commensurate with its economic power, may eventually succumb to the temptation of becoming a political and military superpower. Will the hawks succeed? No unambiguous answers can be given but at the moment the wind seems to be blowing in their favour. Domestic obstacles to a significant acceleration in the Japanese military build-up do not seem to be unsurmountable.

The 'Peace' Constitution

Obviously, the most significant obstacle to the rearmament of Japan so far has been Article 9 of the Japanese Constitution 'renouncing war'. This reads as follows:

> Aspiring sincerely to an international peace based on justice and order the Japanese people forever renounce war as a sovereign right of the nation and the threat of force as means of settling international disputes.
> In order to accomplish the aim of the preceding paragraph, land, sea and air forces, as well as other war potential, will never be maintained. The right of belligerency of the state will not be recognized. [1]

These provisions of the Constitution have been interpreted differently by different groups. For instance, the main opposition party, the Japan Socialist Party (JSP), considers the SDF unconstitutional and is opposed to the Japan-US security arrangements. On the other hand, the ruling party, the LDP, has not only argued that the Constitution permits the right of self-defence and that the SDF are constitutional[2] but also has attempted to broaden the meaning of self-defence. However, there are some elements in the LDP who consider Article 9 as a barrier to the expansion of the SDF and aim at the amendment of the Constitution.

The first major attempt to broaden the meaning of self-defence was made as early as 1954 by the Hatoyama Administration. Prime Minister Hatoyama made a statement before the House of Representatives Cabinet Committee in June 1955 that 'It is not unconstitutional to maintain the minimum war potential necessary for self-defense.'[3] Before this the government had maintained that 'Article 9 of the Constitution prohibits the maintenance of war potential, whether for aggression or self-defense. In this sense, war potential means the ability to conduct modern warfare. It is not unconstitutional to maintain a force that does not amount to war potential.'[4] The Hatoyama Administration further suggested that the right of self-defence extended to attacking 'enemy bases for purposes of self-defense'.[5] Although Hatoyama did not believe in the unconstitutionality of the SDF, he intended to amend the Constitution to transform them into a legitimate army. However, the process of constitutional amendment in Japan is rather difficult. Article 96 on amendments requires that:

> Amendments to the Constitution shall be initiated by the Diet, through a concurring vote of two-thirds or more of all the members of each House, and shall thereupon be submitted to the people for ratification, which shall require the affirmative vote of a majority of all votes cast thereon, at a special referendum or at such election as the Diet shall specify.[6]

The Hatoyama Administration was not in a position to muster a two-thirds majority in either of the Houses of the Diet and as such the amendment could not be proposed. Since then the LDP has favoured the policy of building up defence power within the framework of the present Constitution.[7] Their stand has also been supported by the Japanese Supreme Court. This became clear in what has come to be known as the Sunagawa incident. This case started with the arrest of seven protestors who were a part of the demonstration held in July 1957 at Sunagawa against the expansion there of the US airforce base.[8]

The District Court found that the stationing of the US forces in Japan under the Japan-US Security Treaty violated the spirit of the Constitution's preamble as well as Article 9.[9] The Supreme Court overturned the lower court decision and contended that the Japanese Constitution 'does not renounce the inherent right of a sovereign nation to self-defense, nor does it demand defenselessness and nonresistance'.[10] It further suggested that 'As long as the collective security function of the United Nations is insufficient for Japan's protection, for a security agreement to be concluded with another country is not in contradiction to the preamble's pacifism.'[11]

The government's position about the constitutionality of the SDF was further supported by a judicial decision when in August 1976 the Sapporo High Court annulled the District Court ruling that the Self-Defense Force Law and the SDF ran counter to Article 9 and were unconstitutional.[12] In a more recent case in February 1977 the Mito District Court gave a ruling that self-defence capability is constitutional so long as it does not exceed certain limits.[13]

This question of limits is the one which can be loosely interpreted. In fact, by now this has been substantially expanded. In a speech delivered by Prime Minister Ohira on the occasion of the 23rd Commencement of the Defense Academy on 18 March 1979, he emphasised: 'What forms its root is the perfection and consolidation of defense power, and our country's defense power must be what can truly become deterrent power.'[14] The use of the term 'deterrent power' has serious implications. In terms of military strategy a 'deterrence can be achieved either through the development of a strong defense or through the threat of punishment. In the first case, the aggressor is deterred by the prospect that he will not succeed. In the second case, he is deterred by the threat that the retaliation he will suffer will outweigh any gains he may achieve.'[15] In current Japanese thinking (as well as in official pronouncements as reflected in recent Defense White Papers) the USSR poses the real threat to Japan. If what Prime Minister Ohira said is taken literally, Japan is now thinking of creating a military machine which will serve as a real 'deterrent' to the USSR. How can such a defence force be a 'moderate' one?

It is also debatable that a 'moderate high-quality defense force' which will serve as a deterrent to the USSR 'will not pose a threat to other countries'. There is a further question which needs to be answered. Can a conventional force serve as a real deterrent to the USSR? In this context, Prime Minister Ohira's statement at an Upper House Plenary Session may have serious implications. He is reported to have said that 'A minimum number of necessary nuclear weapons for self-defense is not something to be prohibited.'[16] The connection between the statement with regard to deterrence and the possession of nuclear arms did not go unnoticed. As the *Tokyo Shimbun* underlined, 'Japan's consolidating its defense power to the extent that it will strictly become "deterrent power" in the nuclear age can be said to be a serious matter when it is considered concretely.'[17]

It must be remembered that Japan adheres to the 'three non-nuclear principles' but at the same time the government contends, as reflected in Ohira's statement above, that the possession of nuclear weapons for self-defence is not prohibited. It is not being suggested that the Japanese government has decided to possess nuclear weapons. However, such statements clearly indicate how the Japanese government is stretching the constitutional provisions under Article 9. On 30 January 1978, Hideo Sonoda, the Director-General of the Cabinet Legislation Bureau, is reported to have said, 'it would have posed a threat had Japan alone possessed machine guns in an age of bamboo spears. There should be changes in the limits of self-defense power which is permitted under Article 9, Paragraph 2 of the Constitution, in accordance with the progress of science and technology at any given time.'[18]

Soon after on 14 February 1978 the JDA submitted to the House of Representatives Budget Committee a written elucidation of what the Agency considered as a 'war potential'. It stated that 'The limit beyond which defense power must not be increased under the restrictions set forth in Article 9, Paragraph 2 of the Constitution is a relative one that can change in accordance with various conditions such as the international situation and the level of military technology at a given time.'[19] Thus a clear indication was given that the Constitution could be further stretched if, in the opinion of the Japanese government, changes in the international situation warranted it. The JDA felt that F-15 fighter-interceptors or P-3C anti-submarine aircraft being acquired by Japan were for defensive purposes and therefore were permissible under the Constitution. Only weapons such as the ICBMs and long-range bombers, which were intended exclusively for attack on enemy territory, contravened the constitutional provision of Article 9.[20] More recently, Seisuke Okuno, the Justice Minister in the Suzuki government, is reported to have said that the LDP as a whole favours a revision of the Constitution in the campaign for the 1983 Upper House election.[21] Soon after Prime Minister Zenko Suzuki told a Diet Committee that 'his administration has no plans to propose an amendment to the war-renouncing constitution in the 1983 House of Councillors election campaign'.[22]

Nevertheless, if Article 9 does become a real restraint on the expansion of Japanese military power one suspects that the pressures for the constitutional amendment will increase. The 'hawks' have been asking for that for some time. As early as 1969 the Chairman of the Joint Staff Council, Admiral Itaya, categorically said:

> The state does not exist because there is a Constitution. There is a Constitution because there is a state . . . If it is absolutely necessary for the survival of the state, the Constitution should be interpreted accordingly. If this cannot be done, the Constitution should be revised.[23]

The ground for a constitutional revision, if need be, is already being prepared by some leading LDP personalities. Yasuhiro Nakasone, the former party Secretary General of the LDP, considered to be a 'hawk' on defence issues, not only suggests that 'the Constitution contains elements that are no longer in keeping with reality' but also questions the legitimacy of the present Constitution itself since it 'was drawn up based on occupation policy at a time when the Japanese did not have complete free will, review is also warranted from the standpoint of a democratic constitution'.[24] He stresses:

> In the case of an independent, democratic constitution, those who draft it and those to whom it is applied must both be groups with a sense of common identification; and this in turn must be based on free will. The process by which the Constitution was drafted was dictated by GHQ.
>
> During the occupation it was impossible not only to enact but even to submit legislation to a plenary session of the Diet without permission from GHQ. We were indirectly threatened with being purged if we made any complaints. It was under such circumstances that the present Constitution was enacted.[25]

Naturally, the amendment to the Constitution will require the consent of the opposition parties and the people. Japanese 'pacifism' and the sanctity of Article 9 were preserved because of the intellectuals as well as the masses rallying round the *Kakushin* parties in the 1960s. All indications are that the *Kakushin* forces are losing ground to the conservative forces.

In a public opinion poll conducted by *Asahi* in December 1980 as many as 44 per cent respondents favoured an amendment to the Constitution in order to clearly recognise the SDF as against 41 per cent who opposed such an amendment.[26] If the orchestrated campaign regarding the 'Soviet threat' by the 'hawks' and the defence establishment in Japan continues at the present rate it is almost certain that the people's resistence to a constitutional amendment will not last very long.

In the remaining pages of this chapter we will examine some of the factors which might carry weight in the coming years.

The Changing Attitude of the Political Parties

Among the opposition parties the Japan Socialist Party (JSP) and the Japan Communist Party (JCP) have both considered the SDF to be unconstitutional and have opposed the US-Japan Security Treaty but their views on defence have differed significantly. The JSP advocates the theory of 'unarmed neutrality' but the JCP believes in neutrality backed by defence capability.[27] The Democratic Sociality Party (DSP) and the *Komeito* (Clean Government Party) hold more moderate views on the SDF and the Japan-US Security Treaty. The *Komeito* doubts the constitutionality of the SDF but does not desire an immediate disbandment of the SDF or the abrogation of the treaty.[28] Like the JCP, it does not believe in unarmed neutrality. It also supports the idea of a global security system under the auspices of the UN. In October 1975 the *Komeito* outlined a new policy demanding abrogation of the Japan-US Security Treaty by mutual consent of the two parties and for the treaty to be subsequently replaced by a friendship and a non-aggression treaty.[29]

Unlike the other three political parties, the DSP does not consider the SDF unconstitutional. It is not against the Japan-US Security Treaty but dislikes the stationing of foreign troops in Japan. In a symposium held in November 1975 the DSP confirmed that it acknowledged 'the functions of the existing Japan-US Security Treaty for the present' but at the same time called for the 'elimination of the perpetual US military presence in Japan'.[30]

Recent evidence suggests that the appeal of the radical left is declining among the people. One of the main reasons has been an increasing disenchantment with socialism, particularly as a result of the growing feud between the USSR and the PRC.[31] This feeling of disillusionment must have been further aggravated by the Vietnamese invasion of Kampuchea and the attack on Vietnam itself by the PRC. Besides, the supporters of the leftist parties 'with more information about the realities in socialist countries have come to take a more realistic political stand than before in the face of the increasing pressures from the economic slump. They have begun to seek constructive reform of the present free market economy system instead of trying to transform it into a socialist system.'[32]

The structural changes in Japanese society which have intensified 'middle-class' values have also led to a reaction against idealism and militancy. This trend of the Japanese people towards conservatism was reflected in the 1979 gubernatorial elections in fifteen prefectures. Of the 152 mayors elected in April 1979, 103 were either directly backed by the LDP or by a centralist coalition of the *Komeito* and the DSP.[33] This also happened in those areas such as Hokkaido, which were traditionally considered to be the stronghold of the socialists. This trend of movement away from the JSP was further confirmed by the general election in October 1979. The JSP could win only 107 seats against 123 in 1976. They also lost, though marginally, in their share of votes, from 20.7 per cent in 1976 to only 19.7 per cent in the 1979 elections.[34] The conservatives, the LDP and the New Liberal Club (NLC), a splinter group of the former, between them lost 14 seats compared with 1976, though they marginally increased their share of the popular vote. Both the centralist parties *Komeito* and the DSP gained some seats as well as a share of the popular vote. However, the JCP made the largest gains with 22 more seats than it had in 1976 but its share of the popular vote remained much the same. This seemed to be a clear hint for the JSP that the voters were expecting an 'effective leadership in the opposition camp' which was not forthcoming because of internal strife between the left and right wings of the JSP.[35] The JSP failed to improve its position in the June 1980 elections, while the LDP gained 284 seats in the lower house against only 248 in the 1979 elections. Much of this gain was mainly at the cost of the *Komeito* and the JCP. The LDP and other conservative elements such as the New Liberal Club (NLC) and independent conservatives gained a combined total of 330 seats out of a total of 511 in the lower house.[36]

These reverses in local as well as national elections have forced the JSP to come to an agreement with the *Komeito*, and the two parties have now agreed to have a joint platform. The result of the agreement was that the JCP has been excluded from the coalition talks. Under pressure from the *Komeito*, the JSP had to concede that it would not call for an immediate and unilateral abrogation of the Japan-US Security Treaty. It had to accept the *Komeito* line that the termination of the treaty has to be implemented through diplomatic negotiations with the USA. The JSP also conceded that the SDF may be retained at present under effective civilian control. However, both parties agreed that studies ought to be undertaken to reorganise the SDF or reduce its size if this was feasible. No clear-cut policy agreement was reached with regard to construction of nuclear power plants.[37]

In the meantime the *Komeito*-DSP agreement has created further problems for the JSP. This agreement calls for the maintaining of the Japan-US Security Treaty, the approval of the SDF and the promotion of atomic power generation, although these provisions ran somewhat counter to *Komeito*'s traditional policies. However, the *Komeito* is tending to move nearer to the *Komeito*-DSP line.[38] The JSP, with its ambitions to create a viable opposition, is hoping to have a JSP-*Komeito*-DSP coalition. This may mean that the JSP would have to make further concessions on its principles of unarmed neutrality and opposition to the SDF, the Security Treaty and atomic power generation. This was clearly reflected in the draft of a major policy document produced by the JSP's 'diplomacy and defense project team' headed by Secretary General Tagaya, entitled 'Prospects For a Non-aligned and Neutral Japan and the Ensuring of Peace in the Multi-Polarization Age'. It is interesting to note, as *Mainichi* reported, 'that "non-armament", which had been the basis of the JSP's policies ever since the establishment of the Party has disappeared from the title, and that such expressions as "anti-Security Treaty" and "anti-SDF" have also disappeared completely'.[39]

This capitulation of the JSP to the centralist line on the SDF and the US-Japan Security Treaty is a clear indication that the political climate has changed in favour of the defence forces.

The Intellectual Climate

It is well known that in the immediate postwar years in Japan, major monthly magazines 'which both guide and reflect the prevailing intellectual atmosphere'[40] were full of articles condemning pre-war Japanese thinking as well as the social structure which gave rise to militarism. They looked more and more into Western values such as democratic ideals, political freedom and individual rights to provide the basis for a future Japanese society. It is in this context that Article 9 became 'the most dramatic symbol of the new Constitution'[41] for the left. Particularly at the time of the finalisation of the Japan-US Security Treaty, the intellectual revolt culminated in the creation of a united front by the progressive and Communist writers to oppose war, the Security Treaty and the SDF.[42] As Seki suggests. 'It was in this intellectual climate that the demonstrations against the proposed revision of the Japan-US security pact, centred around scholars, organized students and labour unionists were staged across Japan in 1960.'[43]

It was for fear of hostile public reaction that not only was the planned visit of President Eisenhower cancelled but the Japanese Prime Minister Kishi was forced to resign. Later when in 1961 the US government asked Japan to allow US nuclear-powered submarines to call at Japanese ports, the request was refused by the Japanese government.[44]

The opposition to rearmament continued to be strong until about 1969, which was the peak of the anti-establishment campus revolt by Japanese students. This coincided with almost the last serious effort by the opposition to undermine the rearmament of Japan. In 1968 the JDA decided to buy the F-4 Phantom as the mainstay fighter for the Japanese Air Force. The JSP contended that the F-4 had a bombsight and an in-flight refuelling facility, which posed a threat to other countries and was therefore unconstitutional. The government gave way by promising to remove the bombsight as well as the in-flight refuelling facility.[45] (In the late 1970s the mood of the country has so changed that when the decision to buy a more sophisticated aircraft such as the F-15 was taken, nobody seriously suggested that the bombsight or the in-flight refuelling facilities ought to be removed.[46])

Although some changes in the attitude of intellectuals could be perceived even during the 1960s, the major change has taken place since the ending of the Vietnam War and particularly in the aftermath of the oil crisis. 'The ending of the Vietnam War and the American withdrawal from the Indo-Chinese Peninsula opened the eyes of the Japanese to the long-ignored problem of national defense. Then the oil crisis brought home the recognition that Japan's prosperity was rather like a "fragile blossom" stimulating reappraisal of the utopian attitudes prevailing until then.'[47]

Several factors have been suggested as explanations to the 'rightward shift'.[48] An article on 'The Political Structure of the Rightward Shift' in *Asahi Shimbun* on 28 September 1977 listed at least three factors explaining the inertia among the Japanese intellectual left.

First, the growing rivalry between the Japanese socialists and the Communists and the continuing infighting within the two camps created a sense of disillusionment among supporters. In addition, the deepening of the feud between the USSR and the PRC eroded the very legitimacy of socialist thought. Second, the arguments with which the 'rightward shift' could be countered are somewhat outdated and stale and therefore they do not excite intellectuals. Finally, many scholars have begun to question post-war values.

One such article by Shimizu[49], a radical who spearheaded the anti-base struggles at Uchinada and Sunagawa in the 1950s and the 1960 demonstration opposing the revision of the Japan-US Security Treaty, has attracted considerable attention in intellectual circles. In this article Shimizu argues that the post-war notions of justice and righteousness were guided by two major axioms: 'To do away with the *Tenno* [Emperor] system and establish a republican system and to abolish capitalism and establish a socialist or Communist society.'[50] These two axioms were the product of 'the psychology of revenge'[51] on the Peace Preservation Law of 1925 which prohibited organised activity aimed at destroying the *Tenno* system and capitalist institutions. In its revised form it prescribed capital punishment or life imprisonment for such activities. Shimizu does not find the sense of revulsion against this law irrational. But on the other hand, he argues that the Law itself was enacted as a 'self-defense measure'[52] against the Comintern. He suggests that such restrictive laws were already operating in the West:

> No government could stand idly by while a branch of the Comintern was set up on its own soil, with funds, directives, personnel and even arms supplied by Moscow and with Soviet diplomats engaging in clandestine activities as Comintern members. Indeed no government should ignore such a state of affairs.[53]

In spite of these threats to Japan, there were some 'courageous intellectuals with a strong sense of justice, but not prudent enough to discern that the Comintern was a tool of Soviet foreign policy'[54] who became activists to promote Comintern-directed Communist movements. Many such intellectuals were convicted. A number of them were 'converted' and released. In Shimizu's views this 'conversion' happened because these leftist individuals 'reverted to commonsense'. He feels that 'They must have realized at last how preposterous it was to try to convince themselves that what mattered was the security and victory of the Soviet Union and that Japanese citizens should work to help bring about Japan's defeat for the sake of the defense of the Soviet Union.'[55] Shimizu asks why should the record of such a conversion become a source of shame? The alternative to what they did was to continue to blindly believe in the Comintern thesis and sacrifice Japan for the security and development of the USSR.

Obviously, the article is aimed at underlining that there is nothing shameful in changing one's mind if commonsense dictates that such a change is in the interest of society and of the country. It is difficult to say whether this represents a rationalisation and apology for his own conversion. However, at present the article must comfort the 'progressive' intellectuals who feel less inclined to rock the boat of the establishment at a time when the same 'Soviet threat' is lurking round the corner.

The fact remains that Shimizu's conversion is alarming in several respects. He not only advocates the acquisition of nuclear arms by Japan but argues that without adequate military power Japan is not even a sovereign state.[56] To him the 'influence a country has in international politics is determined mainly by its military strength. Economic strength has much less impact. It is only natural that the term "economic giant" has a hollow ring in postwar Japan, when military power is tabooed and therefore political power is not easily generated.'[57] In fact, he questions the legitimacy of post-war thought, which has centred around Article 9 of the Constitution, as well as democracy itself. He argues that 'the Article 9 was imposed on Japan in a "trade-off" for the emperor system wrested from Japan most of its essence as a state. First, by being forced to accept a draft constitution concocted by the United States, Japan was clearly robbed of an important condition of being a state. Second, by accepting Article 9 Japan claimed unequivocally to both its own people and the world at large that it was no longer a state. Article 9 soon became the most important document of post-war Japanese thought, which thus began with the admission that Japan was not a state.'[58] He finds it strange that even today 'politicians of all persuasions in their utterances in the Diet, university professors in their articles for high-brow periodicals, and newspaper writers in their editorials all endorse this idea, never questioning the legitimacy of the postwar thought that denied Japan its status as a state.'[59] To him 'a constitution forced on Japan while under occupation by foreign troops cannot remain valid forever.'[60] On this particular point, as we have already seen, Nakasone has views similar to those of Shimizu. The latter, however, has doubts even about democracy in Japan. In an interview with Hajime Haraga, an *Asahi* reporter, he seems to have indicated that ordinary people did not care the least about democracy:

In the press and publication circles, there was probably what is called post-war democracy. However, before going into that, I think that we can say, in a general way, that there are two worlds in Japan, that is, the world which is created by the words of the intellectuals, such as in influential journals and publications, and the world of the silent majority, who are working diligently, and who do not know how to write their views and have no opportunity to give speeches. All the arguments on just causes, in the post-war years were supplied by the world of the former. Post-war democracy was created and backed up by the authority and power of the Occupation Forces. For the silent majority, there were probably such aspects as their being consoled and saved by it in the period of confusion, but in the end, it simply ends in their saying 'Oh, I see'.[61]

It is difficult to assess whether Shimizu represents the main stream of political thought in Japan. It is alleged by many in Japan, as the *Asahi* reporter put it, that Shimizu always wishes to be in the limelight.[62] On the other hand, there is no doubt that Japan has begun to question 'Western' values and 'is taking a new look at the merits and wisdom of Japanese society'.[63] This is reflected in the current boom in Japanese historical and ethnological studies. However, there may be a risk involved in this revival of interest in the past, particularly for Japan, where there is a tendency to exaggerate the 'uniqueness' of the country. Probably this is what gave rise, at least partly, to ultra-nationalism in the past. Respect for the past may tempt people to provide rationalisation for past mistakes, a tendency that is not completely absent in Japan. A glimpse of this can be had from a dialogue between Kenji Miyamoto, the Chairman of the JCP, and Kakuei Tanaka, who later became Prime Minister, in 1969 in the course of a symposium organised by a leading newspaper. On being asked by Miyamoto how he would characterise the war Tanaka replied:

. . . I do not want to dig up things that have gone down in history. Moreover . . . this is not the question for partisan debate. I don't think it was such a simple war in the history of the Japanese nation. During the occupation it was simply regarded as a war of aggression by Japan, and that was that. But it was not that simple. . . At that time we Japanese had virtually no natural resources. There were some one hundred million of us then, and when we tried to get cheap import we got kicked around by high tariffs. We tried to emigrate, and we got slapped with exclusion. Our export goods were discriminated against. Didn't we hit the very bottom in the depression? Still the upshot was we went on to assault Imphal, Guadal canal and Sydney, and tried to take one third of the earth. That was aggression. That was going too far. But after the Sino-Japanese War, everything that came thereafter including the days when the Japanese nation was spitting blood . . . you may say in one sentence, 'was that not a war of aggression?'.[64]

Unfortunately a number of factors that Tanaka suggested had led Japan to go to war still exist. Japan still does not have many natural resources, her exports are discriminated against and there is a serious risk of unemployment. As self-defence Japan is building one of the most sophisticated armed forces in the region. Is not there a risk that her growing self-confidence and economic power may force her in a similar direction? This is what Denis Healey was worried about in the early 1970s.[65] It is highly unlikely that Japan will commit direct aggression again but on the other hand it may interfere militarily in regional disputes and internal strife within the countries of the region. Japanese naval presence on grounds of keeping sea-lanes safe for Japanese trade may become common. Regional security treaties under Japanese 'hegemony' may be made, enabling Japan to support convenient regimes financially and militarily (particularly by supplying military hardware). There is a feeling in some quarters in Japan that she is already involved in some kind of tacit alliance of the three powers USA-Japan and the PRC on the lines of NATO, with Japan taking a similar place as West Germany. This feeling has been strengthened since the signing of the Sino-Japanese peace treaty. There is also a feeling that Japan is preparing to fill the military vacuum after the US departure (or reduction in the US presence) from the region. This feeling has become more credible because of the increasing co-ordination between the military leadership of the two countries and the recent joint exercises of the two forces. It may not be a rapid 'militarisation' of Japan but it is a slippery slope that Japan is walking. With a growing mood of conservatism inside the country and with an orchestrated campaign about the Soviet threat the risk of putting a foot wrong is not impossible.

While it is true that there is a definite trend towards 'conservatism' among intellectuals in Japan, it does not mean that progressive thinking has completely disappeared. For instance, *Sekai* continues to publish pacifism-oriented articles.[66] However, the emphasis has changed. In the 1950s the emphasis was more on unarmed neutrality based on a conviction that no country would like to invade a nation committed to a 'Peace' constitution. It opposed both the SDF and the Japan-US Security Treaty. In the 1960s the articles published in *Sekai* began to concede that invasion was possible but Japan ought to rely not on the SDF or the Security Treaty. Instead it should invite the UN peace-keeping forces into Japan to protect the security and the integrity of the country.[67] In recent years the number of such articles has declined significantly. Those which are published stress passive resistence to demoralise the aggressors. For instance, in an article published in *Sekai* in August 1978 Mitsuo Miyata wrote:

> In the defense debate of the past, the external threat of hostile forces of a political nature was taken for granted. An analysis

of the dangers of the present world shows, however, that this
concept of the enemy, as well as the whole ideology of 'friend
versus foe' no longer has meaningful content. The most
imminent danger today is not military but 'social' threats. For
instance, how can we protect ourselves from air pollution and other
forms of environmental destruction − very real threats that the
industrialized world has engendered and turned against itself?[68]

Although he himself does not consider military aggression as a real
threat, he suggests measures for passive resistance against direct
aggression:

> Group sit-ins, demonstrations, hunger strikes, and so forth of course
> deserve consideration, but they should be assigned an appropriate
> place in the overall resistance picture. The invaders' intention of
> controlling society and people's way of life must be thwarted in a
> quicker and less dramatic manner. For example, refusal to obey
> the occupation's unlawful orders whether by civil servants or by
> plant workers, is more important that many more flamboyant
> activities.[69]

In Miyata's model of unarmed defence two basic tactics play an
important part. First, an attempt should be made to reduce the
advantages to be gained by the occupying force, and second, an
invasion force should be demoralised, possibly even before aggression
takes place. The first tactic would involve nullifying the usefulness of
mines, railways and factories. As an example of this kind of activity
he quotes the Swedish case, when the people rigged their iron mines
for destruction in the event of the planned Nazi *Polarfuchs* and then
leaked the plan to the Germans. The attack never came. Among the
second type of activity (i.e. demoralising the adversary) he suggests
that the enemy forces may be reminded of loved ones back home, or
the emptiness of war, etc.[70]

Admittedly, such a strategy against foreign aggression is somewhat
idealistic. Passive resistance works but success depends largely on the
nature of the enemy. For instance, Mahatma Gandhi's non-violent
resistance against the British worked, whereas the same weapon has had
absolutely no effect on the South African government's policy on
apartheid. This idealistic view on meeting the aggression is now
increasingly being criticised in Japan as 'pipe-dream pacifism'.[71]

Here it may be interesting to mention a recent exchange between
Michio Morishima, a leading Japanese economist (now living in London),

and Yoshihiko Seki, a leading Japanese political scientist. On 15 September 1978 Seki wrote for the *Sankei Shimbun*'s Seiron column an article entitled 'Measures to cope with "Emergencies" are Natural'.[72] A further clarification was later published in *Hokkaido Shimbun* on 29 January 1979. Seki basically argued that mere good intentions do not prevent aggression. Unilateral pacifism may, in fact, encourage foreign aggression. With a view to substantiating his contention, Seki cited Chamberlain's appeasement policy which enabled Hitler to invade Poland in 1939. Therefore, he argued, the Japanese 'government and the people must make efforts for defense in preparedness for an emergency'.[73]

Morishima suggested that this article shocked him.

Upon reading this treatise, I received a really very severe . . . shock. That is because, when I came to England from Japan about ten years ago, I did not think that Mr. Seki was such an advocate of national defense, even though he may not have been a pacifist. I do not know him personally, but I had thought from before that, ideologically, Mr. Seki was not so far removed from me. Has Japan changed that much? I even felt afraid of returning to Japan.[74]

He further asked:

Will armaments really defend a nation? If one were to list the examples of armed forces' defending the nation and the examples of their leading their nation to destruction, it cannot necessarily be said that the former examples outnumber the latter examples. We must not forget the fact that it was not just Nazi Germany alone, but that the Japanese Imperial forces also devastated our national land completely.[75]

He also cited the example of the Shah of Iran, who was forced to leave the country in spite of the arsenals of weapons he had accumulated to protect himself.

Therefore Morishima suggested that if ever the Russians invaded Japan, which he does not believe to be likely, the Japanese people ought to 'meet them calmly, holding a white flag and a red flag. Even under Soviet rule, a socialistic but tolerable economy could certainly be created if only we meet defeat with dignity.'[76] He further argued that a dignified surrender by the SDF might ensure, in exchange, a right to political self-determination. Morishima did not think, as do many other Japanese as well as Americans, that the USA will come to the rescue of Japan. The wisdom of this line of argument was seriously questioned by Seki, who suggested that the Eastern European experience did not indicate that there was any hope of retaining freedom or even maintaining current living standards. He stressed:

> We were happier 30 years ago under the occupation rule of the U.S., a free and democratic country. Turning over this country to the new invader and making it an Eastern Europe in the Far East, we would not be able to maintain today's standards of living.[77]

Therefore even though there was an imminent danger of defeat against the Russian invading army, Seki argued that Japan must put up a stiff resistance for 'say two weeks until the U.S. comes to help'.[78]

The Morishima-Seki debate has attracted considerable intellectual attention in Japan. A number of articles both for and against a defence build-up have appeared in several journals. For instance, writing in *Bungei Shunju* in July 1980 Michitaro Tanaka gave a new twist to the argument by suggesting that Japan ought to rearm in the interest of world peace. He argued that in view of the tipping of the military balance in favour of 'socialist states' and against 'free countries', restoring the balance 'has become an urgent priority. Japan's defense must be considered within this context. The defense issue is becoming increasingly important not only for Japan but for world peace, and Japan only causes its neighbors trouble by not taking its defense seriously.'[79] Against this, Jiro Kamishima in an article in *Sekai* in July 1980, while conceding that 'Japan, as a mighty economic power, is obligated to assume some kind of central role in the international political arena'[80] argued that this 'role should not be one of pretending to act like the military superpowers or following obediently in their footsteps. Instead Japan must make full use of the original political assets it has itself built up over the years. Japan's point of departure, in other words, must be demilitarization.'[81] In his view, both the USA and the USSR 'desperately need alternative policies' to replace a continued escalation of military build-up but 'they are finding it difficult to come up with such policies by themselves. This is why Japan's cooperation is essential, and it is also why Japan must not give its agreement to the American call for a powerful Japanese military.'[82] Support for Morishima's views have also come from Shigeto Tsuru, who, like Shimizu, was against the SDF, the Japan-US Security Treaty and the US bases in Japan. Tsuru, writing in *Asahi Janaru*, argues in favour of unarmed neutrality and advocates the transformation of Japan into an international centre for cultural, aesthetic, educational, medical and health activities for people all over the world, particularly for the developing countries.[83] According to him, Japan ought to increase her assistance to developing countries and to refugee relief.

Another twist to this debate was given by Naohiro Amaya, the Vice-Minister for international affairs of the MITI, in an article in *Bungei Shunju* in March 1980 where he argues that Japan has two choices: to live as a merchant or as a warrior. In his views if 'Japan chooses to continue treading the path of a mercantile nation in international society, it must apply wholeheartedly to the merchant's trade. This means that, when necessary, Japan must go begging to the oil-producing nations; that if circumstances compel Japan must grovel before the military nations. Japan also must be wise enough to calculate the strengths and weaknesses of oil-producing and military nations, to perceive correctly the trends of the world and of history, and to choose risk-minimizing options. And when money will be helpful, Japan needs the gumption to pay handsomely.'[84] If, on the other hand, the Japanese people decide to live by the code of Samurai 'it is necessary to have two swords. To preserve Japan's reputation as a warrior in the international arena, Japan must expand its military even at the cost of a large tax increase. Moreover, since swords are not worn as mere ornaments, Japan must be prepared to draw them if necessary. For instance, if safe transit through the Persian Gulf is threatened, Japan has to be prepared to run to the scene sword in hand.'[85] Amaya further argued that as 'the export of military hardware is an important means of military diplomacy, Japan's current restrictions on arms exports will have to be rescinded forthwith.'[86] To Amaya, if Japan became a totally 'warrior' nation, the cost would be enormous, but 'Japan will be able to select totally new courses of action in, for example, its diplomatic efforts to procure natural resources from abroad.'[87] This view has been challenged by Masamori Sase in an article published in *Bungei Shunju* in April 1980. Sase argued that it was illusory to think that a militarily powerful Japan will find it easier to make diplomatic efforts to acquire natural resources.[88] After all, 'Several nations are militarily more powerful than Japan, yet diplomatically they have just as much difficulty in acquiring resources as does Japan.'[89] Thus the debate on whether to greatly enhance the defence capability or to gradually move towards unarmed neutrality still continues.

The two lines — those of Morishima and Seki — typically represent the two poles of the current defence debate. Unilateralists such as Shimizu are still in the minority. The Seki line is very close to the current 'overt' official JDA line, which puts faith in the Japan-US treaty and hopes that the SDF will fight the battle in a defensive capacity while the offensive will be taken by the US forces. As we shall see later, public opinion is increasingly moving nearer this line.

On the other hand, Morishima's argument represents the traditional *Kakushin* views which have certainly lost ground in recent years and, as we have seen, at least for tactical reasons, even the JSP has given up the opposition to the SDF and the Japan-US treaty. In fact, even those who take a more 'realistic' view of the situation and are more in agreement with the Seki line are worried about the increasing influences of the 'hawks'. For instance, Masamichi Inoki, the Director of the Peace and Security Research Institute, who was invited by *Seiron* to comment on the Morishima-Seki exchange and who argued in favour of an increase in the defence budget, warned that:

> However, it is also true that, recently, the voices of 'national defense advocates' have come to mount suddenly in our country. My impression is that there is no presence more dangerous to Japan's security than these 'national defense advocates'. It is extremely troublesome if they have forgotten completely that the armed forces, in the past, multiplied like cancer cells and destroyed the Japanese Empire. In the past, the expression 'alienation between the armed forces and the people' was often used. 'National defense advocates' are the new type of forces for 'alienation between the armed forces and Japan', which drive a wedge between the people and the Self-Defense Forces. There is nothing more harmful than the 'advocates of national defense' for the fostering of *strong defense power, deeply rooted among people*. It will be a big problem if security were to be separated from the goal of peace.[90] (Italics mine).

Other intellectuals seem to be questioning the wisdom of an orchestrated campaign to convince the people of the Russian threat. Commenting on the events in Japan during the period up to the formal decision on the guideline for Japan-US joint operations at the meeting of the Japan-US Consultative Committee on Security, which was held on 27 November 1978, Hiroharu Seki, Professor of International Politics at Tokyo University, wrote:

> As a matter of fact, the allergic manipulation of public opinion in both Japan and the US during this period, to inflame the sense of Soviet threat, was beyond forbearance. In the background of this, there was also a play of contacts between the hawk faction-oriented defense experts of the two countries and those surrounding them. *The Japanese people's sound common-sense on true security*

*was thus at a crisis of collapse due also to the creation of linkage
politics of the hawk faction beyond the border.*[91] (Italics mine).

Similar views were expressed in October 1978 by Chihiro Hosoya, the
Professor of International Politics at Hitotsubashi University, in *Chuo
Koron*:

> Manipulations from within and outside the country to fan a 'sense
> of the threat of the Soviet Union' will probably become more active.
> This will create a very favourable environment for endeavoring for a
> drastic expansion of self-defense power. There is something ominous
> in the fact that voices seeking the strengthening of defense power are
> becoming louder, with the further mounting of defense arguments,
> recently. Of course, the way of nation's defense should be thorough-
> goingly discussed. However, the expansion of defense power, which
> will become linked with the revival of a 'military big-power' Japan,
> will disturb the stability of Northeast Asia, and we must avoid the
> 'dangerous road' of making the various Southeast Asian nations
> recall the nightmare of Japanese militarism and of fanning their
> sense of guardedness towards Japan.[92]

Such campaigns are already having some effect, thought not a pronounced
one, on public opinion. A poll in December 1978 showed that 86 per cent
of those responding supported the retention of the SDF.[93] This
proportion in 1972 was only 71 per cent and in 1976 only 78 per cent.
In a public opinion survey commissioned by the JDA in 1977 83 per cent
of respondents argued that the SDF should be modernised in line with
progress in science and technology. In another nationwide poll conducted
by the Japan Public Opinion Survey Association in December 1978[94]
51 per cent of the people found that the SDF was not a violation of
the Constitution against only 19.5 per cent who considered it a violation.
Also, 64.7 per cent of the people were against the amendment of
Article 9 of the Constitution to change the SDF into a regular armed
force. Nearly 73 per cent of the respondents felt that the Japan-US
Security Treaty was of some service to the country. Almost half
(46.7 per cent) felt that maintaining the Peace Constitution was the
most effective way of ensuring Japan's security. With regard to the
question on 'legislation of emergency' only 10 per cent felt that it was
needed in the near future. Another about 38 per cent thought that the
problem should be studied. On exporting weapons, 47 per cent of
the people suggested that it was undesirable. The same year, the
Nationwide Public Opinion Survey by *Yomiuri Shimbhun* indicated

that nearly three-quarters of the people did not desire Japan to possess nuclear weapons. However, nearly 53 per cent considered the Soviet Union to be a threat to Japan. At the same time some 38 per cent of respondents felt that in an emergency the USA would not defend Japan under the Japan-US Security Treaty. But at the same time only a third of those responding suggested that, in the event of US withdrawal from South Korea, Japan should strengthen its own independent defence structure. Nearly 46 per cent of people suggested that in the case of maritime disputes relating to the extent of territorial waters or fisheries, Japan should utilise diplomatic negotiations. Only 8.5 per cent supported the strengthening on the MSDF.

Taking all these into account, it is clear that the ordinary Japanese accepts the *status quo* relating to the SDF and the US-Japan Security Treaty, and is not in favour of strengthening them. The orientation of the Japanese people towards peace is pretty much intact. The 'hawks' have a long way to go before they can sell the idea of a constitutional amendment or a substantial increase in the defence budget. But the people seem to be genuinely concerned about the Soviet threat, and, though it has not reached an alarming stage, it provides a very favourable environment for the 'hawks'.

On the other hand, there are some tendencies which may have implications for the future. In the Second Survey of National Character conducted by the Institute of Statistical Mathematics in 1958, 55 per cent of respondents favoured democracy;[95] in a similar poll in 1973 only 43 per cent of the people found democracy good; another 46 per cent gave a conditional reply that it depended on time and circumstances.[96] It was surprising that in 1973 there were only 30 per cent who said totalitarianism was not good. A third, in fact, considered that the answer depended on time and circumstances. Does this mean that the tolerance of the Japanese people for 'totalitarianism' has increased in recent years? In the absence of comparable data for 1958 no definite answer can be given. However, recent surveys suggest that the Japanese are now attaching less importance to individual rights and freedom than before.[97] This is much more pronounced among the age groups between 20 and 24. The recent survey also showed that the tendency towards conformism and the respect for Japanese traditional values such as filial piety (*oyakoko*), gratitude (*ongaeshi*), etc. has increased.

This may reflect a growing self-confidence based on the recent economic success *vis-à-vis* the West. It is also likely that with more and more people travelling abroad they have come to appreciate both the strengths and the weaknesses of those foreign countries. On the other hand, it may be a reflection of the re-emergence of national chauvinism. This is reflected in a substantial increase in the number of people who consider themselves superior to the Westerners: in 1973 this number was 39 per cent against only 20 per cent for 1958.

The Japanese sense of superiority towards developing countries seems to have grown as well. This also applies to neighbouring countries such as Korea. In a survey on cultural friction conducted in Japan and South Korea, two-thirds of the respondents agreed that the Japanese people have a sense of superiority towards South Korea even today.[98]

The Japanese leadership is highly critical of Japanese behaviour towards neighbouring countries. For instance, in an interview Tamio Kawakami, the International Bureau Chief of the JSP and member of the Lower House of the Japanese Parliament, laments that:

Japanese people are visiting the southern seas, and they are raising monuments, one after another, as a memory to Japanese military personnel. I think that before long, several dozens and several hundreds of such monuments will be raised there. Do we not need to consider fully how people in the area will think of this? . . . Should we not take into consideration fully why monuments have not been erected in the memory of Japanese military personnel on the China Continent, where over 700,000 men died, if it were a beautiful thing, really? It is not logical of us to do a thing which we are not permitted to do in China, in the southern seas.[99]

Similar views have been expressed by Yoshikazu Sakamoto, Professor of International Politics in Tokyo University. He enumerates some of the main criticisms voiced by the medium and small Asian nations:

. . . Male tourists are especially unpopular. They become engrossed in buying goods and human beings, on the one hand, while showing complete indifference to the culture and way of life of the native people.
. . . in the pattern of behaviour of the Japanese people living in these areas, their closed nature and their sticking together by themselves are especially conspicuous. They look down on the native people as if they were inferior, and they do not try to learn the local language . . . In addition to the superiority complex generally harbored by the Japanese people, there is the fact that no matter how outstanding and fine a record a local employee may have, he is never appointed to a decision-making position . . .[100]

Sakamoto stresses that in addition to the pattern of personal attitudes and behaviour there are some structural problems relating to the nature of Japanese investment, trade and aid that hurt the developing countries in regions and lead to the resentment of the local people against Japan. In his view, 'In the final analysis, what Japan is actually doing in the medium and small nations of Southeast Asia has the strong colouring of "economic aggression".'[101] Many South-east Asian scholars feel that 'the Greater South East Asia co-prosperity sphere actually exists today'.[102]

Admittedly, such complaints by the countries on the receiving end may be somewhat exaggerated, but the fact remains that a resource-poor country such as Japan has to depend on the goodwill of the developing countries in the region and elsewhere. Some goodwill can be bought by aid and other legal and illegal payments to the local elite, but much of this goodwill has to be earned by mutual respect. However the 'congenital big-power orientation'[103] of Japan will always hinder the development of mutual respect and understanding between Japan on the one hand and the developing countries on the other.

This is one of the main reasons that Japan has not made any real progress in her UN diplomacy and was rebuffed in 1978 by the Third World countries in an effort to secure a non-permanent seat in the Security Council for the fifth term. On being admitted to the UN in December 1956 Japan formulated three foreign policies: (1) the use of the UN as the main instrument of Japanese diplomacy; (2) co-operation with the free nations; and (3) the promotion of Japan's national interest as part of the Afro-Asian bloc.[104] Except for a couple of years after her admission, Japan did not really live up to the third principle. Even in the early 1960s, it was clear that Japan was increasingly aligning herself with the USA and the Western European bloc. Japan's close co-operation on all major international issues with the USA in the UN has often irritated the Afro-Asian bloc. For instance, on the South African question, Japan votes with the Third World on rhetorical motions — condemning apartheid, expressing solidarity with political prisoners, setting up scholarship schemes for refugees, etc. — but on motions concerning economic issues, such as condemning the operations of Western corporations in South Africa, Japan either votes with the Western countries or abstains.

On one occasion the Third World felt completely let down by Japan, and this was on the question of the New International Economic order. In the initial stages Prime Minister Tanaka promised Japan's support for the Charter in joint declaration with Mexico, but when the Charter was put to the vote in the General Assembly in 1974 Japan abstained.[105]

The Japanese attempt to acquire a non-permanent seat permanently has been widely interpreted as an effort to gain a status as a major power. It must be noted that there are only ten non-permanent seats in the Security Council, of which only five are allocated to Asia and Africa. Election to these seats is for two years. By now, Japan has been elected five times, the last occasion being 20 October 1980. On completion of her current term in the Security Council she would have kept one of the five seats for ten years in twenty-five years of membership of the UN. Developing countries consider this to be a callous disregard of the fact that nearly 90 African and Asian countries have to share those five seats. Her claim that the Japanese government was eager to win a non-permanent seat on the Security Council was with a view to living up to Japan's international pledge to give priority to its expanded role in the international body is far from convincing. The Scandinavian countries have played a significant role in the UN without having a permanent seat on the Security Council. Why, then, should this be a necessary precondition? When Japan failed to gain the seat in 1978 Foreign Minister Sonoda expressed his views that he would consult West Germany on the matter of jointly pursuing the possibility of their securing permanent seats.[106] Admittedly, a restructuring of the UN is long overdue. It is possible that if such a restructuring takes place Japan might get a permanent seat, but this is not certain. Except on the criteria of total GNP and therefore her financial contribution to the UN budget, Japan does not stand a better chance than many other countries. It would be much more difficult for West Germany to get one because the EEC alone could not hope to get three permanent seats. In any restructured UN one of the main criteria would be a fair regional representation. Latin America, Africa and the Arab countries do not have any representation while Asia has one with the PRC. So it is likely that before another permanent seat is allocated to Asia (i.e. Japan) other regional claims have to be met. But even if Japan hopes to get a seat, this is hardly the way to go about it. By declaring her intention to align with West Germany at the total neglect of the Third World countries she has already alienated those countries who do control a substantial majority in the General Assembly, and any country not being fully supported by the Third World will have difficulty in getting such a permanent seat even if it is created.

Japan's trouble lies in her projecting the traditional concept of the hierarchial order of things from her domestic world to the outer world of nations. Most Third World nations have recently gained their political sovereignity, not necessarily economic independence, and are sensitive to any encroachment of this newly won 'self-respect'. Japan should understand this feeling better than the Western nations, because since the Meiji Restoration she herself has been fighting to regain respectability and equality with her Western partners, particularly the USA. Developing countries are in search of some kind of respectability, and any overt expression of superiority alienates them. Unless Japan begins to treat them as equals there is little hope for the genuine co-operation which she badly needs to keep the flow of scarce raw materials going.

However, a multi-dimensional approach to Japanese security as reflected in the concept of 'comprehensive national security' (in which a positive diplomatic effort to build a peaceful international environment is a step in the right direction. The question remains whether under US pressure Japan is sucked into some kind of Asian NATO with the USA and the PRC as partners. Such a step would certainly lead to an accelerated pace of military build-up which a resource-poor 'middle power' such as Japan, even though economically feasible, could not sustain for a long time. Even the raw material and energy requirements of a large military machine would be such as to threaten the supply sources of the West. If such a situation ever arose the Japanese alliance with the West would not prevent the West from taking retaliatory action in the political and strategic spheres as they are presently doing to her in the economic areas. What Japan has to fear most is not a threat of foreign aggression but the enemy within, the 'congenital big-power orientation'. Some options open to Japan in the 1980s are analysed in the next chapter.

Notes

1. Quoted in J.K. Emmerson, *Arms, Yen and Power: The Japanese Dilemma*, pp.50-51.
2. Ibid., pp.128-9.
3. K. Murakami, 'The Postwar Defense Debate in Review', *Japan Echo*, vol. V. no. 4 (1978), p.20.
4. Ibid.
5. Ibid., p.21.
6. The Constitution of Japan, quoted in G.M. Beckmann, *The Modernization of China and Japan*, p.683.
7. Murakami, 'The Postwar Defense Debate', p.21.
8. Ibid., p.21n.
9. S. Hayashi, 'Supreme Court Rulings on Constitutional Issues', *Japan Echo*, vol.5, no. 3 (1978), pp.27-8.
10. Ibid., p.28.
11. Ibid.
12. Ibid.
13. Ibid.
14. *Tokyo Shimbun*, 21 March 1979.
15. R.G. Speed, *Strategic Deterrence in the 1980's*, p.7.

222   *The Strains on Japanese Pacifism*

16. *Tokyo Shimbun*, 21 March 1979.
17. Ibid.
18. Murakami, 'The Postwar Defense Debate', pp.29-30.
19. Ibid., p.30.
20. Ibid.
21. *The Japan Times Weekly*, 14 Feb. 1981, p.2.
22. Ibid.
23. Quoted in J. Halliday and G. McCormack, *Japanese Imperialism Today: Co-Prosperity in Greater East Asia*, pp.90-1.
24. Y. Nakasone, 'Towards Comprehensive Security', *Japan Echo*, vol. V. no. 4 (1978), p.38.
25. Ibid., pp.37-8.
26. *The Japan Times Weekly*, 17 Jan. 1981, p.3.
27. *Japan Echo* (editorial) vol. III, no. 3 (1976), p.48.
28. Emmerson, *Arms, Yen and Power*, pp.110-11.
29. *Japan Echo* (editorial) vol. III, no. 3 (1976), p.48.
30. Ibid.
31. R. Shiratori, 'Ghosts Linger in Political Party System', *The Japan Times Weekly*, 22 Sept. 1979, p.5.
32. Ibid: see also K. Murata, 'The Decline of the Left', *The Japan Times Weekly*, 21 April 1979, p.3.
33. *The Japan Times Weekly*, 28 April 1979, p.1.
34. *The Japan Times Weekly*, 13 Oct. 1979, p.1.
35. M. Shimizu, 'Centrists Exude Confidence in National Politics', *The Japan Times Weekly*, 28 April 1979, p.4.
36. *The Japan Times Weekly*, 28 June 1980, p.1.
37. *The Japan Times Weekly* (editorial), 19 Jan. 1980, p.12.
38. *Tokyo Shimbun*, 25 July 1980.
39. *Mainichi*, 26 July 1980, pp.1-2.
40. Editorial comment on 'Shifting Intellectual Trends', *Japan Echo*, vol. V, no.3 (1978), p.93.
41. D.C. Hellman, 'Japanese Security and Postwar Japanese Foreign Policy' in R.A. Scalapino (ed.), *The Foreign Policy of Modern Japan*, p.331.
42. Y. Seki, 'Democracy and Japanese Intellectuals: The Concept of Democracy in Post-war Japan as Reflected in Magazine Articles', *Japan Report*, 1 July 1978, p.3.
43. Ibid.
44. Murakami, 'The Postwar Defense Debate', p.24.
45. Ibid., p.26.
46. Ibid., p.30.
47. Seki, 'Democracy and Japanese Intellectuals', p.4.
48. *Asahi Shimbun*, 28 Sept. 1977, quoted in *Japan Echo* (editorial) vol. V, no. 4 (1978), p.7.
49. I. Shimizu, 'Questioning Post-War Values, *Japan Echo*, vol. V, no. 3 (1978).
50. Ibid., p.96.
51. Ibid.
52. Ibid., p.101.
53. Ibid.
54. Ibid.
55. Ibid., p.107.
56. I. Shimizu, 'The Nuclear Option: Japan, Be a State!' *Japan Echo*, vol. VII, no.3 (1980): see also 'Nuclear Weapons For Japan – Why Not?', *The Japan Times*, 10 Aug. 1980. Both articles are abridged translations of the original article published in *Shokun*, July 1980.
57. Shimizu, 'The Nuclear Option', p.40.
58. Ibid., p.34.

59. Ibid., p.35.

60. Ibid., p.42.

61. *Asahi*, 18 June 1980.

62. 'Letter from Reporter Haraga to Ikutaro Shimizu – Always Riding on the Current of the Times', *Asahi*, 18 June 1980, p.3.

63. S. Sato *et al.*, 'Beyond Conservative vs. Kakushin Politics', *Japan Echo*, vol. V, Special Issue (1978), p.30.

64. Quoted in T. Kataoka, 'Waiting For Pearl Harbor: Japan Debates Arms', mimeographed, 1979, pp.55-6.

65. See page 31.

66. *Japan Echo*, Editorial comment on 'The Defense Debate Flares Up', vol. V, no. 4 (1978), p.16.

67. Ibid.

68. M. Miyata, 'The True Meaning of Defending the Country', *Japan Echo*, vol. V, no. 4 (1978), pp.41-2.

69. Ibid., pp.42-3.

70. Ibid., p.44.

71. M. Inoki, 'Active Discussion on Security should be Initiated: Commenting on Morishima-Seki Exchange of Peace Debate', *Seiron*, April 1979.

72. In July 1978 the Chairman of the Joint Staff Council, General Hiroomi Kurisu, made a public statement that the SDF was not empowered to act on their own initiative even in the cases of emergencies such as a surprise landing of enemy forces. He further suggested that in such cases of emergency the SDF officers would not wait for orders from Tokyo but would act 'supra-legally' to cope with the situation (*The Japan Times Weekly*, 5 Aug. 1978.) Under the SDF law, if the Lower House is not in session the Prime Minister, in consultation with the House of Councillors, has to take the decision. The controversy led to the dismissal of General Kurisu. The JDA has been asked to undertake a study of the nature of amendments that are needed to meet such emergencies. The Leftists argue that if such a legislation is passed it might revive some of the legal provisions of the pre-1945 State Total Mobilisation Law which heavily infringed on civil liberties and other human rights (K. Murata, 'Specter of Wartime Laws: Infringement of Basic Human Rights by Emergency Legislation Feared', *Japan Times Weekly*, 2 Sept. 1978, p.3). The interesting fact was that the JSP and JCP did not get as much support in the major monthlies as would have been the case twenty years ago. This is further evidence of the growing 'conservative' mood in the country.

73. Quoted in Inoki, 'Active Discussion on Security'.

74. Morishima, quoted in Inoki, ibid.

75. Ibid.

76. T. Tokuoka, 'Japan – Red or Dead', *New York Times*, 2 Sept. 1979.

77. Ibid.

78. Ibid.

79. M. Tanaka, 'Reflections on Three Recent Events', *Japan Echo*, vol. VII, no. 3 (1980), p.23.

80. J. Kamishima, 'The Tradition and Realism of Demilitarization', *Japan Echo*, vol. VII, no. 3 (1980), p.31.

81. Ibid.

82. Ibid., pp.31-2.

83. *Japan Echo* (editorial), vol. VII, no. 3 (1980), p.15: see *Japan Quarterly*, Oct.-Dec. 1980 for a complete English version of this article.

84. N. Amaya, 'Japan As a Mercantile Nation', *Japan Echo*, vol. VII, no. 2 (1980), p.59.

85. Ibid., p.60

86. Ibid.

87. Ibid.

88. M. Sase, 'Refuting the Mercantile Nation Theory', *Japan Echo*, vol. VII,

no. 2 (1980), p.67.

89. Ibid.

90. Inoki, 'Active Discussion on Security'.

91. H. Seki, 'Changing Asia and Defense Diplomacy: Requests toward the Ohira Cabinet', *Sekai*, Feb. 1979.

92. C. Hosoya, 'Course for "All-Directions", Japan to Take', *Chuo koron*, Oct. 1978.

93. J. Lewis, 'A Hard Look at the Real World', *Far Eastern Economic Review*, 3 Aug. 1979, p.16.

94. *Tokyo Shimbun*, 6 Jan. 1979.

95. Z. Suetuna *et al.*, *Annals of the Institute of Statistical Mathematics Supplement*, p.32.

96. C. Hayashi, 'Japanese Attitudes and Party Preference', *Japan Echo*, vol. V special issue, 1978, p.75.

97. *The Japan Times Weekly*, 12 Jan. 1980, p.3: also K. Murata, 'Conservative Japanese: Survey Shows Traditional Values, Attitudes Returning', *The Japan Times Weekly*, 4 Aug. 1979, p.3.

98. *Sankei*, 28 Dec. 1978.

99. T. Kawakami, in an interview with Yoshimasa Miyazaki, a political affairs commentator, *Jiyu*, March 1979.

100. Y. Sakamoto, 'The Way of Life for Japan: Status of the People of an Intermediate Nation', *Sekai*, Jan. 1979.

101. Ibid.

102. Ibid.

103. M. Nakajima, 'Diplomacy as Defense Strategy', *Japan Echo*, vol. VI, no. 1 (1979), p.62.

104. S. Matsumoto, 'Japan's Voting Behaviour in the United Nations' in H. Itoh (ed.), *Japanese Politics – An Inside View*, p.188.

105. J. Nishikawa, 'Towards a New International Order', *Japan Echo*, vol. VI, Special Issue (1979), p.62.

106. *The Japan Times Weekly*, 18 Nov. 1978, p.1.

8 JAPAN'S OPTIONS FOR THE FUTURE

It is not always easy to discern what the official view in Japan is with regard to the future of Japanese defence commitments at home and abroad. Statements by government officials and members of the Cabinet have been often conflicting and evasive. Even on important issues such as the revision of the Constitution, no clearcut policy seems to have emerged. For instance, on 27 August 1980 Justice Minister Seisuke Okuno told the Diet that 'he wanted the controversial war-renouncing Article 9 of the present Constitution to be revised or totally dropped'.[1] A similar remark was made earlier by Yoshio Sakurauchi, the Secretary-General of the LDP, the party in power. The same evening Prime Minister Zenko Suzuki told newspaper reporters that the government would 'strictly and sincerely' adhere to the Constitution irrespective of the 'personal' views of Cabinet members and the party leader.[2] In spite of a categorical statement by the Prime Minister, Okuno reiterated the need for a revision of the Constitution in February 1981 and added that the LDP may propose an amendment to the Constitution in the campaign for the 1983 Upper House election. In his view, the LDP as a whole favoured a revision of the Constitution. Commenting on Okuno's statement, the Prime Minister once again confirmed that 'his administration has no plans to propose an amendment to the war-renouncing Constitution in the 1983 House of Councillors election campaign'.[3] Similarly, on the question of Japan's participation in UN peace-keeping activities abroad, in August 1980 Foreign Minister Masayoshi Ito contradicted the views of senior officials of his own ministry, who had suggested earlier that 'the sending of SDF men could not be ruled out in the future'.[4] Ito suggested that the 'Japanese government was not considering sending and cannot send under the existing law, Self-Defense Force men abroad for United Nations peace-keeping activity'.[5] However, the Cabinet clarified the issue further on 28 October 1980 by saying that it would be unconstitutional for the SDF to take part in UN peace-keeping forces if their duties involved military action but 'the participation of the Self-Defense Forces in UN forces is not forbidden under the Constitution if their purpose and duties do not involve military action'.[6]

Another important subject on which official statements have been rather conflicting is the question of defending the sea-lanes. On

21 October 1980 Joji Omura, the chief of the Defense Agency, told the Diet that 'the government would give "serious consideration to the defense of the sea lanes, including the constitutional problems involved" in order to safeguard sea traffic and secure the oil supply from the Middle East'.[7] Later in the day, Kiichi Miyazawa, the chief Cabinet secretary, argued that 'the nation's right to self-defense should be exercised in a limited manner and in a limited area under the current interpretation of the Constitution'.[8] At least, by implication, he suggested that the Constitution restricted the operation of the SDF in the neighbourhood of Japan and not as far as the Middle East. On 15 November Prime Minister Suzuki told a Diet Committee that there was no constitutional limitation to the SDF with regard to protecting 'Japanese merchant ships on the high seas against attack despite their primary mission of defending Japan's land, territorial waters and air space'.[9] In his view 'the SDF forces' at present were 'incapable of protecting Japanese vessels in the Persian Gulf and the Indian Ocean'.[10] He further added that 'he had no intention of altering the MSDF's target of assuring the security of waters for several hundred nautical miles from Japanese coasts and the sea routes serving Japan for up to 1000 nautical miles from Japan'.[11]

As in the case of the Japanese government's attitude towards the defence issue, the Japanese diplomatic position is also ambiguous. In the words of Kenichi Ito, a retired Japanese diplomat, 'In Japan, the philosophy of opportunism is dominant.'[12] In his view, one of the recent outstanding examples of 'opportunistic diplomacy' and indecisiveness was the Japanese government's attitude to the purchase of Iranian oil by Japanese multinationals in spite of the trade embargo requested by the US government. Initially, the Japanese government seemed to defend the action of Japanese petroleum companies. The then Foreign Minister, Saburo Okita, on 12 December 1979 made a statement in Tokyo arguing that 'the American people do not fully understand the "specificities" of the Japanese economy, which heavily depends on overseas energy sources'.[13] He further hoped that 'the U.S. will better understand Japanese petroleum firms had no choice but to use boycotted Iranian oil to make up for a sharp decrease in supplies by American major oil companies to them'.[14] Similarly, a senior MITI official defended the oil purchase by the Japanese companies by saying that 'spot crude purchases cannot be helped to some extent at a time when international oil companies are increasingly cutting supplies to this country'.[15]

In the meantime public criticism of Japan was mounting in the USA. Several newspapers carried headlines suggesting that Japan was obstructing US efforts to secure the release of the hostages in Iran. On 11 December 1979 a draft resolution was presented to the US Senate signed by thirteen members, asking the Japanese government to take 'resolute measures so that Japanese enterprises will not resort to such actions in future'.[16] The following day speaker O'Neill attacked Japan in the following words:

> We would like to 'teach' Japan [the faith among allies] in the field of trade. Despite the fact that there was the 'ignominious day' [meaning Japan's surprise attack against Pearl Harbor], did not the US kindly and magnanimously help Japan to become an economic big power? Despite this fact, it is now taking actions which obstruct US efforts for securing of the release of the hostages. In this kind of situation [like the Iranian crisis], one either becomes an ally or becomes an enemy.[17]

On the same day a bill to impose a penalty tariff of 50 per cent on imports from countries not co-operating with the USA in the Iranian boycott was submitted to the House of Representatives. In the face of growing US criticism and an increasing trade retaliation, the Japanese government panicked, and on 14 December MITI's Councillor Naohiro Amaya, in a formal press conference, conceded that 'It is regrettable that some Japanese enterprises hastily purchased large amounts of Iranian oil, at high prices, disregarding the guideline on spot oil transactions established by the Japanese government'[18] and confirmed that 'it is our policy to give strict guidance in the future so that Japanese enterprises will act in an orderly manner in the future, and that they will not repeat actions which may hamper the settlement of the hostage problem'.[19] This was a complete reversal of the original official stand within a week.

Another important recent issue on which the Japanese government reversed its stand was the question of the fate of the South Korean dissident leader Kim Dae Jung, who was sentenced to death allegedly for crimes against the state. On 10 September 1980 the Japanese Foreign Minister Masayoshi Ito expressed his concern on the trial and said that 'its outcome could damage Tokyo-Seoul relations badly'.[20] Chief Cabinet Secretary Kiichi Miyazawa voiced similar concern in a meeting with reporters but added that 'Japan should be careful not to make statements that could be interpreted by the South Korean government as Japanese interference in the proceedings of a South Korean court.'[21] Prime Minister Suzuki reiterated in his first policy speech on 3 October 1980 that the government will continue to express its 'concern' about Kim's fate.[22]

In November the Prime Minister told the South Korean ambassador that 'Tokyo would find it difficult to maintain cooperative relations with Seoul if Kim Dae Jung was executed.'[23] He also threatened that in the event of the execution taking place 'the call among the Japanese for expanded ties with Pyonyang would gather momentum'.[24] Naturally this brought a wave of protest in South Korea. The South Korean Defense and Diplomatic Affairs Committee of the Legislative Council 'expressed anger at Japan's arrogance which they took as "naked blackmail" designed to intervene in the domestic affairs of Korea'.[25] In response to such criticisms Prime Minister Suzuki conceded that 'he would for the time being refrain from speaking on the fate of South Korean dissident leader Kim Dae Jung under sentence of death in Seoul'.[26] However, the government maintained 'that the South Korean news reports were misleading and considerably distorted'.[27] Such ambiguities, contradictions and reversals have led to the Japanese people nicknaming Japanese diplomacy as a 'hit-or-miss diplomacy'. In a nationwide public opinion survey held by *Yomiuri Shimbun* in February 1980 56 per cent of respondents called Japanese diplomacy a 'hit-or-miss diplomacy'.[28]

Nevertheless, broad outlines of Japanese security and diplomatic postures are emerging. Several official and private study groups have considered the Japanese options for the 1980s and recommended appropriate action. Such recommendations have not so far been accepted by the government but the composition of these groups is such that these groups will have a significant effect on official thinking. Among them some of the following are the most important:

1 The Report on Comprehensive Security prepared by the Comprehensive National Security Study Group created by the then Prime Minister Masayoshi Ohira in April 1979. The group was headed by Masamichi Inoki, the President of the Research Institute For Peace and Security. It submitted its report on 2 July 1980.
2 The Report of the External Economic Policy Research Group under the chairmanship of Professor Tadao Uchida. This group was considered to be Prime Minister Ohira's 'think tank' on external economic problems. The Report was submitted to the Prime Minister on 21 April 1980.
3 The Report on Security Policy for the 1980s prepared by the Foreign Ministry's Security Measures Planning Committee under the chairmanship of Administrative Vice Minister Takashima. The Report was announced officially on 27 July 1980.

Among the other reports we must mention the Nomura Research Institute's report entitled 'Changes in the International Environment and Japan's Responses — Advice for the 21st Century'; the JSP's draft report on the 'Prospects For a Non-Aligned and Neutral Japan and the Ensuring of Peace in the Multi-Polarization Age'; and the report on 'Strengthening of the Nation's Security and Defense Power', prepared jointly by the LDP's Security Research Council and the National Defense Committee.

With the exception of the JSP Report, all the others support the idea of strengthening the defence capability and reinforcing the Japan-US security arrangement. However, there is a clear recognition of the fact that security in its narrow sense, i.e. military capability to defend Japan's sovereignty by itself, will not be enough in coming years. Economic security, i.e. uninterrupted access to the sources of raw materials, fuel and food, has to be a major component of a 'Comprehensive Security Policy'.

The common theme of the above reports is that 'We are living in an age when 'Pax Americana" is nearing an end without any substitute order taking its place . . . When an order is shaken, danger is great. Unlike the past, when we could rely on the sound functioning of the system, the present calls on us to work for the system's maintenance and to make self-reliant efforts to compensate for imperfections in the system.'[29] It is stressed that in the changed situation when the military as well as the economic power of the USA has suffered a relative decline 'the days are gone when Japan could count on a system maintained single-handedly by the United States, be it in terms of military security, politics and diplomacy, or the economy. Japan must now contribute to the maintenance and management of the system as an influential member of the free world. There has been a shift from a world of "Pax Americana" to a world of "peace maintained by shared responsibilities".'[30]

According to the Report on Comprehensive National Security, comprehensive national security ought to consist of efforts at three levels both for security in the narrow sense and for economic security:

Security Policy in a Narrow Sense[31]

  (i) First-level efforts: creation of a more peaceful international order.
     International co-operation
     Co-operation with countries that may become enemies, i.e.
     arms control and confidence-building measures.
  (ii) Second-level efforts: intermediary measures
     An alliance or co-operation with countries sharing common political

       ideals and interests.
(iii) Third-level efforts: Self-reliant efforts
       Consolidation of denial capability; i.e. capability to prevent the easy
       establishment of a *fait accompli*.

Economic Security Policy

  (i) First-level efforts: management and maintenance of the inter-
               dependent order
       Maintenance of the free-trade system
       Resolution of the North-South problem
 (ii) Second-level efforts: intermediary measures
       Promotion of friendly relations with a number of nations that are
       important to a nation's economy.
(iii) Third-level efforts: Self-reliant efforts
       Stockpiling
       A certain degree of self-sufficiency
       Basically, the maintenance of the nation's economic strength, i.e.
       maintaining productivity and competitive export power.

This long list of policy measures clearly indicates that economic
considerations – the need for markets, for raw materials and fuel and
for food – will play a significant role in determining the future foreign
policy of Japan. Attempts at promoting economic co-operation,
particularly with the oil-producing countries and the resource-rich
Third World countries, is likely to be intensified. It is argued that

> Japan has completed its modernization in less than one hundred
> years in a context that is completely different from Europe
> culturally and ethnically. This is a source of great encouragement
> for developing nations and also is the reason for their aspiration
> to learn especially from Japan's experience. Many countries are
> hopeful of assistance from Japan also because it is a reliable economic
> power that can be counted on to be free of political ambitions. It can
> even be said that Japan's world historic mission is to play a leading
> role in creating an order between the North and the South.[32]

However, the Comprehensive National Security Study Group assigned
a prominent role to military means. It argued that 'Military capability is
a major factor governing the foreign policy of each country.'[33] While
conceding that 'it is hardly possible to protect economic security by
direct use of military force, such as by occupying oil fields, but this
possibility cannot be totally discounted, and military measures must be

taken into consideration'.[34] Thus the 'Weaknesses in the field of economic resources are offset with strengths in the field of military resources.'[35] The group firmly believed that Japan ought to make 'self-reliant efforts in defense'.[36] On this issue of strengthening military capability, the Foreign Ministry report (mentioned above) holds similar views. It argued that it was 'necessary for Japan, as well as the NATO countries, to seek to strengthen the defense capabilities from the broad global perspective, and such an effort will lead to ensuring Japan's own security'.[37] The LDP's Security Research Council stressed that Japan, 'which has become an economic big power, to contribute to world peace and fulfil its role in the easing of tension in the arena of international politics in a positive way *as a truly independent nation*, it is important to foster the spirit of patriotism to defend one's own country by oneself, and to consolidate the domestic structure of self-defense' (italics mine).[38] Here the LDP's Security Research Council identified true independence with strengthening of defence. However, the External Economic Policy Research Group categorically suggested that 'rather than to raise ratio of military expenditures to the GNP to more than at present, greater efforts should be made to make contributions through peaceful means, such as the increasing of assistance, technological cooperation and the opening of the market'.[39] It also recommended that Japan 'In co-operation with the U.S. and the European nations' must contribute 'in a positive way, to the international economic structure [which will include the Third World and the Socialist bloc], centering on the principles of freedom and reciprocity and it must share the costs necessary for this'. It warned that in carrying out international co-operation 'direct military co-operation, such as the raising of the ratio of military expenditure to the GNP to a level higher than at present, should not be hastily expanded', and Japan ought to make more 'positive contributions than other nations in the field of co-operation other than in military field, such as in the economic, diplomatic, cultural, scientific and technological fields'.[40] The JSP's Report on the 'Prospects for a Non-aligned and Neutral Japan' was highly critical of the Japanese Government and the LDP policy line of 'the large-scale strengthening and the increasing of the war-response structure of the SDF . . . is clearly intended as a response to the present state of the nuclear armaments expansion race between the US and the Soviet Union. However, it will only have the effect of making today's international crises more serious.' According to this report the 'strengthening of the "non-aligned and neutral" forces, which are critical towards both the US and the Soviet Union, will become the decisive force for blocking of the nuclear armament expansion race'.[41]

Even a cursory look at this debate shows that there is almost unanimity among the experts on the role of economic forces in the comprehensive security of Japan. By and large, they seem to agree on the need for 'peaceful' diplomacy through economic and cultural co-operation with the Third World countries to enable Japan to obtain raw materials and fuel which she so badly needs. But the views on the future military and political role of Japan varies considerably, ranging from an independent nuclear deterrent (the Shimizu line) on the one extreme to unarmed neutrality (the Morishima line)[42] on the other. At least, at present and possibly for the foreseeable future (perhaps another ten years), both the Shimizu and Morishima lines are not likely to be generally accepted by Japan. It is possible, however, that Japan may possess nuclear weapons within a decade. Therefore given the Japanese glorification of the 'Samurai' traditions and her 'congenital big-power orientation' the Shimizu line may be a more realistic representation of Japan in the coming decades. The Morishima line may be too idealistic to be true.

Under the circumstances, the real option for Japan in the 1980s is a choice between three alternatives:

(1) Continuing with the present Japan-US security arrangement and moderately enhancing military capability;
(2) Developing an independent defence capability;
(3) Non-alignment with moderate military capability.

Each of these options has some merits and demerits. It must be remembered that perceptions of these merits or demerits largely depend on the judgement of the analyst and therefore are highly subjective. There would not be a unanimity of views even within a country.

Japan-US Alliance

Undoubtedly, Japan's military alliance with the USA has brought significant economic gains. As mentioned earlier, the USA not only provided huge economic and military aid but also, at least initially, allowed almost unlimited access for Japanese goods into US domestic markets. Wartime procurement by the US forces resulting from the Korean and Vietnam wars also brought considerable economic advantages to Japan. However, the economic contribution of the alliance can easily be exaggerated. Unless the USA became a

completely closed market, Japanese products would have some access
to their market anyway. It was at best a matter of time. As seen earlier,
some of the major European powers and their colonies refused to grant
most-favoured-nation treatment to Japan in 1955, but gradually the
situation became normal, and Japan developed reasonable trading
relations with these countries. Besides, the Japan-US alliance did not
prevent the USA from forcing 'voluntary' restraints on Japan as early
as 1957. Account has to be taken of the fact that, as a direct result of
the alliance, Japan had to delay normalisation of her trade relations
with the PRC. The alliance also stood in the way of Japan's
developing closer trade relations with the USSR and the Eastern
European countries. Besides, Japan had to suffer more direct losses
to trade in recent years because of US insistence on a trade embargo
on the USSR after her invasion of Afghanistan, and on Iran in the wake
of the hostage crisis. Allowance has also to be made for the financial
sacrifice that Japan is making by not charging for the use of Japanese
soil for US bases. In fact, she pays a significant part of the cost of
stationing US troops in Japan.

Whether the security arrangement between the two countries has
really provided safeguards against Soviet invasion is a debatable issue.
It would have deterred the USSR if she had aggressive intentions. There
is no obvious reason why the USSR would be interested in taking over a
resource-poor densely populated country, except perhaps for bases for
an attack on the PRC. The industrial capacity, if left intact, could be
a prize but the industries could be made to work only if uninterrupted
foreign supplies of raw materials and food continued to flow in. In the
event of a large-scale invasion of Japan by the USSR supplies of raw
materials and food from outside the Communist world would be
stopped, making it untenable to run the industries and even to feed the
people, particularly if the Japanese population did not co-operate
with the occupying forces. Under the circumstances, to see in the USSR
an inevitable or a potential threat is being a victim of European and
US prejudices. As already mentioned, some Japanese as well as US
experts feel that much of the Soviet military presence in the Far East
is 'defensive'.

Some argue that the Russians have always been on the receiving
end of foreign interference, even before the 1917 Revolution, which has
given them a 'persecution complex'. The Russian 'perception of being
encircled increased as a result of the following series of events: the
interference by Western powers immediately after the 1917 revolution,
their delay in officially recognizing the Soviet government (well into
the 1920's, the encirclement of the 1930's) . . ., Hitler's invasion in

the '40s, the containment policy of the West immediately after World War II, the disgrace of Cuba in the '60's and the formation of an encirclement network by the U.S., NATO, Japan and China since the early '70s'.[43] If one accepts that the USSR's military build-up is mainly defensive and is in response to her encirclement then it can be easily argued that the Japan-US security arrangement was not all that important for Japan.

Some Japanese emphatically deny that 'Japan has taken a free ride on the United States for its own military security'.[44] 'On the contrary', they argue that 'by entering into the Japan-U.S. security arrangements, Japan has undertaken a role in the American world strategy, contributing to U.S. objectives in the Far East. This is a free ride for America, not Japan.'[45] Whether one accepts this analysis or not, the fact remains that by continuing to remain a willing partner to the US alliance (or the Western alliance) Japan is more prone to a Soviet invasion or a pre-emptive nuclear strike. The growing realisation that the USA will not risk a nuclear war with the USSR to defend her allies has certainly reduced the usefulness of the Japan-US security arrangement.

The Japanese alliance with the USA has meant that Japan has foregone the right to be critical of the USA even on moral grounds. For instance, while Japanese criticism of the USSR on her invasions of Poland, Hungary, Czechoslovakia and, more recently, Afghanistan has been vocal, criticism of US action in Vietnam, or, for that matter, her covert or overt interference in Latin American countries, is at best muted. Admittedly, there is much more freedom and openess in the USA and other Western European countries, and no-one who believes in freedom of thought and belief would support the 'totalitarian' methods widely practised in the Communist countries. However, one has to remember that in their self-interest, the Western democracies have consistently supported undemocratic and repressive regimes all over the world. Japan, for fear of offending the major partner in the alliance, has always condoned such actions.

On the other hand, the USA — the major partner, at least in recent years — has not felt the need to consult her allies. They are simply told what the USA has decided and are expected to fall into line. One of the US decisions which affected not only the Western alliance but the entire world was the unilateral new economic policy announced by President Nixon on 15 August 1971, which suspended the convertibility of the dollar into gold or other reserve assets and imposed a temporary import surcharge of 10 per cent.[46] Another decision — which the Japanese regarded as a betrayal — was Kissinger's trip to the

PRC in 1971 without Tokyo's knowledge.[47] This was in spite of the fact that 'For two decades Japanese leaders had shaped their China policy to conform to Washington's.'[48] Similar examples of unilateral decisions by the Carter Administration can also be mentioned. Within a few months of his inauguration, President Carter announced the withdrawal of US groundforces from South Korea without consulting her allies.[49] More recently, the boycott of the Moscow Olympics in 1980 and economic sanctions against Iran were forced on the US allies against their will. Commenting on the Nixon Administration, George Ball, who served as Under-Secretary of State under Presidents Kennedy and Johnson, suggests that the recent US foreign policy has used the 'established alliance relationships primarily to increase United States leverage'.[50] He stresses that:

> The concept underlying such a strategy was Ptolemaic, pre-Copernican; it perceived the United States as the center of the cosmos with other nations in orbit around it. Rejecting the fiction of equality that would require to factor the views of our allies into common decisions, we would expect our allies to follow our lead without grumbling while we measured their value to us by the degree to which the uncritically supported our actions. We would try, in the terms of an historical parallel, to convert the Delian League into the Athenian Empire.[51]

This tradition of non consulting allies is not a particularly new one. One of the most blatant cases of such a disregard was the abrupt cancellation of the US Lend-Lease arrangement with the UK on 21 August 1945, which threw the British government into a panic. President Truman 'directed the Foreign Economic Administrator to take steps immediately to discontinue all Lend-Lease operations and to notify foreign governments receiving Lend-Lease of this action'.[52] The British government was neither consulted nor was it given prior notice.[53] When Prime Minister Attlee complained that the abrupt American decision had put Britain 'in a very serious financial position', a figure associated with the Truman Administration called this a 'cry-baby act'.[54] The Lend-Lease arrangement with the USSR had already been terminated in May 1945 as abruptly as that with the British.[55] It is important to note that the British, the closest of the US allies, were treated not much better than the potential enemy (the USSR). Nor did the alliance prevent John Foster Dulles from repudiating British and French efforts to seize the Suez Canal in 1956[56] — a US attempt to eliminate or at least minimise British influence in the Middle East.

In view of these examples it seems highly unlikely that the USA will in future consult Japan, or for that matter other allies, on equal terms. The Japanese leadership does not question the US leadership of the alliance but it does wish to be consulted on major issues. This is clear in the following statement of Kiichi Miyazawa, Foreign Minister in the Ohira Administration:

> No one objects to the US being the leader. Thus, that the US will take the leadership has been more or less agreed to. However, because we are now in a different age from the age of *Pax Americana*, concerning the problem of what joint policy we should decide on, we cannot take any policy simply because the US has decided on it, but rather we cannot help take joint work. Although the US understands this logically, the nation tends to avoid such hassles.[57]

Such views are shared by others. For instance, Yasuo Takeyama, the Managing Director of the editorials of *Nihon Keizai Shimbun*, expressed similar sentiments:

> The evaluation of detente with Soviets differs between the U.S. and Western Europe, which most directly benefits from detente. But if Europe pursues an independent foreign policy, it should be within the common framework to safeguard democratic values. The U.S. in return should accept the reality that a relationship between autonomous allies is healthier and more productive than one based on fading U.S. hegemony . . .
>
> Japan, though not accepted yet as a full-fledged member of the alliance, should be consulted in depth when the strategy and foreign policy of the alliance are formulated.[58]

Successive US administrations have promised closer co-operation in policy formulation but it has so far remained an unattained goal. Itaru Yano, a professor at Kyoto University, argues that the USA (as well as the USSR) is a 'nation of psychology',[59] and suggests, at least by implication, that decisions in the USA are taken in haste and rather in an impulsive manner, and therefore right decisions cannot easily be taken.[60] The USA is a complex society with varying social and political traditions and it is difficult to generalise about her but the US view of the world and of her role in the world is a rather simplistic one. This is exemplified in Kissinger's statement that Americans greatly

admire anyone who is 'acting alone'. 'Americans admire the cowboy
leading the caravan [sic] alone astride his horse, the cowboy entering
a village or city alone on his horse, without even a pistol, maybe
because he doesn't go in for shooting. He acts, that's all; aiming at the
right spot at the right time.'[61]

Kissinger's view that the lonely cowboy symbolises American
society has been probably rightly ruled out as a fantasy inspired by
'spaghetti Westerns' by George Ball. However, even serious thinkers
have commented on the rather simplistic view of the world that the
US leadership has. Arnold Toynbee, a leading British historian, writing
in 1965 comments:

> For the past twenty years the government and people of the United
> States have been acting on the belief that communism is on the
> march for the conquest of the world and that it is the manifest
> destiny of the United States to save the world from suffering this
> fate . . . Americans have believed that America has practically the
> whole human race on her side in her anti-Communist stand . . . This
> picture is not founded on facts.
> . . . The revolt of the 'native' majority of mankind against the
> domination of the Western minority — this, and not the defense
> of freedom against communism by the leading Western country,
> the United States, is the real major issue in the world today . . .
> Is the United States St. George fighting against the dragon? Or is
> the [sic] Goliath fighting David? The question is important, because
> St. George is a winner but Goliath is not. The [US] President manifestly
> believes that he is speaking with Churchill's voice — the Churchill of
> 1940 — but to the ears of people who have suffered Western
> domination in the past, his voice sounds like the Kaiser's and
> Hitler's.
> . . . The American picture of aggressive ecumenical communism
> is a mirage, but the reality which America is up against today is
> something much more formidable. She is up against the determination of
> the non-Western majority of mankind to complete its self-liberation
> from Western domination.[62]

This rather simplistic view of the world of two camps, the 'free world
and the communist world' has often led the US leadership to take
decisions which have been detrimental to their own as well as to the
world's interests. One of the outstanding examples of this was the US
decision to back Chiang Kai-shek rather than Mao Tse-tung in 1944.
As Barbara Tuchman suggests, 'Their [the Chinese Communists under

Mao] future alignment in international affairs was not, in 1944,
necessarily fixed. What course Chinese communism might have taken if
an American connection had been brought to bear is a question that
lost opportunities have made forever unanswerable. The only certainty
is that it could not have been worse.'[63] Similarly, if the US
Administration had not abruptly cancelled the Lend-Lease arrangement
with the USSR in 1945 and had assisted Russian economic reconstruction
as she helped not only her allies but also her former enemies (West
Germany, Italy and Japan) the world in all probability may have been
a safer place today.

It seems, therefore, that an unquestioned acceptance of US policy
decisions by her allies may not be always desirable, particularly when
the interests of the other countries in the alliance are not the same,
and when the consequences of a policy blunder fall more heavily on her
allies rather than on the USA.

The debate in Japan over the boycott of the Moscow Olympics and
more so of the Iranian crisis clearly highlighted the Japanese dilemma.
While the Japanese still continue to be loyal — a reflection of the
'group consciousness' of the Japanese — they distinctly perceive that the
USA does not fulfil the obligations of a leader of the group to consult
before reaching a policy decision. This is very much against the Japanese
ethic of 'consensus decision-making'. The Japanese leadership has
conceded wholly or partially on all major issues — car imports, NTT,
agricultural imports, banking restrictions — involving potential trade
conflict with the USA; it agreed to increase defence expenditure and
to undertake a qualitative improvement of the SDF, and it also
supported, though reluctantly, the boycott of the Moscow Olympics
and the economic sanctions against Iran. Japan values the alliance, or
at least the US market, so much that she officially apologised to the
American people for sanction-breaking on Iranian oil by Japanese
companies, knowing full well that such sanction-breaking is commonly
practised by US and European multinationals.

In return she is blamed for lack of faith[64] and receives ever-
increasing pressure for further concessions, so much so that Kiichi
Saeki, the Director of the Nomura Institute, calls Japan-US relations
'a one-sided love-affair on the part of Japan'.[65] This has led to some
disenchantment in Japan with the USA. Even moderates like
Saburo Okita, the then Foreign Minister in the Ohira cabinet, conceded
that even though Japan-US co-operation is the basis of foreign policy
of Japan in the 1980s 'cases where Japan thinks on its own and acts
by itself will increase'.[66] On the other hand, there are 'hawks' who
advocate that 'ultimately, Japan should aim for an autonomous

defense of the Western Pacific'.[67] They also argue that 'In order to
counter the possibility of Soviet nuclear blackmail, Japan must possess
strategic nuclear weapons of the order of the French *force de frappe* . . .
Nuclear arms cannot be avoided if we are to pursue the goal of an
autonomous defense posture. We may acquire the full panoply of
conventional weapons and employ them with combatworthy armies,
but without strategic nuclear capability we will be dependent on the
United States just the same. Nuclear armament is the logical capstone
of autonomy and self-reliance in defense in today's world.'[68]

The Independent Nuclear Deterrent

Possessing an independent nuclear deterrent will certainly fulfil Japan's
most cherished ambition of being considered a superpower in its own
right. It may also provide Japan with the freedom to take an
independent line in international disputes. It is also possible that she
would have much greater leverage over the USSR in the settlement of
mutual disputes. However, this would require a considerably large nuclear
arsenal at the disposal of Japan. She certainly has the technical and
industrial capacity to produce this but the economic cost would be
considerable. Estimates differ, but anything between $124 to 162
billion was spent on defence in 1979 by the USSR; in 1980 the
USA spent nearly $142.7 billion dollars. To possess any meaningful
deterrent Japan will have to match Soviet expenditure on defence
and not be content with the scale of the French nuclear capability,
which is at best a symbol of defiance to US supremacy in NATO.
Besides, Japan will have to possess long- and medium-range missiles
to reach the industrial heartland of the USSR. Even if Japan spends
only half of the USSR's military budget, her defence expenditure
will have to jump from nearly $11 billion to $70 billion, or nearly
7 per cent of the Japanese GDP. This burden, if politically acceptable,
would not necessarily be excessive, given the health of the Japanese
economy. However, the resource requirement for such a major
rearmament programme would be immense. Japan already imports
more than her fair share of the world's scarce resources. For
instance, in 1978 she imported nearly 14.6 per cent of the world's
exports of oil against only 5.9 per cent for West Germany and 6.9 per
cent for France. Similarly, she imported as much as 40.5 per cent of
the total world import of iron ore against only 16.2 per cent for West
Germany, 4.4 per cent for France, 5.4 per cent for the UK and 4.6 per
cent for Italy. Thus Japan imported at least a third more iron ore

than the combined total of the four major EEC countries (Table 8.1).

Table 8.1: Major Countries' Share of Imports as a Proportion of Total World Imports, 1978 (Unit %)

	Japan	USA	France	Italy	UK	West Germany
Energy	13.7	18.9	6.8	6.0	3.6	7.4
Coal	26.9	1.5	11.3	5.5	1.1	4.1
Crude oil	14.6	18.3	6.9	6.6	4.2	5.9
Natural gas	9.3	17.5	10.4	9.5	2.3	19.5
Iron ore	40.5	14.0	4.4	4.6	5.4	16.2
Copper	23.9	11.4	6.6	7.7	8.8	15.5
Lead	5.0	18.4	3.2	10.3	20.6	10.8
Zinc	8.5	26.5	8.2	3.9	8.2	10.1
Tin	19.8	31.7	8.0	4.5	5.6	10.7
Aluminium	17.6	22.9	8.2	5.6	4.8	11.4
Nickel	9.5	28.6	7.1	4.0	14.9	12.6

Source: JETRO, *White Paper on International Trade 1980*, p.40, Table 4.2.

It is difficult to visualise many countries, particularly those which are by and large 'client' states of the USA, continuing to provide scarce resources on this scale to a militarised Japan, for it is almost certain that the USA does not wish to see Japan develop into a military superpower. There is a worry 'about the possibility that Japan, when it will have strengthened its armaments, may walk in a direction beyond the United States' control. This position prevails strongly among scholars knowledgeable of Japan who are close to the US Government.'[69] It is important to note in this connection that 'both the fuels and non-fuel mineral industries are generally dominated by companies from the United States, and to a lesser degree from Great Britain'.[70] In the event of Japan developing into a major military power against the wishes of the USA the latter may prevent US companies from selling minerals and other scarce resources, including foodgrains. Any independent nuclear deterrents which are perceived as undermining US world supremacy will certainly bring about retaliatory action and will therefore be counterproductive. A major military build-up in Japan will, as the US Arms Control and Disarmament Agency argues, in all probability be seen as a threat to the USSR and even to the PRC over the longer term. Therefore it is possible that a rapid and significant Japanese military build-up could even contribute to a Sino-

Soviet *rapprochement.*[71]

There may be some domestic opposition to such a programme of Japanese militarisation. For instance, given the present attitude of the Japanese to conscription, it is possible that mobilising the requisite number of people for the SDF may prove to be difficult. As the US Arms Control and Disarmament Agency suggests, 'In the absence of conscription, an effort to attract more recruits would obviously require the Japanese Government to incur considerable costs to make the military more competitive . . . This would certainly require much larger allocation of government revenues which could constrict other forms of government spending and add to the size of the overall military burden.'[72] There may also be difficulty in procuring enough land for airfields, military housing, depots and new production sites for the SDF.[73] The Japanese continue to be sensitive to using land for military purposes, and to placate them the government in recent years had to spend a lot of money on 'base countermeasures' (i.e. programmes for noise-prevention or subsidies for the local civilian population). These countermeasures accounted for as much as 15 per cent of the total defence budget in 1978.[74]

Thus both economic and political consequences, though not easily predictable, will most likely be unfavourable. On the other hand, such a militarisation of Japan may not provide the security she will be looking for. A close proximity to the Asian mainland itself makes it easier for the USSR to reach the heartland of Japan in a pre-emptive or a retaliatory strike. Most Soviet bombers, particularly the Backfires, can reach any part of Japan with ease. So can the medium-range ballistic missiles (MRBMs).[75] Besides, much of the population and the industrial capacity is highly concentrated in Honshu. As Hiroshi Kimura suggests, Japan is 'an unusually and frighteningly centralized country where everything important is concentrated in certain areas. Political and administrative functions are concentrated in Tokyo and the population, industrial facilities, mass media and educational institutions are centered chiefly along the Pacific Coast, stretching from the Tokyo-Yokohama area to the Osaka-Kobe area via Nagoya. If you destroy this nerve-centre belt, you can capture Hokkaido as well as Kyushu and Shikoku without much difficulty.'[76] Since no part of Japan is farther than seventy-five miles away from the sea she lacks strategic depth; in terms of military strategy she would have to rely on a forward defence involving pre-emptive strike.[77] In such cases attack is the best defence. At least for the present this line of argument is not acceptable to the majority of the Japanese people. Besides, such a strategy will incur the displeasure of most of her neighbours and possibly even her allies.

Lack of strategic depth makes effective air defence and early warning systems problematical. As Momoi suggests 'no site in Japan is distant enough to provide more than twenty-minute warning'.[78] Besides, to guard against simultaneous attack from land and sea she would 'need to have a 360-degree ballistic missile early warning system (BMEWS) . . . not even the United States is capable of installing such a system'.[79] It can, in fact, be argued that a major military build-up in Japan will increase her vulnerability — both in terms of military as well as economic security — rather than ensure her security, particularly against the Soviet threat.

But will the nuclear deterrent enhance her capacity to influence power politics on the world arena? There are sceptics on this question as well. Masanori Sase argues that 'it is illusory to think that becoming a military nation will make Japan's diplomatic efforts to acquire natural resources "much simpler". Several nations are militarily more powerful than Japan, yet diplomatically they have just as much difficulty in acquiring resources as does Japan . . . If Japan were to carry a bigger sword, its diplomatic efforts could well change to some extent. But unless we are prepared to blow ourselves to bits our efforts to obtain natural resources will not change much. We must not entertain illusions about power politics.'[80]

Thus even if Japan became a military superpower — which is highly unlikely in view of her high dependence on imported food, fuel and strategic minerals — her diplomatic leverage with other major powers may improve marginally, but the price of this marginal gain will be high in terms of an increased vulnerability to a pre-emptive nuclear strike.

Non-alignment

Given Japan's lack of resources as well as her strategic vulnerability, the most viable option for the country is to become a non-aligned nation. Because of its adherence to a 'Peace Constitution' she has a unique position in the world. She has shown that a determined nation can regain self-respect and influence even without military power. This is where her 'comparative advantage lies'. Jiro Kamishima rightly argues that Japan should not act like the military superpowers or follow obediently in their footsteps. 'Instead Japan must make full use of the original political assets it has itself built up over the years, as a result of her peace-orientation.'[81]

There are obvious disadvantages to a policy of non-alignment. Its immediate implication would be to abrogate the Japan-US security arrangement and to ask the USA to withdraw her forces from Japan.

This would certainly incur the wrath of the USA, particularly as the Reagan Administration is currently seeking a closer military alliance with and a significant increase in military budgets by the US allies. It is almost certain that initially it would be seen as a betrayal by an 'ungrateful' ally, and demands for trade retaliation would be made. Since effective action on this front will be constrained because of GATT regulations, the real damage to trade may not be substantial. The USSR and Eastern European countries are an expanding market for high-technology products, and a non-aligned Japan will have greater freedom to trade with these countries. Therefore if there is any decline in Japan's trade with the USA, at least some of it will be compensated for by an increase in demand from the Communist bloc. Japan may also be able to meet some of her resource needs from Soviet sources, particularly from Siberia. The USSR has become 'the world's largest producer of oil, gas, iron ore and steel, lead, cadmium, mercury, silver and manganese, and the second largest producer of aluminium, copper, zinc, magnesium and gold'.[82] Besides, Siberia, 'the largest untapped mineral reserves in the world',[83] remains unexplored and undeveloped. A Japanese detente with the USSR would not be particularly welcome to the PRC, but a clear declaration of non-alignment will, at least partially, pacify them.

On the political and military front a withdrawal of US forces from Japan may conceivably result in an increased risk of Soviet adventurism. On the other hand, since a non-aligned Japan would not be a threat to the USSR, the risk of a Soviet military threat to Japan may be reduced. In the wake of the Soviet invasion of Afghanistan it is difficult to be optimistic, but it is probable that the *real* cost of the Afghanistan invasion — in terms of hardware and personnel, as well as the world's displeasure, particularly that of the Third World — will in the future deter the USSR from adventurism. Since the USSR needs advanced technology to keep up with the West in the technological and armaments race and for the economic development of Siberia, she may even attempt to placate a non-aligned Japan by handing over the four northern islands. 'In fact, there are few Soviet foreign policy experts who argue the four islands off Hokkaido are essential for Soviet security. The Soviets may regard them as negotiable in future.'[84]

Politically, non-alignment will in all probability be an asset for Japan. Three major issues which alienate the West from other nations, particularly the Third World, are the West's attitude towards the Soviet bloc, the Islamic countries (especially the Arab World) and the South African regime. On all these three issues, European and US attitudes are the product not so much of rational political and economic calculations but of the continuation of old prejudices. Fisher, a leading British historian, commenting on the European attitude towards Russia in the mid-nineteenth century wrote:

> The vast size of the Russian Empire, the scale of its armaments, its slow but apparently irresistible expansion over the Asian plateau, its reputed designs on Constantinople, created more particularly in England with her Oriental interests, a vague but persistent feeling of alarm, which was combined with a vehement aversion from the whole political system of which Russia was the principal prop and pillar in Europe. To the contemporaries of Palmerston and Thackeray no feelings of admiration or regard mitigated the sinister impression aroused by the name of Russia.[85]

This traditional fear of and aversion to Russia were increased after the Russian Revolution of 1917, when the experiments in Communism threatened the very existence of capitalism.

> One of the first acts of the Bolshevik revolution was to nationalize the country's minerals and fuel industries. This was the first time that foreign companies were fundamentally challenged by the people of an exploited nation, and their reaction was swift, uncompromising, and violent. Backed by their home governments, who feared the spread of this menacing example, they sought to destroy the new Soviet government, and to regain control of the nationalized industries . . . The United States, Britain and France, along with the 'White Russian' army, invaded the Soviet Union in an attempt to bring down the government. Although defeated, they succeeded in flooding the mines and burning the smelters and processing plants, leaving the entire mineral industry in ruins. They also instituted a trade, credit and supplies blockade.[86]

Another complicating factor has been the attitude of US immigrants from the Communist countries. Many of them — or their parents and grand-parents — suffered great persecution both by the Czarist and the succeeding regimes and the hate harboured by these oppressed people has been passed on to successive generations. A combination of all these factors has meant that the West is incapable of taking an objective stand in their relationship with the USSR. Similarly, the attitude of the West suffers from a traditional lack of objectivity in its relationship to Islam. As Godfrey Jansen, the Levant correspondent of *The Economist*, wrote recently:

Today Islam and the modern Western world confront and challenge each other. No other major religion poses such a challenge to the West... This is so because Islam has confronted the West militarily, off and on, for 1,500 years, and the present is an 'on' period. The political contest has been continuous for the past 180 years, at least; spiritually the two systems have challenged each other for about a century, and economically for the past 20 years.[87]

He suggests that in addition to political and economic rivalry there is 'a mutual repulsion at a deep spiritual and philosophical level between Islam and Western society'[88], and that the prospects for mutual understanding and accommodation are not very bright, at least in the foreseeable future.

The relationship between the West and the Islamic countries, especially the Arab countries, is further complicated by the Western sense of guilt with regard to the 'holocaust'. This sense of guilt forces them to make more concessions to the state of Israel, often to the detriment of Arab interests. The economic leverage of the Jewish communities in the West, particularly in the USA, is a further reason for biases in the Western attitude against the Arabs. There has been some change in the attitude of the West European nations towards the Arabs because of the increasing threat of their use of the oil weapon if the Arab-Israeli dispute had lingered on. This pro-Arab stance has been criticised by the US Administration, which does not like its allies to take an independent stand on the issue. Instead of allowing peaceful diplomacy, the US administration is forcing her European allies to co-operate in the Rapid Deployment Force (RDF), which is supposedly being stationed in the Persian Gulf area to protect Arab allies such as Saudi Arabia from Soviet adventurism. However 'there is a broad impression throughout the Gulf area that the Rapid Deployment Force cannot protect Saudi Arabia; there is an equally strong impression that the U.S. might use it to seize control of the Saudi oil fields. The feeling is that the RDF, combined with the U.S. advisory team in Saudi Arabia, is more than adequate to make a quick grab for the oil facilities in the Northeast provinces and the U.S. might well do this in the event of another oil embargo.'[89]

The Western attitude is rather ambivalent on the South African policy of apartheid. Most Western democratic governments proclaim their distaste for apartheid but do not like to put economic, political or moral pressure on the white minority government of South Africa. They also continue to have trading and other economic relations as well as sporting and cultural links with South Africa. The governments,

particularly of the USA, the UK and France, have often voted against
or abstained on UN resolutions condemning South Africa or calling
for economic sanctions, in spite of the fact that South Africa has
undermined a joint European-US effort to defuse the Namibia crisis.
It is strange that the same governments which have in the past vetoed
the idea of economic sanctions against South Africa or of discontinuing
sporting and cultural links did not hesitate to impose such sanctions
against Iran and the USSR. This inconsistency has often hurt Third
World, especially African, feelings and has certainly alienated the Third
World from the West. It is almost certain that this inconsistency on the
part of the West has pushed many developing countries into the
Soviet fold.

On all three issues — the USSR, Islam and South Africa — Japan is
fortunate not to have past legacies. It is possible for her to play a more
objective role than the West, which is a victim of its past. A non-aligned
Japan could conceivably be a powerful instrument to defuse these
issues: in so doing it would not only be helping the Third World but
also the West. The US demands for compliance with policies unilaterally
decided by the USA not only annoys her allies but also puts them into
situations where they cannot provide effective mediation, even if they
so desire. This was clearly demonstrated in the Iranian hostage crisis.
Japan wished to mediate but, because of Japan's need to conform to US
sanctions, she was not trusted by the Iranian leadership. Ultimately, it
was mainly Algeria, a non-aligned nation, which succeeded in settling
the issue. This aspect is clearly recognised by some Japanese scholars.
Jiro Kamishima argues that 'the United States and the Soviet Union
lack an adequate perceptual framework for viewing the future evolution
of the world. Though they desperately need alternative policies, they
are finding it difficult to come up with such policies by themselves.
This is why Japan's cooperation is essential, and it is also why Japan
must not give its agreement to the American call for a powerful
Japanese military.'[90]

Non-alignment does not necessarily mean unarmed neutrality.
Switzerland is a case in point; in spite of its neutrality it has a reasonable
defence capability, though it is nothing like adequate against an enemy
as powerful as the USSR. If such a limited defence capability gives a
degree of confidence to the Japanese people it ought to be maintained.
But this should not rule out the possibility of alternative arrangements,
such as a UN force. The effectiveness of the UN in solving political
problems has often been questioned. But what Fisher said of the League
of Nations — that it 'can be no better than the member states of which
it is composed'[91] — is also true of the UN. Unfortunately, even the

founder-nations have often undermined the UN's authority. The other major problem is that the UN voting power is so constituted that not only the Third World but also the developed countries such as Japan often find it frustrating to operate within the system. This is another major field in which a non-aligned Japan can make a real contribution. She can, in co-operation with West Germany, Canada, Australia, the Scandinavian countries as well as the Third World, reopen the issue of UN voting rights so that that organisation becomes much more democratic. A formula that does not ignore financial contributions but at the same time does not put excessive weight on it, while ignoring all other criteria such as population, regional representation, etc., could be found to make the participation of nations more meaningful. Some kind of weighted voting to appease the superpowers, though in principle undesirable, could still be defensible, but the rights of veto given to medium-sized powers such as Britain and France while Japan, West Germany or Canada enjoy no such privileges are simply anachronistic. A non-aligned Japan involved in such an active diplomacy in the UN to make that organisation more effective will not be Amaya's 'Tradesman Country', distributing money or indulging in the art of flattery with a view to prospering.[92] She would be fighting for the cause of world peace, which she has adhered to for three decades, and in which the majority of Japanese people still believe. It is by pursuing this positive role of enhancing the prospects of world peace that Japan may be able to attain the objective of becoming the 'number one' of the twenty-first century. Japan brought disaster upon herself during World War II by emulating the former imperialist designs of the West. Those who do recommend her to tread the same path cannot be her real friends.

Summing Up

In conclusion it can be predicted with a reasonable degree of confidence that the inability of the West to introduce rapid structural changes in their respective economies will inhibit their rates of growth and their overall economic performance, while the cohesion of Japanese society will continue to help her in attaining a reasonable rate of growth in the foreseeable future. As the gap between their economic and export performances widens, pressures on Japan from the West, particularly from the USA, for further trade concessions will continue. So would be the demands for increasing military expenditure and for sharing the cost of the defence of the 'free world' which is often viewed as a means of creating demand for military hardware produced by the US military-industrial complex as well as a device to divert Japanese efforts away from directly productive purposes to the largely unproductive field of defence.

It can also be predicted that the failure of the West, particularly the USA, to economise substantially on fuel and other mineral resources while their stocks are becoming badly depleted will result in increasing confrontations between the richer countries and the resource-rich Third World, as the latter, with a view to slowing down the depletion, takes increasing control of its assets. The West's inaction on the Arab-Israeli dispute and the covert or overt support of South Africa will increasingly inhibit North-South relations. While the resource-rich Third World countries will attempt to use their newly acquired economic power to obtain concessions from the West on such issues as South Africa or the Arab-Israeli conflict, the West would become increasingly anxious about losing its unquestioned supremacy in world affairs. This would lead them more and more to look for military options, or at least threats. In response, the Third World, though already disenchanted with the USSR, will have no other option but to look to the USSR for protection. The latter, worried about her encirclement, will take this as an excuse to continue to extend her influence overseas, which in its own turn will exacerbate West-East confrontation.

Japan will inevitably be caught in the middle. Its very dependence on foreign sources of supply of fuel and minerals will prevent her from taking sides in the North-South confrontation which the continuance of the Japan-US alliance will impose on her. Non-compliance with US policy decisions will, as in the case of the Iran hostage dispute, incur US wrath and may result in increasing import restrictions on Japanese goods in the USA and in the EEC.

Similarly, if Japan takes a more militant posture, as many of her 'hawks' advocate, in the West-East confrontation she would not only have to sacrifice her ideals of peace but she would also have to risk Soviet displeasure, and the threat to her military security would increase. Such a dilemma on various fronts is not easy to answer. So far, Japan has taken a low profile, which is reflected in her policy of 'comprehensive security' and which calls for only a modest increase in military expenditure. But if the pressure from the West for trade concessions and more active military participation continues the hawks within Japan will gain influence, particularly if increasing trade concessions lead to a significant increase in unemployment. Under such circumstances it could legitimately be argued that increased military expenditure and relaxation on the export of armaments would generate employment opportunities in Japan.

If such a situation arises it is difficult to predict what the likely outcome would be. As argued above, non-alignment may be the right answer to the Japanese dilemma, but her 'congenital big-power orientation' may inhibit such an action. The alternative, an emergence of Japan by the end of this century as a military superpower, armed with sophisticated nuclear weapons, cannot be ruled out. After all, this is what Premier Tojo, who is now enshrined in Yasukuni Shrine and is therefore 'listed among the gods',[93] had predicted just before his execution. He wrote:

Saraba nari koke no shita nite ware matan
yamato shima neni hana kaoru toki

This is farewell
I shall wait beneath the moss,
Until the flowers again are fragrant
In this island country of Japan.[94]

Notes

1. *The Japan Times Weekly*, 30 Aug. 1980, p.1.
2. Ibid.
3. *The Japan Times Weekly*, 14 Feb. 1981, p.2.
4. *The Japan Times Weekly*, 16 Aug. 1980, p.1.
5. Ibid.
6. *The Japan Times Weekly*, 1 Nov. 1980, p.1.
7. *The Japan Times Weekly*, 23 Oct. 1980, p.1.
8. Ibid.
9. *The Japan Times Weekly*, 15 Nov. 1980, p.1.
10. Ibid.
11. Ibid.
12. K. Ito, 'Age of My-Home Diplomacy Has Ended: My Empirical Theory of Japanese Diplomacy', *Asahi Journal*, 15 Feb. 1980.
13. *The Japan Times Weekly*, 15 Dec. 1979, p.1.
14. Ibid.
15. Ibid.
16. Y. Komori, 'Angry America and "Chrysanthemum and the Sword"', *Bungei Shunju*, Feb. 1980.
17. Ibid.
18. N. Amaya, 'Grumblings on a Shop-clerk of Japan, a Tradesman Country', *Bungei Shunju*, March 1980. This article was also published in an abridged form in *Japan Echo*, vol. VII, no.2, under the title 'Japan as a Mercantile Nation'.
19. Ibid.
20. *The Japan Times Weekly*, 13 Sept. 1980, p.1.
21. *The Japan Times Weekly*, 20 Sept. 1980, p.1.
22. *The Japan Times Weekly*, 11 Oct. 1980, p.2.
23. *The Japan Times Weekly*, 29 Nov. 1980, p.1.

24. Ibid.
25. Ibid.
26. Ibid.
27. Ibid.
28. *Yomiuri*, 15 March 1980.
29. The Comprehensive Nation Security Group, *Report On Comprehensive National Security* (English version) (1980), p.34.
30. Ibid., p.31.
31. Ibid., p.21.
32. Ibid., p.33.
33. Ibid., p.23.
34. Ibid.
35. Ibid.
36. Ibid., p.32.
37. Ministry of Foreign Affairs Security-Policy Planning Committee, *Outline of First Round Discussions* (mimeographed 1980), p.15.
38. *Nihon Keizai*, 6 April 1980, pp.2 and 4.
39. *Nihon Keizai*, 22 April 1980.
40. Ibid.
41. *Mainichi*, 26 July 1980.
42. This was originally the JSP line but for political exigencies has come to be modified recently (see pages 206-12).
43. H. Kimura, 'Relax – The Russians are not Coming', *The Japan Times Weekly*, 22 Nov. 1980.
44. J. Kamishima, 'The Tradition of Realism of Demilitarization', *Japan Echo*, vol. VII, no.3 (1980), p.30.
45. Ibid.
46. L.B. Krause and S. Sekiguchi, 'Japan and the World Economy' in H. Patrick and H. Rosovsky (eds.), *Asia's New Giant: How the Japanese Economy Works*, p.435.
47. A.D. Barnett, *China and the Major Powers in East Asia*, p.113.
48. Ibid.
49. F.B. Weinstein, 'Conclusions and Policy Recommendations' in F.B. Weinstein (ed.), *US-Japan Relations and the Security of East Asia*, p.270.
50. G.W. Ball, *Diplomacy For a Crowded World*, p.9.
51. Ibid.
52. *The New York Times*, 22 Aug. 1945, quoted in R.N. Gardner, *Sterling-Dollar Diplomacy*, p.184.
53. Ibid., p.185.
54. Ibid.
55. T.G. Paterson, *Soviet-American Confrontation*, p.22.
56. Ball, *Diplomacy*, p.134.
57. K. Miyazawa, in an interview with *Sankei*, 29 April 1980, p.8.
58. Y Takeyama, 'The U.S.-Japanese Partnership', *The Wall Street Journal*, 4 Sept. 1980.
59. *Sankei*, 23 April 1980.
60. Ibid. Yano quotes a passage by Eric Hoffer, the author of *The Passionate State of Mind*, suggesting that: 'The frivolousness of the American people results from the fact that they act fast, easily. One needs time in order to contemplate things. Maturing takes time, too. Persons who are in a hurry can neither think, nor grow, nor become corrupt. They stay permanently in a state of stupidity.' (*Sankei*, 23 April 1980.)
61. Ball, *Diplomacy*, p.13.
62. A. Toynbee, quoted from *Vancouver Times*, 11 May 1965 (reprinted from the *London Observer*) by D. Dellinger, *Revolutionary Nonviolence*, pp.63-4.
63. B.W. Tuchman, *Stilwell and the American Experience in China, 1911-45*

(6th printing), p.622.

64. In a public opinion poll conducted on the American views on the reliability of Japan as an ally of the USA, only 18 per cent categorically replied that Japan could be trusted. (See *Sankei*, 20 May 1980.)

65. Saeki Kiichi, in an interview with Yasuo Hariki, the chief editor of *Zaikai*, reported in *Zaikai*, 22 April 1980.

66. *Tokyo Shimbun*, 3 Jan. 1980.

67. T. Kataoka, 'The Concept of the Japanese Second Republic' *Japan Echo*, vol. VII. no. 1 (1980), p.88.

68. Ibid., p.96.

69. *Sankei*, 9 March 1980.

70. M. Tanzer, *The Race For Resources. Continuing Struggles over Minerals and Fuels*, p.22.

71. US Arms Control and Disarmament Agency, *Japan's Contribution to Military Stability in Northeast Asia*, p.61.

72. Ibid., p.56.

73. Ibid., p.58.

74. Ibid.

75. M. Momoi, 'Are there any Alternative Strategies for the Defense of Japan?' in Weinstein (ed.), *US-Japan Relations*, p.79.

76. Kimura, 'Relax – The Russians are not Coming', p.4.

77. Momoi, 'Are there any Alternative Strategies?' p.79.

78. Ibid., p.83.

79. Ibid., p.83.

80. M. Sase, 'Refuting the Mercantile Nation Theory', *Japan Echo*, vol. VII, no.2 (1980), p.67.

81. Kamishima, 'The Tradition of Realism', p.31

82. Tanzer, *The Race for Resources*, p.212.

83. Ibid., p.215.

84. J. Suzuki and M. Kawahira, 'Soviet Military Power has its Limits', *The Japan Times Weekly*, 13 Sept. 1980, p.2.

85. H.A.L. Fisher, *A History of Europe*, vol. II, p.1030.

86. Tanzer, *The Race for Resources*, p.211.

87. G. Jansen, 'Moslems and the Modern World', *The Economist*, 3 Jan. 1981, p.21.

88. Ibid., p.23.

89. A.K. Mansur, 'The American Threat to Saudi Arabia', *Survival*, (Jan./Feb. 1981), p.38.

90. Kamishima, 'The Tradition of Realism', pp.31-2.

91. Fisher, *A History of Europe*, p.1275.

92. See Amaya, 'Grumblings of a Shop Clerk'.

93. K. Tsurumi, *Social Change and the Individual*, p.125.

94. Quoted in R.J.C. Butow, *Tojo and the Coming War*, p.536.

BIBLIOGRAPHY

Abegglen, J.C. and Rapp, W.V. 'The Competitive Impact of Japanese
Growth' in Cohen, J.B. (ed.) *Pacific Partnership: United States-
Japan Trade* (1972), Japan Society, Inc., Lexington, Mass.

Ackerman, E.A. *Japanese Natural Resources* (1949), GHQ, SCAP,
Tokyo.

Ahearn, R. 'Japan-U.S. Trade Imbalance: Issue Brief No. IB 78025',
Congressional Research Service, US Library of Congress, 1979,
Washington DC.

Akimoto, H.* 'Era of Heavy Unemployment Coming', *Shukan
Yomiuri*, 1978, Tokyo.

Alexander, S. 'Europe Unites to put Skids under Nissan', *Sunday
Times Business News*, 8 Feb. 1981, London.

Aliber, R.Z. 'U.S.-Japanese Economic Relationship: Economic
Structure and Policy in the 1960's, 1970's and 1980's' in Kaplan
M.A. and Mushakoji, K. *Japan, America and Future World Order*
(1976), The Free Press, NY.

Allen, G.C. *How Japan Competes: An Assessment of International
Trading Practices with special Reference to 'Dumping'* (1978),
Hobart Papers, Institute of Economic Affairs, London.

——, *Japan's Economic Expansion* (1965), Allen and Unwin,
London.

Amaya, N.* 'Grumblings of a Shop-clerk of Japan, a Tradesman Country',
Bungei Shunju, March 1980, Tokyo.

——, 'Japan As a Mercantile Nation', *Japan Echo*, vol. VII, no. 2
(1980).

Appleyard, B. 'Understanding the Japanese Market', *The Times*,
22 Dec. 1980, London.

Arakawa, J. 'Japanese Distribution Channels are Flexible and Changing',
The Japan Economic Journal (Supplement), 11 April 1978, Tokyo.

Baldwin, R.E. 'Measuring Trade and Employment Effects of Various
Trade Policies' in Baldwin, R.E. *et al* (eds.) *Evaluating the Effects
of Trade Liberalization* (1979), Graduate Institute of International
Studies, Geneva and Trade Policy Research Centre, London, A.W.G.
Sijthoff, Leiden.

——, and Murray, T. 'MFN Tariff Reductions and LDC Benefits under
the GSP', *The Economic Journal*, vol. 87, no.345, March 1977, London.

252

Bale, M.D. and Greenshields, B.L. *Japan: Production and Imports of Food – An Analysis of the Welfare Cost of Protection*, USDA Foreign Agricultural Economic Report No. 141, 1977, Washington DC.

Ball, G. *Diplomacy for a Crowded World: An American Foreign Policy* (1976), Bodley Head, London.

Barnet, R. and Muller, R.E. *Global Reach: The Power of the Multinational Corporation* (1974), Simon and Schuster, NY.

Barnett, A.D. *China and the Major Powers in East Asia* (1977), Brookings Institution, Washington DC.

Beckmann, G.M. *The Modernization of China and Japan* (1965) Harper International, NY.

Blechman, B.M. *et al. The Soviet Military Build-up and U.S. Defense Spending* (1977), Harper & Row, NY.

Boltho, A. *Japan: An Economic Survey* (1975), Oxford University Press, London.

Bonavia, D. 'Another Turnabout in China', *Far Eastern Economic Review*, 12 Dec. 1980, Hong Kong.

British Parliamentary Report, Cmnd. 8449, 1897, HMSO, London.

Bronfenbrenner, M. 'Japan's Galbraithian Economy', *The Public Interest*, no.21 (1970), Carnegie-Mellon University, Pittsburg.

Butow, R.J.C. *Tojo and the Coming War* (1961), Stanford University Press, Stanford.

Caves, R.E. and Uekusa, M. *Industrial Organisation in Japan* (1976), Brookings Institution, Washington DC.

Cohen, J.B. (ed.) *Pacific Partnership: United States-Japan Trade* (1972), Japan Society Inc., Lexington, Mass.

Colby, W. in an interview with O. Yoshida, *Sankei*, 6 April 1989, Tokyo.

Comprehensive National Security Group. *Report on Comprehensive National Security* (1980), Tokyo.

Crawcour, S. 'The Japanese Employment System', *Journal of Japanese Studies*, vol.4, no.2 (1978).

Crawford, M. 'So What's New about Fortress America?', *Sunday Times*, 5 Sept. 1971, London.

Dahlby, T. 'Japan's Paternalism is Put to the Test', *Far Eastern Economic Review*, 9 March 1979, Hong Kong.

Dale, C. 'Great Strides in Drug Technology', *Financial Times*, 6 Nov. 1979, London.

Dale, R. 'Make-or-break Time for a New World Trade Order', *Financial Times*, 16 Jan. 1978, London.

Davies, D. 'Japan '78: Overview', *Far Eastern Economic Review*, 23 June 1978, Hong Kong.

Dellinger, D. *Revolutionary Nonviolence* (1970), Bobbs-Merrill, NY
Dickson, M. 'Regenerating the Nuclear Option', *Financial Times*,
    4 Feb. 1981, London.
Dore, R. *Education in Tokugawa Japan* (1965), Routledge & Kegan Paul,
    London.
——, *British Factory-Japanese Factory* (1973), Allen & Unwin, London.
Drysdale, P. 'An Organisation For Pacific Trade, Aid and Development:
    Regional Arrangements and the Resource Trade', Australia-Japan
    Economic Relations Research Project, Australian National University
    (mimeo), 1978, Canberra.
—— and Patrick, H. 'Evaluation of a Proposed Asian-Pacific Regional
    Economic Organisation', Australia-Japan Economic Relations
    Research Project, Australian National University (mimeo), 1979,
    Canberra.
Dutt, R.P. *India Today* (1947), People's Publishing House, Bombay.
Dyson, F. *Disturbing the Universe* (1979), Harper & Row, NY.
Economic Planning Agency *Economic Survey of Japan* (1967), Tokyo.
—— *Economic Survey of Japan* (1967), Tokyo.
—— *Economic Survey of Japan* (1970), Tokyo.
—— *Economic Survey of Japan* (1978), Tokyo.
Emmerson, J.K. *Arms, Yen and Power: The Japanese Dilemma* (1971),
    Dunellen, NY.
Enthoven, A.C. and Smith, K.W. *How Much Is Enough? Shaping the
    Defense Programme, 1961-69* (1971), Harper & Row, NY.
FAO *FAO Production Year Book, 1979* (1980), Rome.
Fisher, H.A.L. *A History of Europe*, vol. II (1935), Fontana, London.
Funabashi, Y. 'Slowly Turning to the Right' (Part 8), *Asahi*, 20 March
    1978, Tokyo.
Galenson, W. and Odaka, K. 'The Japanese Labour Market' in H. Patrick
    and R. Rosovsky (eds.) *Asia's New Giant: How the Japanese Economy
    Works* (1976), Brookings Institution, Washington DC.
Gallios, P. 'United States Strategy and the Defense of Europe', in H.A.
    Kissinger (ed.) *Problems of National Strategy* (1965), Praeger, NY.
GAO, (US) *United States-Japan Trade: Issues and Problems* (1979),
    United States, General Accounting Office, Washington DC.
Gardner, R.N. *Sterling-Dollar Diplomacy* (1956), Clarendon Press,
    Oxford
General Agreement on Tariffs and Trade (GATT) *International Trade,
    1964* (1965), Geneva.
Gonzaga, L. 'The Headaches caused by Over-visibility', *Far Eastern
    Economic Review*, 23 March 1979, Hong Kong.
Halliday, J. and McCormack, G. *Japanese Imperialism Today:*

Co-Prosperity in Greater East Asia (1973), Pelican, Harmondsworth.

Hamilton, A. 'Japanese Trade: Time to Rethink', *Business Observer*, 26 Feb. 1978, London.

Hanson, R. 'A Major Force Emerges', *Financial Times*, 6 Nov. 1979, London.

—— 'High Hopes for the Future', *Financial Times*, 6 Nov. 1979, London.

—— 'Japan's New Industries', *Financial Times*, 6 Nov. 1979, London.

—— 'In-Car Electronics', *Financial Times*, 6 Nov. 1979, London.

—— 'Growing Force in World Markets', *Financial Times*, 3 Dec. 1980, London.

Harrison, S.S. 'The United States, Japan and the Future of Korea' in Weinstein, F.B. (ed.) *U.S.-Japan Relations and the Security of East Asia* (1978), Westview Press, Boulder.

Hayami, Y. 'Trade Benefits to All: A Design of the Beef Import Liberalization in Japan', quoted in *Task Force Report* (1979), Government Printing Office, Washington DC.

Hayashi, S. 'Supreme Court Rulings on Constitutional Issues', *Japan Echo*, vol. 5, no.3 (1978), Tokyo.

Hazelhurst, P. 'Soviet Anger over Japan Campaign', *The Times*, 9 Feb. 1981, London

Healey, D. 'The Japanese Threat', *Sunday Times*, 3 Oct. 1971, London.

Hellman, D.C. 'Japanese Security and Postwar Japanese Foreign Policy' in Scalapino, R.A. (ed.) *The Foreign Policy of Modern Japan* (1977), University of California Press, Berkeley.

Higashi, C. 'U.S. Foreign Policy and Auto Wars', *Look Japan*, 10 April 1980, Tokyo

Hirschmeier, J. 'The Japanese Spirit of Enterprise, 1867-1970', *The Business History Review*, vol. XLIV, no.1 (1970), Cambridge, Mass.

—— and Yui, T. *The Development of Japanese Business, 1600-1973* (1975), Harvard University Press, Cambridge, Mass.

Hosoya, C. 'Course for "All-Directions", Japan to Take', *Chuo koron*, Oct. 1978, Tokyo.

Hubbard, G.E. *Eastern Industrialisation and Its Effects on the West* (1978), Oxford University Press, London.

Inoki, M.* 'Active Discussion on Security should be Initiated: Commenting on Morishima-Seki Exchange of Peace Debate', *Seiron*, April 1979, Tokyo.

International Institute for Strategic Studies. *The Future of Strategic Deterrence*, Part I, 1980, IISS, London.

—— *The Military Balance: 1980-1981* (1980), IISS, London.

International Monetary Fund. *The Rise in Protectionism* (1978), IMF,

Washington DC.
—— *Annual Report on Exchange Arrangements and Exchange Restrictions, 1979* (1979), IMF, Washington DC.

Ito, K.* 'Age of My-Home Diplomacy Has Ended: My Empirical Theory of Japanese Diplomacy', *Asahi Journal*, 15 Feb. 1980, Tokyo.

Iwai, A.* 'Present State of Labour Movement and JSP's Tasks', *Gekkan Shakaito*, Nov. 1978, Tokyo.

Iwashima, H. 'Trends in Peace Research and Military Studies in Japan' (1972) quoted in Barnett, *China and the Major Powers.*

Jansen, G. 'Moslems and the Modern World', *The Economist*, 3 Jan. 1981, London.

Japan Defense Agency. *Defense of Japan, 1976* (1976), Tokyo.
—— *Defense of Japan, 1977* (1977), Tokyo.
—— *Defense of Japan, 1978* (1978), Tokyo.

Japan External Trade Organisation. *Japan's Industrial Structure: A Long Range Vision* (1975), Tokyo.
—— *White Paper on International Trade 1976* (1976), Tokyo.
—— *White Paper on International Trade 1977* (1977), Tokyo.
——*White Paper on International Trade 1978* (1978), Tokyo.
—— *White Paper on International Trade 1979* (1979), Tokyo.
—— *White Paper on International Trade 1980* (1980), Tokyo.

Johnson, S.E. and Yager, J.A. *The Military Equation in North East Asia* (1979), Brookings Institution, Washington DC.

Joint Struggle Committee for People's Spring Struggle, *White Paper on the 1980 Spring Struggle* (1980), Sohyo, Tokyo.

Kahn, H. *The Emerging Japanese Superstate* (1971), Andre Deutsch, London.

Kamishima, J. 'The Tradition and Realism of Demilitarization', *Japan Echo*, vol. VII, no.3 (1980).

Kamiya, F. 'The Prospects for Peace in Korea' in Weinstein, F.B. (ed.) *US-Japan Relations and the Security of East Asia* (1978).

Kase, H. 'Defense Lifeline of Japanese Archipelago', *Jiyu*, Jan. 1979, Tokyo.

Kataoka, T. 'Waiting For Pearl Harbor: Japan Debates Arms', unpublished, 1979.
—— 'The Concept of the Japanese Second Republic', *Japan Echo*, vol. VII, no.1 (1980), Tokyo.

Kawakami, T.* in an interview with Yoshimasa Miyasaki, a political affairs commentator, *Jiyu*, March 1979, Tokyo.

Keohane, R.O. and Nye, J.S. *Power and Interdependence: World Politics in Transition* (1979), Little, Brown and Co, Boston, Mass.

Kimura, H. 'Relax — The Russians Are Not Coming', *The Japan Times*

Weekly, 22 Nov. 1980, Tokyo.

Kissinger, H.A. 'The Search for Stability', *Foreign Affairs*, July 1959, Washington DC.

Kojima, K. 'An Organisation for Pacific Trade, Aid and Development: A Proposal', Australia-Japan Economic Relations Research Project, Australian National University (mimeo) (1976), Canberra.

Komori, Y.* 'Angry America and "Chrysanthemum and the Sword"', *Bungei Shunju*, Feb. 1980, Tokyo.

Krause, L.B. and Sekiguchi, S. 'Japan and the World Economy' in Patrick, H. and Rosovsky, H. (eds.) *Asia's New Giant: How The Japanese Economy Works* (1976), Brookings Institution, Washington DC.

Kubo, T. 'The Meaning of the U.S. Nuclear Umbrella for Japan' in Weinstein, F.B. (ed.) *US-Japan Relations* (1978).

Kurihara, K. *The Growth Potential of the Japanese Economy* (1971), Johns Hopkins University Press, Baltimore.

Lal, D. *Market Access for Semi-Manufactures from Developing Countries* (1979), Graduate Institute of International Studies, Geneva and Trade Policy Research Centre, London, Sijthoff, Leiden.

Lall, S. 'Transfer Pricing by Multi-National Manufacturing Firms', *Oxford Bulletin of Economics and Statistics*, 1973, Oxford.

—— 'Financial and Profit Performance of MNC's in Developing Countries: Some Evidence from an Indian and Columbian Sample', *World Development*, vol. 4 (1976), Oxford.

—— 'Transfer Pricing and Developing Countries: Some Problems of Investigation', *World Development*, vol. 7 (1979), Oxford.

Leifer, M. *Conflict and Regional Order in South-east Asia,* Adelphi Papers, no.162 (1980), London.

Lewis, J. 'The SDF's New, Sharp Teeth', *Far Eastern Economic Review*, 16 Jan. 1981, Hong Kong.

Lockwood, W.W. *The Economic Development of Japan* (1955), Oxford University Press, London.

Magaziner, I.C. and Hout, T.M. *Japanese Industrial Policy* (1980), Policy Studies Institute, London.

Mansfield, M.* in an interview with T. Miyamoto and J. Kusano, *Sankei*, 7 Jan. 1980, Tokyo.

Mansur, A.K. 'The American Threat to Saudi Arabia', *Survival*, Jan./ Feb. 1981, London.

Matsumoto, S. 'Japan's Voting Behaviour in the United Nations' in Itoh, H. (ed.) *Japanese Politics – An Inside View* (1973), Cornell University Press, Ithaca.

Matsumura, Z. 'Economic Growth and Foreign Exchange Reserves' in Yau, J. (ed.) *Monetary Factors in Japanese Economic Growth* (1970), Research Institute for Economic and Business Administration, Kobe University, Kobe.

Meacher, M. 'Peculiar Japanese Distribution Attitude Forms Non-tariff Barrier', *The Japan Economic Journal* (Supplement), 11 April 1978, Tokyo.

Merritt, G. 'Why Japan's Car Barrier is so Difficult to Breach', *Financial Times*, 7 Nov. 1980, London.

Ministry of Foreign Affairs, Security Policy Planning Committee *Outline of First Round Discussion* (1980), Tokyo.

Ministry of International Trade and Industry. *Japan's Industrial Structure – A Long Range Vision, 1976 edition* (1976).

—— *Japanese Markets: The Myth and the Reality* (1977), Issued by Director, Information Centre, Embassy of Japan, London.

—— *Japan's Industrial Structure – A Long Range Vision, 1978 edition* (1978), Tokyo.

—— *Economic Cooperation of Japan 1978* (1978), Tokyo

Miyata, M. 'The True Meaning of Defending the Country', *Japan Echo*, vol. V., no. 4 (1978), Tokyo.

Miyazawa, K. in an interview with *Sankei*, 29 April 1979, Tokyo.

Momoi, M. 'Are There Any Alternative Strategies for the Defense of Japan?' in Weinstein (ed.) *US-Japan Relations.*

Morita, M. 'Japan's Despised Seat Warmers', *The New Vanguard*, Nov. 1978, Sarawak.

Murakami, K. 'The Postwar Defense Debate in Review', *Japan Echo*, vol, V, no.4 (1978), Tokyo.

Murata, K. 'Specter of Wartime Laws: Infringement of Basic Rights by Emergency Legislation Feared', *The Japan Times Weekly*, 2 Sept. 1978, Tokyo.

—— 'The Decline of the Left', *The Japan Times Weekly*, 21 April 1979, Tokyo.

—— 'Conservative Japanese: Survey Shows Traditional Values, Attitudes Returning', *The Japan Times Weekly*, 4 Aug. 1979, Tokyo.

—— 'The Soviet Threat: It is a Subject of Many Discussions in Mass Media', *The Japan Times Weekly*, 24 Jan. 1981, Tokyo.

Myrdal, A. *The Game of Disarmament* (1976), Pantheon Books, NY.

Nakajime, M. 'Diplomacy as Defense Strategy', *Japan Echo*, vol. VI, no.1 (1979), Tokyo.

Nakamae, T. 'Good Managers or Sharp Traders?', *Guardian*, 4 July 1977, London.

Nakane, C. *Japanese Society* (1970), Penguin, Harmondsworth.

Nakasone, Y.L. 'Towards Comprehensive Security', *Japan Echo*, vol. V, no.4 (1978), Tokyo.

Nanto, K.D. 'Automobiles Imported From Japan', Issue Brief Number IB 800 30, Congressional Research Service, US Library of Congress, 1980, Washington DC.

Nathan, J.A. and Oliver, J.K. *The Future of United States Naval Power* (1979), Tokyo.

Nishikawa, J. 'Towards a New International Order', *Japan Echo*, vol. VI, Special Issue (1979), Tokyo.

Noda, K. 'Postwar Japanese Executives' in Komiya, R. (ed.) *Postwar Economic Growth in Japan* (1966), University of California Press, Berkeley.

Nukazawa, K. 'Japan's Emerging Service Economy and the International Economic Implication', unpublished, 1979, Rockefeller Foundation, NY.

Oba, S. 'Anglo-Japanese Trade — Some Practical Aspects', *The Japan Economic Journal* (Supplement), 11 April 1978, Tokyo.

Odaka, K. 'An Analysis of the Personal Consumption Expenditure in Japan, 1892-1967' (1974) quoted in Wallich, H.C. and Wallich, M.I. (1976).

Ohta, H. 'Recent U.S.-Japan Economic Relations: An Overview', *US-Japan Trade Council Report 13* (1979), Washington DC

Organisation for Economic Co-operation and Development. *The Industrial Policy of Japan* (1972), Paris.

—— *Development Cooperation Review, 1973* (1973), Paris.

—— *OECD Economic Surveys: Japan* (1980), Paris.

—— *Development Cooperation Review, 1980* (1980), Paris.

Paterson, T.G. *Soviet-American Confrontation* (1973), Johns Hopkins University Press, Baltimore.

Patrick, H. and Rosovsky, R. (eds.) *Asia's New Giant: How the Japanese Economy Works* (1976).

—— 'Japan's Economic Performance: An Overview' in Patrick and Rosovsky (eds.) *Asia's New Giant* (1976).

Pechman, J. and Kaizuka, K. 'Taxation' in Patrick and Rosovsky (eds.) *Asia's New Giant* (1976).

Ramsey, D. D.R. 'Cautious Approach to Setting Up Abroad', *Financial Times*, 26 July 1977, London.

Reischauer, E.O. *The Japanese* (1978), Belknap Press of Harvard University Press, Cambridge, Mass.

Richardson, D. 'World Missile Directory', *Flight International*, vol. 11 (1977).

Richardson, L. 'Nuclear Power in Japan — The New Age Turns Sour', unpublished, 1978.

Roningen, V. and Yeats, A. 'Nontariff Distortions of International Trade: Some Preliminary Empirical Evidence', *Weltwirtschaftliches Archiv*, no.4 (1976).

Rubin, P.J. 'Flair for Design Work', *Financial Times*, 6 Nov. 1979, London.

Saeki, K.* in an interview with Yasuo Hariki, the chief editor of *Zaikai*, reported in *Zaikai*, 22 April 1980, Tokyo.

Sakamoto, Y.* 'The Way of Life for Japan: Status of the People of an Intermediate Nation', *Sekai*, Jan. 1979, Tokyo.

Sakanaka, T.*, the editor of *Asahi Shimbun*, in a dialogue with Shinohara, a member of the *Asahi Shimbun* editorial committee, reported in *Asahi*, 7 Feb. 1980, Tokyo.

Sase, M. 'Refuting the Mercantile Nation Theory', *Japn Echo*, vol. VII, no. 2 (1980), Tokyo.

Sato, S. *et al.* 'Beyond Conservative vs. Kakushin Politics', *Japan Echo*, vol. V (Special Issue) (1978), Tokyo.

Schmidt, H. *The Balance of Power: Germany's Peace Policy and the Superpowers* (translated by Edward Thomas) (1971), William Kimber, London.

Scott-Stokes, H. 'It's All Right to Talk Defense in Japan', *The New York Times Magazine*, 11 Feb. 1979, NY.

Seaborg, G. *Man and Atom* (1971), E.P. Dutton & Co., NY.

Sebald, W.J. and Spinks, C.N. *Japan: Prospects, Options and Opportunities* (1967), American Enterprise Institute, Washington DC.

Seki, H.* 'Changing Asia and Defense Diplomacy: Requests toward the Ohira Cabinet', *Sekai*, Feb. 1979.

Seki, Y. 'Democracy and Japanese Intellectuals. The Concept of Democracy in Post-war Japan as Reflected in Magazine Articles', *Japan Report*, 1 July 1978.

Sheridan, K. 'A Review of the Japanese National Economic Plans, 1956-1986' (mimeo) (1977), Australia-Japan Economic Relations Research Project, Australian National University, Canberra.

Shimizu, I. 'Questioning Post-War Values', *Japan Echo*, vol. V, no.3 (1978), Tokyo.

—— 'The Nuclear Option: Japan, Be a State!', *Japan Echo*, vol. VII, no.3 (1980), Tokyo.

—— 'Nuclear Weapons For Japan – Why Not?', *The Japan Times Weekly*, 16 Aug. 1980, Tokyo.

Shimizu, M. 'Centrists Exude Confidence in National Politics', *The Japan Times Weekly*, 28 April 1979, Tokyo.

Shinohara, M. *Structural Change in Japan's Economic Development* (1970), Kinokuniya Bookstore Co. Ltd., Tokyo.

Shiratori, R. 'Ghosts Linger in Political Party System', *The Japan Times Weekly*, 22 Sept. 1979, Tokyo.

Simison, R.L. 'After Coaxing Japanese Car Makers to U.S., UAW Finds They Resist Union Organizing', *The Wall Street Journal*, 30 July 1980, NY.

—— 'Ford Fires an Economist', *The Wall Street Journal*, 30 July 1980, NY.

Sinha, R. 'Japan's Aid to Developing Countries', *World Development* vol. 2, no. 8 (1974), Oxford.

Smith, C. 'Japan Admits High Imports Mark-up', *Financial Times*, 2 Dec. 1977, London.

—— 'Large Market is Growing Rapidly', *Financial Times*, 6 Nov. 1977, London.

—— 'Sectors Growth Rate Outstrips that of Manufacturing Industry', *Financial Times*, 29 Oct. 1980, London.

—— 'Fears of Nightmare Deficit Vanish', *Financial Times*, 3 Dec. 1980, London.

Sohyo. *White Paper on The 1980 Spring Struggle*, Joint Struggle Committee for the People's Spring Struggle, *Sohyo News*, 1980, Tokyo.

Speed, R.D. *Strategic Deterrence in the 1980's* (1979), Hoover Institution Press, Stanford.

Streeten, P.P. and Lal, S. *Main Findings of a Study of Private Foreign Investments in Selected Developing Countries* (UNCTAD, TD/B/C. 3/111), 1973.

Suetuna, Z. et al. *Annals of the Institute of Statistical Mathematics Supplement* (1961), Tokyo.

Swearingen, R. *The Soviet Union and Postwar Japan* (1978), Hoover Institution Press, Stanford.

Tachibana, T. 'What Must Be Done?', *Japan Echo*, vol. III, no.4 (1976), Tokyo.

Tanaka, M. 'Reflections on Three Recent Events', *Japan Echo*, vol. VII, no.3 (1980), Tokyo.

Takeyama, Y. 'The U.S.-Japanese Partnership', *The Wall Street Journal*, 4 Sept. 1980, NY.

Takubo, T.* 'U.S. Studies on "Emergency in the Far East – Analysis of U.S. Naval Institute Report"', *Bungei Shunju*, Dec. 1980, NY.

Tanzer, M. *The Race For Resources: Continuing Struggles over Minerals and Fuels* (1980), Monthly Review Press, NY.

Tasker, R. 'The Ugly Japanese Image is Still Very Real', *Far Eastern Economic*

Review, 23 March 1979, Hong Kong.

Tokuoka, T. 'Japan — Red or Dead', *New York Times*, 2 Sept. 1979, NY.

Tokuyama, J. 'Japan's Role in the Pacific Era', *Japan Echo*, vol. VI, no. 1 (1978), Tokyo.

Toynbee, A. quoted from the *Vancouver Times*, 11 May 1965 (reprinted from the London *Observer*) by Dellinger, D. *Revolutionary Nonviolence* (1970).

Treverton, G. 'China's Nuclear Forces and the Stability of Soviet American Deterrence' in IISS, *The Future of Strategic Deterrence*, Part I (1980), London.

Trezise, P.T. and Suzuki, Y. 'Politics, Government and Economic Growth in Japan' in Patrick and Rosovsky (eds.) *Asia's New Giant* (1976).

Tsuda, M. 'Japanese Wage Structure and its Significance for International Comparison', *British Journal of Industrial Relations*, vol. III, no.2 (1965), London.

Tsunoda, R. *et al. Sources of Japanese Tradition*, vol. I (1969), Columbia University Press, NY.

Tsuru, S. *Essays in Economic Development* (1968), Kinokuniya Bookstore Co., Tokyo.

Tsurumi, K. *Social Change and the Individual* (1970), Bantam Books, NY.

Tuchman, B.W. *Stilwell and the American Experience in China, 1911-45* (6th printing) (1979), Bantam Books, NY.

Turner, L. *Multinational Companies and the Third World* (1973), Hill and Wang, NY.

United Nations. *Yearbook of International Trade Statistics, 1978* (1979), NY.

—— *Monthly Bulletin of Statistics*, vol XXXIV, no.7 (1980), NY.

—— Department of Economic and Social Affairs *Panel on Foreign Investment in Developing Countries*, E.69, IID. 12, 1969, NY.

—— Economic Commission For Asia and the Far East (ECAFE) *Economic Survey of Asia and the Far East, 1948* (1949), NY.

—— *Economic Survey of Asia and the Far East, 1949* (1950), NY.

—— *Economic Survey of Asia and the Far East, 1950* (1951), NY.

United States Arms Control and Disarmament Agency *Japan's Contribution to Military Stability in Northeast Asia* (1980), Washington DC.

—— House of Representatives *Task Force Report on United States-Japan Trade*, prepared for the Subcommittee on Trade of the Committee on Ways and Means, 1979, Washington DC.

US-Japan Trade Council *Yearbook of U.S.-Japan Economic Relations, 1978* (1979), Washington DC.
——— *Yearbook of U.S.-Japan Economic Relations, 1979* (1980), Washington DC.
US National Foreign Assessment Centre *Handbook of Economic Statistics, 1979* (1979), table 1, Washington DC.
Van Alslyne, R.W. *The United States and The East Asia* (1973), Thames and Hudson, London.
Vogel, E.F. *Japan as Number One* (1979), Harvard University Press, Cambridge, Mass.
Walker, T. 'Peking Fears Shift of Policy under Reagan', *Financial Times*, 2 Dec. 1980, London.
Wallich, H.C. and Wallich, M.I. 'Banking and Finance' in Patrick and Rosovsky (eds.) *Asia's New Giant* (1976).
Watanabe, S. 'Technological Linkages between Formal and Informal Sectors of Manufacturing Industries', unpublished, ILO Working Paper, 1978, Geneva.
Weinraub, B. 'Nation's Military Anxiety Grows as Russians Gain', *The New York Times*, 21 Sept. 1980, NY.
Weinstein, F.B. 'Conclusive and Policy Recommendations', in Weinstein (ed.) *US-Japan Relations and the Security of East Asia* (1978).
Whytman, R. 'Officially Japan doesn't have an Army but this is what it has for Self-defence', *Sunday Times*, 5 Feb. 1978, London
Wilkinson, W. 'It's Back to School for Europeans: Subject is Japan', *The Japan Times Weekly*, 1 Sept. 1979, Tokyo.
Williams, C. 'The Pacific Community: A Modest Proposal', Australia-Japan Economic Relations Research Project, Australian National University (mimeo), 1979, Canberra.
World Bank *World Development Report, 1980* (1980), Washington DC.
World Health Organisation. *World Health Statistics* (1979), Geneva.
——— *World Health Statistics* (1980), Geneva.
Yanaga, C. *Japan Since Perry* (1966), Archon Books, Hamden, Conn.
——— *Big Business in Japan* (1968), Yale University Press, New Haven.
Yao, J. (ed.) *Monetary Factors in Japanese Economic Growth* (1970), The Research Institute for Economic & Business Administration, Kobe University, Tokyo.

Note:
*All the quotations from the articles marked with an asterisk are from the translations of the originals from *Daily Summary of Japanese Press*, and *Summaries of Selected Japanese Magazines* produced by the Office of Translation Services, American Embassy, Tokyo.

INDEX